GUIDE TO MANAGEMENT
IDEAS AND GURUS

TIM HINDLE is the author of several best-selling books on management and business. He is a former business and management editor of *The Economist* and was the founder editor of *EuroBusiness*. He has also been editor of *Director* magazine.

OTHER ECONOMIST BOOKS

Guide to Analysing Companies
Guide to Business Modelling
Guide to Business Planning
Guide to Cash Management
Guide to Economic Indicators
Guide to the European Union
Guide to Financial Management
Guide to Financial Markets
Guide to Hedge Funds
Guide to Investment Strategy
Guide to Managing Growth
Guide to Organisation Design
Guide to Project Management
Guide to Supply Chain Management
Numbers Guide
Style Guide

Book of Isms
Book of Obituaries
Brands and Branding
Business Consulting
Business Strategy
Buying Professional Services
The City
Coaching and Mentoring
Doing Business in China
Economics
Emerging Markets
Marketing
Megachange
Modern Warfare, Intelligence and Deterrence
Organisation Culture
Successful Strategy Execution
The World of Business

Directors: an A–Z Guide
Economics: an A–Z Guide
Investment: an A–Z Guide
Negotiation: an A–Z Guide

Pocket World in Figures

GUIDE TO MANAGEMENT IDEAS AND GURUS

Tim Hindle

THE ECONOMIST IN ASSOCIATION WITH
PROFILE BOOKS LTD

Published by Profile Books Ltd
3A Exmouth House, Pine Street, London EC1R 0JH
www.profilebooks.com

Typeset in EcoType by MacGuru Ltd
info@macguru.org.uk

Printed in Great Britain by
Clays, Bungay, Suffolk

A CIP catalogue record for this book is available
from the British Library

Hardback ISBN 978 1 84668 108 0
Paperback ISBN 978 1 84668 607 8
ebook ISBN 978 1 84765 039 9

The paper this book is printed on is certified by the © 1996 Forest Stewardship Council A.C. (FSC). It is ancient-forest friendly. The printer holds FSC chain of custody SGS-COC-2061

FSC

Mixed Sources
Product group from well-managed
forests and other controlled sources

Cert no. SGS-COC-2061
www.fsc.org
© 1996 Forest Stewardship Council

Contents

Part 2 Management Gurus

Introduction

This book provides a short introduction to the management concepts that have most influenced companies over the past century or so, and to some of the more influential people behind them. These people and their ideas are no longer confined to the pages of learned management journals or to the lecture halls of prestigious business schools. Many are mentioned nowadays in the pages of the everyday business press and in general-management training material. Yet few of them are familiar to the average person in an office.

The popularity of these ideas changes over time. They are subject to fashion like everything else. Not long ago the Japanese concept of *kaizen*, or slow gradual improvement, was being studied intensively by managers in the West. But nowadays no one literally has time for *kaizen*. Change it seems is happening so rapidly that only big breakthroughs and dramatic outcomes will do. Even Toyota itself, the epitome of *kaizen*, has declared its allegiance to *kakushin*, the Japanese version of dramatic change.

Bain & Company, a Boston-based consulting firm, provides a barometer of that change in the shape of an annual survey of the most popular management ideas. In 2000, strategic planning, mission and vision statements, and benchmarking headed its list; by 2010, ten years on, benchmarking had pushed strategic planning out of the top slot. Reflecting today's sharper focus on customers, CRM (customer relationship management) came fourth. As ideas drop in and out of fashion, the need to update a book like this increases.

The final selection of ideas and gurus included here was inevitably a personal one. There are 54 gurus in the book, but there could as easily be 154. A small band of them appears in virtually all such lists – a band that is more or less confined to what can be called the "Famous Five": Peter Drucker, Douglas McGregor, Michael Porter, Alfred Sloan and Frederick Winslow Taylor.

Most of these lists are produced by business magazines and management writers like me. But one such list stands out from the rest. In 2003, *Harvard Business Review* asked gurus themselves to name their favourite guru, and they came up with an interestingly different selection – which is not so surprising since it is not unlike asking those shortlisted for the Turner Prize to name their favourite painter. Although the gurus placed

Peter Drucker (predictably) at the top, they put James March in second place and Herbert Simon in third. Tom Peters was nowhere to be seen.

Around my famous five swirl others who have come and gone with the years. In the 1980s, for example, the Japanese had their moment of glory when Kenichi Ohmae, Akio Morita and Japan's adopted Americans, W. Edwards Deming and Joseph Juran, were treated like the Delphic oracle itself. Then there was a moment when Europeans seemed about to burst into vogue – people like Yves Doz (French), Geert Hofstede and Manfred Kets de Vries (Dutch), and Charles Handy (Irish). But then they too faded somewhat, overshadowed again by Americans, who have persistently dominated the field. Out of my list of 54, 34 of them have American nationality. There are more Mormons on the list than there are Britons.

The rising stars having their moment now are Indian, albeit Indians with one foot in the West. C.K. Prahalad was born in Madras, but did much of his early work with Gary Hamel, an American, at the University of Michigan; Sumantra Ghoshal, though born in Calcutta, died in the UK while working at London Business School; and both Pankaj Ghemawat (at IESE) and Rakesh Khurana (at Harvard Business School) were born in India. In the next decade it may be a field that the Chinese, or perhaps even the Russians, turn their minds to. This opens up endless possibilities for new entries in later editions of this book, perhaps on Mahjong strategy or on Gary Kasparov and chessmaster leadership.

There is occasional overlap between gurus and ideas. Just a few men have come to be associated with a single idea – people like Robert Kaplan and the balanced scorecard, for instance, or Dave Ulrich and human resources transformation. Many more of them, however, have been remarkably broad in their thoughts, distinguished particularly for their way of expressing them. In some cases they "own" ideas because they were the first to name them. People like Ted Levitt, Alvin Toffler, William Whyte and even Peter Drucker have shone almost as much for their illuminating writing as for what they were writing about.

For management ideas are rarely rocket science. As GE's Jack Welch once said:

> An idea is not necessarily a biotech idea. That's the wrong view of what an idea is. An idea is an error-free billing system. An idea is taking a process that used to require six days to do and getting it done in one day.

Both the gurus and the ideas in this book can be grouped more or less into one or other of what have been the two main streams of management thinking at least since Noah employed carpenters near Ararat to build him an ark: the idea that management is a science – represented most notably by F.W. Taylor's ideas about "scientific management" – and the idea that management is about motivating – represented most memorably perhaps by Douglas McGregor's Theory Y. This divide also accounts for the two main disciplines that management gurus come from: social science, represented by Elton Mayo, McGregor, Abraham Maslow and Elliott Jaques; and engineering, represented by Taylor, Michael Porter, Michael Hammer and Taiichi Ohno.

This book is designed to lead the interested reader on to further learning through the reading lists that are attached to many of the entries. My original aim was to compile the 100 greatest management ideas and the 100 greatest gurus of the 20th century, an average of one big thought and one big thinker per year being about as much as anyone could hope for. It might have answered the question, who would have won the Oscars (one per year for best thought and one per year for best thinker) throughout the 20th century. A prize which should perhaps be called a Winslow. But it was a list way too long for a single tome.

Lastly, I would like to thank Stephen Brough at Profile Books for believing with me that there was a market for a product like this. And I would also like to thank all the management thinkers and writers referred to in the book. Unfortunately, many of them have suffered from the volumes of mumbo-jumbo that are published as management wisdom every year and that give their genre a bad name. But the fun in writing this book came from the fact that the best of them throw extraordinary flashes of insight on the way that most of us spend the greater part of our waking days. If the book has mirrored just a few of those flashes it will have achieved its aim.

Tim Hindle
January 2012

PART ONE
MANAGEMENT IDEAS

Active inertia

This is an idea closely identified with Donald "Don" Sull, an associate professor at London Business School and a rising star in a new generation of management gurus. Educated almost exclusively at Harvard (first degree, doctorate and MBA), Sull worked in consulting (with McKinsey & Company) and private equity (with Clayton, Dubilier & Rice) before moving to an academic career.

At the core of his idea is the observation that managers often get stuck in a rut, so when an entirely new situation arises they revert to old responses. Active inertia, Sull says, is "management's tendency to respond to the most disruptive changes by accelerating activities that succeeded in the past".

He quotes the example of tyre company Firestone's response to the introduction by Michelin of radial technology. Instead of embracing the new technology and all the changes that it implied, Firestone undertook more of the activities that had worked for it in the past, in the pre-radial era – extending its existing technology, making more tyres on existing equipment and keeping old factories working at full throttle. As Sull puts it, "It just dug itself an even deeper hole."

When managers are in a hole, they should stop digging. But too often, like a car stuck in the mud, they keep the engine turning as if they are on a normal road. They do this partly because they "equate inertia with inaction". But inaction does not have to mean that nothing is going on. When troops are not in battle, they keep themselves in a state of active preparedness. Companies should do likewise.

The focus of Sull's research has been successful companies in uncertain markets. Over a six-year period he monitored more than 20 pairs of comparable companies in a number of what he calls unpredictable industries (telecommunications and software, for example) in unpredictable markets (China, in particular). What he found was that the more successful of each pair consistently responded "more effectively to volatile factors that influenced performance, such as unexpected shifts in regulation, technology, competition and macroeconomics". They did not behave like Firestone. Rather, they exemplified what Sull calls "active waiting", a strategy that he explains as "anticipating and preparing for opportunities and threats that executives can neither fully predict nor control".

We all know the power of waiting quietly for the right moment to pounce upon an opportunity. But Sull's idea is that waiting does not have to be quiet. While they are waiting there are lots of useful things that companies can do – build up a war chest, for instance, streamline operations, carry out scenario planning (see page 157), and so on.

To avoid active inertia, Sull says leaders should not march "headlong toward a well-defined future". Instead, they should "articulate a fuzzy vision ... a fuzzy vision works because it provides a general direction and sets aspirations without prematurely locking the company into a specific course of action".

Further reading

Sull, D., "Why Good Companies Go Bad", Harvard Business Review, July 1999

Sull, D., Revival of the Fittest, Harvard Business School Press, 2003

Sull, D., "Strategy as Active Waiting", Harvard Business Review, September 2005

Sull, D., The Upside of Turbulence, HarperBusiness, 2009

Activity-based costing

Activity-based costing (ABC) is a method of assigning costs to products or services based on the resources that they consume. Its aim, *The Economist* once wrote, is "to change the way in which costs are counted".

ABC is an alternative to traditional accounting in which a business's overheads (indirect costs such as lighting, heating and marketing) are allocated in proportion to an activity's direct costs. This is unsatisfactory in the first place because two activities that absorb the same direct costs can use very different amounts of overhead. A mass-produced industrial robot, for instance, can use the same amount of labour and materials as a customised robot. But the customised robot uses far more of the company engineers' time (an overhead) than does the mass-produced one.

This difference would not be reflected in traditional costing systems. Hence a company that makes more and more customised products (and bases its pricing on historic costings) can soon find itself making large losses. As new technologies make it easier for firms to customise products, the importance of allocating indirect costs accurately increases.

Introducing activity-based costing is not a simple task – it is by no means as easy as ABC. For a start, all business activities must be broken down into their discrete components. As part of its ABC programme, for example, ABB, a Swiss-Swedish power company, divided its purchasing activity into things like negotiating with suppliers, updating the database, issuing purchase orders and handling complaints.

Large firms should try a pilot scheme before implementing the system throughout their organisation. The information essential for ABC may not be readily available and may have to be calculated specially for the purpose. This involves making many new measurements. Larger companies often hire consultants who are specialists in the area to help them get a system up and running.

The easy approach is to use ABC software in conjunction with a company's existing accounting system. The traditional system continues to be used as before, with the ABC structure an extra to be called upon when specific cost information is required to help make a particular decision. The development of business accounting software programs has made the introduction of activity-based costing more feasible.

Setting up an activity-based costing system is a prerequisite for improving business processes and for any re-engineering programme (see page 25). Many firms also use ABC data for the measures required for a balanced scorecard (see opposite).

Activity-based costing became popular in the early 1980s largely because of growing dissatisfaction with traditional ways of allocating costs. After a strong start, however, it fell into a period of disrepute. Even Robert Kaplan (see page 259), a Harvard Business School professor sometimes credited with being its founding father, has admitted that it stagnated in the 1990s. The difficulty lay in translating the theory into action. Many companies were not prepared to give up their traditional cost-control mechanisms in favour of ABC.

In 2007 Kaplan brought out a new book that tried to make activity-based costing easier. Called TDABC (time-driven activity-based costing), it attempted to relate the measurement of cost to time. As Kaplan put it, only two questions need to be answered in TDABC:

- How much does it cost per time unit to supply resources for each business process?
- How much time is required to perform the work needed for a company's products, transactions and customers?

Despite its shortcomings, ABC has many satisfied customers. Chrysler, an American car manufacturer, claims that it saved hundreds of millions of dollars through a programme that it introduced in the early 1990s. ABC showed that the true cost of certain parts that Chrysler made was 30 times what had originally been estimated, a discovery that persuaded the company to outsource (see page 143) the manufacture of many of those parts.

Further reading

Kaplan, R.S. and Cooper, R., "Make Cost Right: Make the Right Decisions", *Harvard Business Review*, September–October 1988

Kaplan, R.S. and Cooper, R., *Cost and Effect: Using Integrated Cost Systems to Drive Profitability and Performance*, Harvard Business School Press, 1997

Kaplan, R.S. and Anderson, S., *Time-Driven Activity Based Costing*, Harvard Business School Press, 2007

Ness, J.A. and Cucuzza, T.G., "Tapping the Full Potential of ABC", *Harvard Business Review*, July–August 1995

Balanced scorecard

Robert Kaplan (see page 259) seems to come up with one big idea per decade. In the 1980s it was activity-based costing (see page 9); in the 1990s it was the balanced scorecard.

The latter was first set out in an article that Kaplan wrote in 1992 for *Harvard Business Review*, along with David Norton, president of a consulting firm. Entitled "The Balanced Scorecard – Measures that Drive Performance", it began with the principle that what you measure is what you get. Or, as the great 19th century English physicist Lord Kelvin put it: "If you cannot measure it, you cannot improve it."

If you measure only financial performance, then you can hope only for improvement in financial performance. If you take a wider view, and measure things from other perspectives, then (and only then) do you stand a chance of achieving goals other than purely financial ones.

In particular, Kaplan and Norton suggested that companies should consider the following:

- **The customer's perspective.** How does the customer see the organisation, and what should the organisation do to remain that customer's valued supplier?
- **The company's internal perspective.** What are the internal processes that the company must improve if it is to achieve its objectives vis-à-vis customers, shareholders and others?
- **Innovation and improvement.** How can the company continue to improve and to create value in the future? What should it be measuring to make this happen?

The idea of the balanced scorecard was embraced with enthusiasm when it first appeared. And it was still among Bain & Company's top ten management tools in 2010. Companies have become frustrated with traditional measures of performance that relate only to the shareholders' point of view. That view is seen as unduly short-termist and too concerned with stockmarket twitches; it prevents boardrooms and managers from considering longer-term opportunities. The balanced scorecard not only broadens the organisation's perception of where it stands today, but it also helps it to identify things that might guarantee its success in the future.

Kaplan and Norton thought the main benefits of the balanced scorecard were that:

- It helps companies to focus on what needs to be done to create a "breakthrough performance".
- It acts as an integrating device for a variety of often disconnected corporate programmes, such as quality, re-engineering, process redesign and customer service.
- It translates strategy into performance measures and targets.
- It helps break down corporate-wide measures so that local managers and employees can see what they need to do to improve organisational effectiveness.
- It provides a comprehensive view that overturns the traditional idea of the organisation as a collection of isolated, independent functions and departments.

Further reading

Kaplan, R.S. and Norton, D.P., "The Balanced Scorecard – Measures that Drive Performance", *Harvard Business Review*, January–February 1992

Kaplan, R.S. and Norton, D.P., *The Balanced Scorecard: Translating Strategy into Action*, Harvard Business School Press, 1996

Kaplan, R.S. and Norton, D.P., "Using the Balanced Scorecard as a Strategic Management System", *Harvard Business Review*, 1996, reproduced July/August 2007

Niven, P.R., *Balanced Scorecard Step-by-Step: Maximizing Performance and Maintaining Results*, John Wiley & Sons, 2002; 2nd edn, 2006

Barriers to entry, exit and mobility

There are barriers preventing firms from entering markets and there are barriers preventing them from leaving. This idea requires that we view markets as fields surrounded by gates of differing sizes and complexity. The gates have to be surmounted by firms wishing to enter or to leave.

To some extent the gates can be both raised and lowered, not just by those inside the fields but also by those outside wishing to enter. Typical barriers to entry include patents, licensing agreements and exclusive access to natural resources. A patented pharmaceutical, for instance, gives the patent holder exclusive rights for a certain period (usually a maximum of seven years) to manufacture and sell that pharmaceutical within a specified market.

The economies of scale (see page 71) that can be gained from being large and established in a particular field can also act as a barrier to entry. If new entrants calculate that they need to sell large volumes before they can hope to be competitive with existing firms, this acts as a deterrent to their ambition. When, for instance, did a new entrant last try to begin manufacturing for the mass car market?

Barriers to entry can be erected by governments. Regulations covering the financial-services industry are designed to act as a barrier to rogues and villains. But inevitably they also deter many honest businesses too. Forty years ago, foreign banks could not operate in the UK unless they had an office within walking distance of the Bank of England, then the industry's regulator. Needless to say, property prices in the City of London's "Square Mile" were among the highest in the world and acted as a powerful barrier to entry for newcomers.

Well-established firms in a particular field or market may be tempted to raise the barriers when they see a newcomer approaching their patch. They can do this, for instance, by lowering their prices, thus making the newcomers' products less competitive. Lowering prices may be an easy option for the incumbents since their prices may have been higher than the free-market level because of the barriers.

Monopolies exist where there are insurmountable barriers to entry. If there were no (or only low) barriers, other firms would enter such markets to participate in the monopoly profits.

Barriers to exit make it more difficult for a company to get out of a particular business than it would otherwise have been. They include things like the cost of laying off staff, and contractual obligations such as the payment of rent. For a classic high-street bank with a large number of staff and a wide network of branches, the barriers to exit from traditional banking businesses can be considerable.

Paradoxically, firms sometimes decide for themselves to erect barriers that hinder their own exit from a market. This can be a strategic ploy designed to convey to their competitors the message that they are committed to that market, and that they are not going to leave it in a hurry.

Old ideas about barriers to entry have been given a new twist with the development of e-commerce (see page 69). By using the internet, firms can sometimes surmount traditional barriers with an ease not previously available. Economies of scale, for instance, do not apply in quite the same way.

Much of the deregulation of the 1980s and 1990s was designed by free-market-oriented governments to lower barriers to entry in industries ranging from airlines to stockbroking. But it had only limited success. A 1996 study of the airline industry by the US government's General Accounting Office, for example, illustrated the complex way in which barriers to entry become tightly woven into the fabric of an industry. The study found that three things – namely, limits on take-off and landing slots at certain major airports; the existence of long-term leases giving airlines the exclusive use of airport gates; and rules prohibiting flights of less than a certain distance – continually impeded new airlines' access to airports.

Despite this, in recent years a number of low-cost carriers have managed to circumvent these barriers to some extent by using secondary airports and by marketing tickets via the internet.

Further reading

Geroski, P., *Market Dynamics and Entry*, Blackwell, 1991

Geroski, P., Gilbert, R. and Jacquemin, A. (eds), *Barriers to Entry and Strategic Competition*, Harwood Academic Publishers, 1990

Karakaya, F. and Stahl, M.J., *Entry Barriers and Market Entry Decisions*, Quorum Books, 1991

Yip, George, *Barriers to Entry: A Corporate Strategy Perspective*, Lexington Books, 1982

Benchmarking

Benchmarking is a way of determining how well a business unit or organisation is performing by comparing it with other units elsewhere. It sets a business's measures of its own performance in a broad context and gives it an idea of what is "best practice". In *The Benchmarking Book*, Michael Spendolini defined benchmarking as a "continuous systematic process for evaluating the products, services or work processes of organisations that are recognised as representing the best practices for the purposes of organisational improvement".

Historically, measures of corporate performance have been compared with previous measures from the same organisation at different times. Although this gives a good indication of the rate of improvement within the organisation, it gives no indication of where the performance stands in absolute terms. The organisation could be getting better and better; but if its competitors are improving even more, then better and better is not enough.

In their book *Benchmarking: A Tool for Continuous Improvement*, C.J. McNair and H.J. Liebfried describe four different types of benchmarking:

- **Internal benchmarking.** This is a bit like the process of quality management, an internal checking of the organisation's standards to see if there is further potential to cut waste and improve efficiency.
- **Competitive benchmarking.** This is the comparison of one company's standards with those of another (rival) company.
- **Industry benchmarking.** Here the comparison is between a company's standards and those of the industry to which it belongs.
- **Best-in-class benchmarking.** This is a comparison of a company's level of achievement with the best anywhere in the world, regardless of industry or national market. The Japanese have a word for it, *dantotsu*, which means "being the best of the best".

Benchmarking is a fluid concept which recognises that the relative importance of different processes changes over time as a business changes. For example, a retailer that shifts from selling through stores to selling over the internet suddenly becomes less concerned about customer parking facilities and more concerned about the performance of its fleet of delivery vans. The importance of benchmarking these respective activities changes similarly.

The process of benchmarking often requires that companies put their measures into some sort of public arena where others can use them for comparison. This is usually carried out by a third party, who puts the data in order and then discloses it in a way that does not reveal the identity of any individual data provider. Firms can, of course, recognise their own data and judge where they stand in the pecking order.

The enthusiasm for benchmarking (it topped Bain & Company's list of popular management tools in both 2008 and 2010) has been fuelled by two things in particular:

- The Japanese development of total quality management (see page 191) and the idea of *kaizen* (see page 109), of continuous improvement. This was a system built on careful measurement of industrial activities, followed by close monitoring of those measures. It not only forced managers to make such measurements; it made their competitors do so too.
- The work of Michael Porter (see page 295) on competitive advantage. This forced firms to think more about their competitors and where they stood in relation to them rather than where they stood merely in terms of their own history.

Further reading

Boxwell, R.J., *Benchmarking for Competitive Advantage*, McGraw-Hill, 1994

Camp, R.C., *Benchmarking: The Search for Industry Best Practices that Lead to Superior Performance*, Quality Resources, 1989; Productivity Press, 2006

Karlof, B., *The Benchmarking Management Guide*, Productivity Press, 1993

McNair, C.J. and Liebfried, K.H.J., *Benchmarking: A Tool for Continuous Improvement*, HarperBusiness, 1992

Brainstorming

Brainstorming is a rather dramatic name for a semi-structured business meeting whose chief purpose is to come up with new ideas for business improvement. It is loosely based on belief in a sort of psychological synergy: that a creative meeting can throw out something more than the sum of its parts, more than the sum of the ideas in the participants' heads.

To be most effective, brainstorming sessions require a trained facilitator and some basic ground rules. Without a facilitator, sessions can degenerate into an effort to find as many negative things as possible to say about each new idea. Ultimately, the idea is cast aside and the group prepares to give the same treatment to the next one.

Formalised brainstorming is based on three basic rules:

- Participants should be encouraged to come up with as many ideas as possible, however wild they are.
- No judgment should be passed on any idea until the end of the session.
- Participants should be encouraged to build on each other's ideas, putting together unlikely combinations and taking each one in unlikely directions.

For those wishing to try out brainstorming, there are a number of helpful hints.

- Identify a precise topic to be discussed.
- If there are more than ten participants split the discussion into smaller groups.
- Make each group choose a secretary to record the ideas that are thrown up.
- Explain clearly the three basic rules above.
- Storm away with ideas, with the secretary listing all those that come up.
- Establish criteria for selecting the best ideas, then evaluate each idea against these criteria.
- Outline the steps needed to implement these best ideas.

Brainstorming is said to have been popularised as a management technique in the early 1940s by Alex Osborn, an American advertising executive. He defined brainstorming as "a conference technique by which a group attempts to find a solution for a specific problem by amassing all the ideas spontaneously thought of by its members". He had four rules: no criticism of ideas; go for a large number of ideas; build on each other's ideas; encourage wild and exaggerated ideas.

At one time the technique was widely used within corporations to help come up with new product ideas or to devise radically new manufacturing processes. The results of brainstorming, however, have frequently been deemed inadequate. Totally unstructured sessions rarely work. But even when basic rules are followed, the results are often disappointing.

Some research suggests that individuals working on their own generally come up with more original and higher-quality ideas. Groups come up with more ideas as such, even though they may be of inferior quality. Groups also go on being productive for much longer; individuals on their own tire easily and dry up. Open-ended group discussions have been found to be particularly helpful in evaluating ideas rather than in generating them. Group feedback seems to be especially useful in this process.

Further reading

De Bono, E., *Serious Creativity: Using the Power of Lateral Thinking to Create New Ideas*, HarperBusiness, New York, 1992; HarperCollins, London, 1992

Goman, C.K., *Creative Thinking in Business*, Kogan Page, 1989

Michalko, M., *Thinkertoys: A Handbook of Creative-Thinking Techniques*, 2nd edn, Ten Speed Press, 2006

Miller, B.C., *Quick Brainstorming Activities for Busy Managers*, AMACOM, 2012

Branding

Originally, branding was the placing on animals (usually by burning) of an identifying mark. In a business context, branding refers to the imposing of a distinctive identity, a brand, on goods and services. Philip Kotler (see page 261), author of *Marketing Management*, a standard textbook, defines a brand as: "A name, term, symbol or design (or a combination of them) which is intended to signify the goods or services of one seller or group of sellers and to differentiate them from those of the competitors."

Firms have recognised the power of brands for many years. One of the most fertile periods for their creation was the 1880s and 1890s, when the names of both Kodak and Kellogg first appeared in shop windows. Their inventors stumbled across a fact not fully recognised until much later: that two of the most powerful elements in a product's name are the guttural sound (and especially the "k" sound) and alliteration (repetition of the same consonant). Think of Pepsi and Coke; Marmite and Google.

Firms with international ambitions must be careful when inventing new brand names. Brillo, a well-known British scouring pad, has a hard time in Italy because Brillo, in Italian, means sozzled. When Chrysler introduced its Nova car into Mexico it forgot that in Spanish *no va* means "it doesn't go".

Of the ten most valuable brands in the world in 2011 no fewer than nine were American. The one exception was China Mobile (in ninth place). There were no European or Japanese names on the list. Nokia, which had been fifth in 2007, was 85th in 2011.

Branding bestows a number of benefits on goods and services:

- **It reassures consumers about the quality of the product.** This allows the producer to charge a premium over and above the value of the basic benefits provided by the underlying product.

  The ability of powerful brands to grab a bigger share of consumers' wallets than lesser-known competing products can give them great value. When Philip Morris bought Kraft, a food company, in 1988 it paid four times the value of Kraft's tangible assets. Most of the 75% spent on intangible assets represented the value of Kraft's powerful brands. When Nestlé bought Rowntree it paid more than five times the book value of Rowntree's assets. Most of that extra (almost £2 billion) was the cost of Rowntree's well-known names, such as Polo, Kit Kat and After Eight.

The confidence that consumers gain from a well-known brand is particularly useful when they do not have enough information to make wise choices about goods and services. Thus Western travellers seek out global brand names when buying drinks and cigarettes, for example, in far-flung corners of the earth. And online shoppers, uncomfortable with the multitude of choices presented to them, often revert to familiar brands.

◼ **It provides an enduring platform on which to develop other businesses.** Brands have considerable staying power. New products can be launched under the same umbrella brand while old ones are gradually withdrawn from the market.

When a branded product becomes number one in its market category it is called a brand leader. One American study found that brand leaders achieve dramatically higher returns on investment than do secondary brands.

When companies have a valuable brand they often attempt to stretch it by attaching it to other products and services. One example is the Mars chocolate confectionery brand, which has been successfully transferred to an ice-cream product. There is a theory, however, that brands can be stretched too far. The expectations that are built up in consumers by one branded product have to be delivered continually by all products bearing the same brand.

Further reading

Adamson, A.P. and Sorrell, M., *BrandSimple: How the Best Brands Keep It Simple and Succeed*, Palgrave Macmillan, 2007

Kotler, P., *Marketing Management: Analysis, Planning, Implementation and Control*, Prentice Hall, 1967; 12th edn, 2006

Lindstrom, M., *Brandwashed: Tricks Companies Use to Manipulate our Minds and Persuade Us to Buy*, Crown Business, 2011

Lodish, L.M. and Mela, C.F., "If Brands are Built over Years, Why are They Managed over Quarters?", *Harvard Business Review*, July–August 2007

Ries, L. and Ries, A., *The 22 Immutable Laws of Branding*, HarperCollins, 1998; Collins, 2002

Business modelling

The use of computer models to simulate different business activities and to assist in decision-making processes is almost as old as IBM itself. Most business modelling nowadays is based on widely available software that allows non-technical general managers to try out different options on (electronic) paper before deciding which one to follow. A retailer, for instance, might have a model to help it choose where to locate a new store. Based on data about the size of the catchment area, the local road networks, parking facilities, demographics and local competitors, the model would come up with the optimal location.

Consultants KPMG say that "to take major [business] decisions without first testing their consequences in a safe environment can be likened to training an airline pilot by having him fly a 747 without first having spent months in the simulator".

Business modelling also helps to democratise decision-making when it is diffused throughout the organisation. *In Reengineering the Corporation*, Michael Hammer (see page 247) wrote:

> When accessible data is combined with easy-to-use analysis
> and modelling tools, frontline workers – when properly trained
> – suddenly have sophisticated decision-making capabilities.
> Decisions can be made more quickly and problems resolved as
> soon as they crop up.

Coincidentally, large airlines are among the biggest users of sophisticated business models. They have to juggle a multitude of different fare structures and handle tricky things like stand-by tickets. Modelling such variables saves them millions of dollars a year.

Other common uses of business modelling include the following:

- Financial planning, with the help of spreadsheets. This quantifies the impact of a business decision on the balance sheet and the income statement.
- Forecasting. Analysing historical data and using it to predict future trends.
- Mapping processes in a visual representation of the resources

required for a task and the steps to be taken to perform it.

- Data mining. Analysing vast quantities of data in order to dig out unpredictable relationships between variables.
- "Monte Carlo" simulation. Putting in random data to measure the impact of uncertainty on the outcome of a project.

The idea of using computer models to support decision-making was given a boost by a popular book published in 1990. *The Fifth Discipline*, written by MIT academic Peter Senge (see page 303), argued that the ability to use models to experiment with corporate structure and behaviour would be a key skill in the future. Senge described computer simulation as "a tool for creating".

Senge also promoted the idea of using modelling to create what he called "Microworlds". These are simplified simulation models packaged as management games. They allow managers to "play" with an issue in safety rather than playing with it first in the real world.

Further reading

Senge, P.M., *The Fifth Discipline: The Art and Practice of the Learning Organization*, Currency/Doubleday, New York, 1990; 2nd revised edn, Random House Business Books, 2006

Tennent, J. and Friend, G., *The Economist Guide to Business Modelling*, 3rd edn, Profile Books, 2011

Business planning

This is the process of putting in writing the hoped-for future financial performance of a new business. It is not just a matter of qualitative fantasising, of asserting "we intend to be innovative market leaders at the forefront of internet technology", for example. It is also a matter of quantitative fantasising, "and we will make a loss of $1.64m in year one, and a profit of $325,000 in year two". The launching of a business idea requires its patron to attribute precise financial numbers to the future cash flow of the business, in the shape of a business plan – numbers, needless to say, that rarely bear any relationship to subsequent reality.

What is the point? There are usually two:

- To obtain funds. Every investor and/or venture capitalist wants to read a business plan to help them assess the likely risk and reward of the project. For the infant business seeking finance, the presentation of the plan is a bit like an actor's audition. There are notoriously bad ones, and a good one is no guarantee of a part. But with a bad one, you are almost sure never to see the footlights.
- To help the business's promoters focus on some fundamental operational issues. For example, what is the likely size of their market? Who is likely to be their main competitor? To some extent the setting of operational targets is self-fulfilling. If the venture is successful, the targets set are the targets reached. They may not be the optimal performance of the organisation, of course, merely a satisfactory one.

Business plans are required not only by new business ventures but also by old businesses trying something new. Proposed mergers and acquisitions require a detailed plan of the future of the merged entity; a venture into a new market requires a business plan; and so too does the winding down or the turning round of an old and tired business.

In an influential article in *Harvard Business Review*, William Sahlman, a professor of business administration, suggested that business plans "waste too much ink on numbers and devote too little to the information that really matters to intelligent investors". What really matters, suggested Sahlman, are four factors that are "critical to every new venture":

- the people;
- the opportunity;
- the context;
- the risk and reward.

A great business plan, Sahlman suggested, is one that focuses on asking the right questions about these four things. It is not easy to compose, however, because "most entrepreneurs are wild-eyed optimists". In any case, as he says, "The market is as fickle as it is unpredictable. Who would have guessed that plug-in room deodorisers would sell?"

Throughout much of the 20th century a business plan was indispensable for any new business venture. But the enthusiasm in the 1990s for downsizing (see page 67) hit corporate planning departments hard. Many of them had made themselves easy targets by concentrating too much on the financial minutiae of future plans rather than looking at the broader picture. The ethos of the internet economy also discouraged planning. With change happening so fast, the argument went, why be prepared when nobody knew what to be prepared for.

Further reading

Cross, W. and Richey, A.M., *The Prentice Hall Encyclopaedia of Model Business Plans*, Prentice Hall, 1998

Friend, G. and Zehle, S., *The Economist Guide to Business Planning*, Profile Books, 2004

Kahneman, D. *et al.*, "Before You Make That Big Decision ...", *Harvard Business Review*, June 2011

Sahlman, W.A., "How to Write a Great Business Plan", *Harvard Business Review*, July–August 1997

Business process re-engineering

The idea of re-engineering was first propounded in an article in *Harvard Business Review* in July–August 1990 by Michael Hammer, then a professor of computer science at MIT (see page 247). The method was popularly referred to as business process re-engineering (BPR), and was based on an examination of the way information technology was affecting business processes.

Subsequently, Michael Porter (see page 295) said:

> *The literature on re-engineering employs the term processes. Sometimes it is a synonym for activities. Sometimes it refers to activities or sets of activities that cut across organisational units. In any case, however, the essential notion is the same – both strategic and operational issues are best understood at the activity level.*

BPR promised a novel approach to corporate change, and was described by its inventors as a "fundamental rethinking and radical redesign of business processes to achieve dramatic improvements in critical measures of performance such as cost, quality, service and speed".

The technique involved analysing a company's central processes and reassembling them in a more efficient fashion and in a way that rode roughshod over long-established (but frequently irrelevant) functional distinctions. Functional silos were often protective of information, for instance, and of their own position in the scheme of things. At best, this was inefficient. Slicing the silos into their different processes and reassembling them in a less vertical fashion exposed excess fat and forced corporations to look at new ways to streamline themselves.

BPR's originators, Hammer and James Champy, maintained that re-engineering had a wider significance than mere processes. It applied to all parts of an organisation, and it had a lofty purpose. "I think that this is the work of angels," said Hammer in one of his more fanciful moments. "In a world where so many people are so deprived, it's a sin to be so inefficient."

Many commentators, however, saw re-engineering as a return to the mechanistic ideas of Frederick Taylor (see page 309, and Scientific management, page 159). Others saw it as a shallow intellectual justification for downsizing (see page 67), a process of slimming down that was being forced on many corporations by developments in IT.

One of the faults of the idea, which the creators themselves acknowledged, was that re-engineering became something that managers were only too happy to impose on others but not on themselves. Champy's follow-up book was pointedly called *Reengineering Management*. "If their jobs and styles are left largely intact, managers will eventually undermine the very structure of their rebuilt enterprises," he wrote with considerable foresight in 1994.

BPR followed a favoured route for popular management ideas: from a university academic's research, via a management consultancy's marketing (Champy was the boss of CSC, a management consulting firm) and a best-selling book, into (briefly) a perceived panacea for all companies' ills. It was helped by the fact that the book's authors (Hammer in particular) were eminently quotable.

BPR was implemented with considerable success by some high-profile organisations. For instance, Hallmark, a card company, completely re-engineered its new-product process; and Kodak's re-engineering of its black-and-white film manufacturing process cut the firm's response time to new orders in half. That was no guarantee of long-term success, however. In January 2012, Kodak filed for Chapter 11 bankruptcy protection from its creditors. The idea was given a boost by the development of ERP (see Enterprise resource planning, page 75). ERP systems enabled a firm's different operations to talk to each other electronically. At last the left hand of the organisation knew what the right hand was up to.

Further reading

Davenport, T., *Process Innovation: Reengineering Work Through Information Technology*, Harvard Business School Press, 1993

Hammer, M. and Champy, J., *Reengineering the Corporation: A Manifesto for Business Revolution*, HarperBusiness, New York 1993; revised updated edn, HarperCollins, 2004

Improving Business Processes, Harvard Business School Press, 2010

Cannibalisation

If a firm introduces a new product or service into a market where there is little scope for further growth, that product or service will either eat into the share of the market's existing products, or swiftly disappear from sight. If some of the existing products are manufactured by the firm that is introducing the new product, the newcomers will cannibalise the old ones; that is, they will eat into the market share of their own kind. For example, it has been estimated that two-thirds of the sales of Gillette's Sensor razor came from consumers who would otherwise have been customers for the company's other razors. Each new blade is cut-throat competition for its predecessors.

There are sound reasons for firms to do such a seemingly stupid thing. In the first place, they may need to keep ahead of the competition. In the chocolate-bar market in the UK, for instance, the decline in Kit Kat's share was arrested by the launch of a new, more chunky bar, which undoubtedly cannibalised the market for the original. Its appeal was to all those people who buy chocolate bars, which includes those who bought the old Kit Kat.

Firms may also choose to cannibalise their own products by producing marginally improved products. The idea is to persuade existing customers to purchase an upgraded version. This is common in the PC market, for example, where Intel's newest, most powerful processor cannibalises the last generation of Intel processors, but in the interests of arresting decline in the total market.

Economists sometimes distinguish between planned and unplanned cannibalisation. Planned cannibalisation is an anticipated loss in sales of an existing product as a result of the introduction of a new product in the same line. In the unplanned version, the loss of sales is unexpected.

Historically, firms have found it hard to cannibalise their own products. They have tried to hang on to declining market shares for too long before deciding to introduce new products that compete with their own. Kodak, for example, refused for years to introduce the 35mm camera for fear of cannibalising its older products. Likewise, years later, it was late to embrace the market for digital imagery. Bausch & Lomb invented the soft contact lens but failed to launch it because the firm did not want to lose the lucrative business of selling the drops that only hard lenses require.

As a result, Johnson & Johnson swept into soft lenses, and the market for hard lenses (and their drops) disappeared.

The internet presented many firms with difficult decisions about cannibalisation. Travel agents, for instance, had to decide whether to offer online services at a fraction of the cost of their traditional branch-based business in order to compete with airlines and other firms that were selling to customers via direct online links. Publishers had to decide how much material (and at what price) to make available electronically.

Deregulation also presents companies with difficult dilemmas about cannibalising products and services that have thrived for years in protected markets. In the airline business, for example, traditional national carriers faced with feisty, low-cost new entrants had to decide whether to join them (and thus compete with themselves) or to remain aloof. British Airways introduced its own low-cost airline called Go (which it sold in 2002). Go competed not only with the new entrants but also (in a carefully controlled way) with BA itself.

Further reading

Kerin, R. and Peterson, R., *Strategic Marketing Problems: Cases & Comments*, 1st edn, Allyn and Bacon, 1978; 10th edn, Pearson Education International, 2004

McGrath, M., *Product Strategy for High-Technology Companies*, 1st edn, Irwin Professional Publishing, 1995, 2nd edn, McGraw-Hill, 2000

Champion

To champion something is to support it, to defend it. We champion the cause of liberty. Hugh Grant, an actor, champions the rights of individuals to privacy from the media.

The word was given a management twist in the late 20th century when companies came to believe that a new project, to gain success, needed a champion, a specific individual within the organisation who would defend it and nurture it through its early days. Without such a person, it was suggested, new projects would wither from lack of devotion.

Donald Schon, a consultant before he became a professor at the Massachusetts Institute of Technology (MIT), once wrote:

> The new idea either finds a champion or dies ... No ordinary
> involvement with a new idea provides the energy required
> to cope with the indifference and resistance that major
> technological change provokes ... Champions of new inventions
> display persistence and courage of heroic quality.

Championing is often applied to people as well: bright, young, talented people within an organisation are deemed to need a champion, someone higher up the corporate ladder who will support them and fight their corner. Many chief executives have risen to the top largely because they have been nurtured through their careers by people in high places.

In their book *In Search of Excellence*, Tom Peters (see page 293) and Robert Waterman argued that successfully innovative companies revolve around "fired-up champions". 3M, the American inventor of the Post-It note, is quoted as saying: "We expect our champions to be irrational."

Champions are not easy people to work and live with. James Brian Quinn, a professor at Tuck School of Business at Dartmouth, spelt out a paradox associated with the type:

> The champion is obnoxious, impatient, egotistic, and perhaps a
> bit irrational in organisational terms. As a consequence, he is not
> hired. If hired, he is not promoted or rewarded. He is regarded as
> not a serious person, as embarrassing or disruptive.

Peters and Waterman maintained that companies need to set up special systems to support and encourage these disruptive people if they are to benefit from their extreme persistence with new ideas (which need not necessarily be their own).

History is spattered with innovations that would never have been successful if they had not been stubbornly supported by one (often rather cranky) individual. Moreover, such support often needs to be for the long term. The Economist once wrote, "All big innovations need to be championed and nurtured for long periods, sometimes up to 25 years."

A widely reported case of championing was that of Spence Silver, an employee of 3M who became unnaturally fond of a glue that was not very good at sticking. "I was just absolutely convinced that it had some potential," Silver is reported as saying. But for many years he was unable to persuade anybody within the organisation to agree with him. He persisted, however, in championing his pet product. As he put it:

> You have to be a zealot at times in order to keep interest alive, because it will die off. It seems like the pattern always goes like this. In the fat times, these groups appear and do a lot of interesting research. And then the lean times come just about at the point when you've developed your first goody, your gizmo. And then you've got to go out and try to sell it. Well, everybody in the division is so busy that they don't want to touch it. They don't have time to look at new product ideas with no end-product already in mind.

Silver's persistence with his "glue that doesn't glue" eventually led to the invention of the Post-It note. The rest, as they say, is history.

Further reading

Nayak, P. Ranganath and Ketteringham, J.M., Breakthroughs!, Mercury, Didcot, 1993; Pfeiffer & Co, San Diego, 1994

Peters, T.J. and Waterman, R.H., In Search of Excellence: Lessons from America's Best-run Companies, Harper & Row, New York, 1982; Profile Books, London, 2004

Change management

Businesses are torn between a desire to define for all time their organisation's structure and strategy, and a recognition that their world is in a constant state of flux. For the larger part of the 20th century they were more focused on the static elements of this dichotomy. But in recent years changes have become more frequent and more dramatic, so much so that a whole branch of management is now devoted to the subject of change itself.

In a classic analysis of the dilemma, Henry Mintzberg (see page 275), a Canadian business academic, described how a student asked him whether he "was intending to play jigsaw puzzle or Lego" with the elements of structure and power that he described in his books and that he put together to make a number of configurations of different organisations. Mintzberg wrote:

> In other words, did I mean all these elements of organisations to fit together in set ways – to create known images [the static state] – or were they to be used creatively to build new ones [the dynamic state]? I had to answer that I had been promoting jigsaw puzzles, even if I was suggesting that the pieces could be combined into several images instead of the usual one. But I immediately began to think about playing organisational Lego. Configuration is a nice thing when you can have it. Unfortunately, some organisations all of the time, and all organisations some of the time, cannot.

Lego stands you in better stead in an ever-changing world.

Rosabeth Moss Kanter (see page 257) is probably best known for her work on change management. Her book *The Change Masters* was labelled as "the thinking man's *In Search of Excellence*", the more popular title by Peters and Waterman that came out a year earlier. Charles Handy (see page 249), another business writer who focused closely on change management, identified "discontinuous change" as the only constant characteristic in today's workplace.

This close examination of the nature of change and the search for a suitable analogy had its critics. In *Beyond the Hype*, Robert Eccles and

Nitin Nohria said that "the primary concern of managers ... should be mobilising action among individuals, rather than endless quibbling about the way the world really is". The philosophical nature of change, they felt, was being discussed more than the question of how to manage businesses and the people in them.

Much of the recent interest in change has focused on Moore's law, the idea that change in IT is exponential, not linear. This has led futurists to predict a time in the not-too-distant future when artificial (non-human) intelligences design a next generation of even more powerful "minds". Will businesses then be run on autopilot?

Further reading

Carr, D.K., Hard, K.J. and Trahant, W.J., *Managing the Change Process: A Field Book for Change Agents, Consultants, Team Leaders, and Reengineering Managers*, McGraw-Hill, 1996

Drucker, P., *Managing in a Time of Great Change*, Butterworth-Heinemann, 1997

Eccles, R. and Nohria, N., *Beyond the Hype: Rediscovering the Essence of Management*, Harvard Business School Press, 1992

Kanter, R.M., *The Change Masters*, Simon & Schuster, 1983

Mintzberg, H., *Mintzberg on management: Inside our Strange World of Organizations*, Free Press, 1989

HBR's 10 Must Reads on Change, Harvard Business Review Press, 2011

Cherry-picking

The idea of cherry-picking applies in a number of business contexts. It refers, for example, to customers who ignore products that are bundled together by a manufacturer (who in the process may disguise cross-subsidies between high-margin and low-margin components of the bundle). Such customers prefer to bundle their products together for themselves, selecting the best value (that is, cherry-picking) from each category of component.

An obvious example is the purchase of music systems. Manufacturers sell music sets, made up of an amplifier, a tuner, an iPod docking station, a CD player and speakers. But many music enthusiasts choose to assemble their own sets, buying their amplifier, CD player, speakers and so on, each from a different producer. Manufacturers try to discourage this by making the price of the complete set competitive. But earnest cherry-pickers can usually find discounted components that enable them to assemble something cheaper.

The term cherry-picking is also applied to the behaviour of new entrants into old industries, firms which try to choose their customers carefully. By calculating which consumers are profitable (and appealing to them while ignoring those who are not) such a firm can sometimes rapidly gain market share. In some cases, cherry-pickers are successful only because traditional firms in the industry do not actually know who their profitable customers are.

Service industries are particularly vulnerable. It is more difficult for them to measure the profitability of individual customers and customer segments. So they are never quite sure which they want to keep and which they want to get rid of. Successful cherry-pickers leave an industry's incumbents with the least profitable customers. They also push up the price to those consumers who are not attractive to them. In car insurance, for example, cherry-picking in the UK pushed up the price prohibitively for young male drivers, the highest-risk group.

A bunch of new airlines set about cherry-picking when deregulation of the skies in Europe and the United States allowed them into the market. Within limits, they were able to choose which routes to operate on. They were unencumbered with the obligations that the traditional national carriers had had to bear in the interests of government policies on transport and/or regional development.

In banking and insurance, cherry-picking newcomers were able to undermine the business of old-timers in just a few years at the end of the 20th century. Firms such as Direct Line, a British telesales insurance business, rapidly won market share by focusing on a narrow (profitable) segment of the market and avoiding costly traditional distribution channels.

The internet made cherry-picking easier in two respects:

- by reducing the cost of entry into particular industries it has made it easier for new entrants to pick at the incumbent's cherries;
- by making it easier for customers to shop around it has helped them to bundle their own products and services – be they music systems or insurance policies.

The success of cherry-picking emphasises something known as the survivorship bias: the tendency of business analysts to judge the past by the record of relatively long-term survivors, ignoring those who drowned or came and went in the meantime.

Further reading

Goetzmann, W. and Jorian, P., "History as written by the winners", *Forbes*, June 16th 1997

Clustering

Clustering is a phenomenon whereby firms from the same industry gather together in close proximity. It is particularly evident in industries like banking. Banking centres in cities such as London and New York have thrived for centuries. Hundreds of banks cluster there, close together and within easy walking distance of each other. This makes it easier for customers to choose between them, and might be thought to act against each individual bank's best interests.

Economists explain clustering as a means for small companies to enjoy some of the economies of scale (see page 71) usually reserved for large ones. An isolated greenfield site in a depressed region where government grants are plentiful may bring a young company immediate benefits. But in the longer term the company may be better off squeezing itself onto an expensive piece of urban real estate in close proximity to a significant number of its competitors.

By sticking together, firms are able to benefit from such things as the neighbourhood's pool of expertise and skilled workers; its easy access to component suppliers (Toyota's suppliers generally cluster round the mother company's factories, wherever they may be); and its information channels (both formal ones like trade magazines and informal ones like everyday gossip in neighbourhood bars). In early industrialised England clusters were common. Staffordshire was the home of many potteries – so many that the region is still known today as "the Potteries". The town of Nottingham was home to many lace-makers, Luton to hatters, and so on.

Modern high-tech clusters often gather round prestigious universities on whose research they can piggyback. Silicon Valley is near Stanford University, for example, and similar high-tech clusters are gathered around MIT near Boston in the United States and around Cambridge University in the UK.

One of the most famous clusters is that of the Hollywood film industry. When the big movie studio system broke up in the 1930s it fractured into a large number of what were essentially small specialist firms and freelancers. Clustering around Hollywood allows each of these small units to benefit as if it had the scale of an old movie studio, but without the rigidities of the studios' wage hierarchy and unionised labour.

In some cases, the ancillary services that grew up to service industrial clusters have remained in position and developed into vibrant new industries long after their original client industry has faded. Near Birmingham in the UK, for instance, the cluster of car-industry service firms that grew up when that city was a force in the industry has become an important element in the development of Formula One and other specialist vehicle businesses.

Clustering is not a phenomenon whose time has passed. Look at California's Silicon Valley. New IT and internet firms continue to gather there in spite of the high prices of local property and the danger of earthquakes. Ironically, these firms find that much of the most valuable information that they obtain comes not electronically but from face-to-face meetings.

Michael Porter (see page 295), a professor at Harvard Business School, has looked at this seemingly paradoxical revival of industrial clusters. In theory, he says, location should no longer be a source of competitive advantage in an era of global competition, rapid transport and high-speed telecommunications. The world's increasingly global businesses should by now be above and beyond geography. Yet clearly they are not.

Porter gives several (non-silicon) examples, including the wine-growing industry in northern California and the flower-growing business in the Netherlands. The Netherlands would not be the natural first choice for anyone starting a flower-growing business today were it not for the fact that the business is already there. This is a huge competitive advantage for a new entrant, who can benefit from such things as the sophisticated Dutch flower auctions, the flower-growers' associations and the country's advanced research centres.

Further reading

Engel, J. and del-Palacio, I., "Global Clusters of Innovation: the Case of Israel and Silicon Valley", *California Management Review*, Winter 2011

Porter, M., "Clusters and the New Economics of Competition", *Harvard Business Review*, November–December 1998

Maggioni, M., *Clustering Dynamics and the Location of High-Tech Firms*, University of Warwick, 1999; Physica-Verlag, 2002

Competitive advantage

Competitive Advantage is the title of a book by Michael Porter (see page 295) which became a bible of business thinkers in the late 1980s. With its echo of the ideas of comparative advantage expounded by David Ricardo, an influential 19th-century economist, it provided managers with a framework for strategic thinking about how to beat their rivals.

Porter argued that:

> Competitive advantage is a function of either providing comparable buyer value more efficiently than competitors (low cost), or performing activities at comparable cost but in unique ways that create more buyer value than competitors and, hence, command a premium price (differentiation).

You win either by being cheaper or by being different (which means being perceived by the customer as better or more relevant). There are no other ways.

Few management ideas have been so clear or seemed so intuitively right. Although there were business and management books that sold more copies in the last two decades of the 20th century, none was as influential as Competitive Advantage.

Behind Porter's idea lay a novel way of looking at the firm as a series of activities which link together into what he called "a value chain" (see page 199). For many, this was the theory's eureka moment. Writers since have developed further concepts based on the metaphor of a linked chain of activities or groups of activities (or their close equivalent, processes – see page 25). Each of the links in the chain adds value – that is, something that a customer is prepared to pay for. Even a company's support activities, such as its training and compensation systems, can be links in the chain and sources of competitive advantage in their own right.

Competitive Advantage was published in 1985 as "the essential companion" to Porter's earlier work, Competitive Strategy (1980). Competitive Strategy considered competition at the industry level, whereas Competitive Advantage looked at it from a firm's-eye view. "My quest", Porter said, "was to find a way to conceptualise the firm that would expose the underpinnings of competitive advantage and its sustainability."

Competitive Strategy (subtitled *Techniques for Analysing Industries and Competitors*) was an aide for ambitious young executives in the planning department to help them come up with grand ideas about what to do next. The book identified five factors that have an impact on a company's profitability: customers, suppliers, substitutes, potential entrants into the industry, and competitors. *Competitive Advantage*, however, was a book for chief executives. Its subtitle was *Creating and Sustaining Superior Performance*. Not only did it promise to enable senior managers to get ahead of the competition, it also promised to help them stay there.

The ideas in *Competitive Advantage* persuaded corporate chiefs to undertake more internal reflection. Previously their firm's identity had been largely described in terms of its relationship to others: its market share, for instance, or its relative size. Porter made corporate navel-gazing respectable. In practice, many firms had difficulty in identifying all the discrete Porterian activities in their organisation, even in cases where they were confident that they knew what they were looking for – and many were not.

In a later book, *The Competitive Advantage of Nations*, Porter looked at how the choice of location by an internationalising business might be a source of competitive advantage. From this issue of location he was drawn on to consider clustering (see page 35) and how business clusters are nowadays "critical to competition".

Further reading

Mintzberg, H., *Strategy Safari: The Complete Guide Through the Wilds of Strategic Management*, FT Press, 2008

Porter, M., "How Competitive Forces Shape Strategy", *Harvard Business Review*, March–April 1979

Porter, M., *Competitive Strategy: Techniques for Analyzing Industries and Competitors*, Free Press, New York, 1980; 2nd edn, Free Press, New York and London, 1998

Porter, M., *Competitive Advantage: Creating and Sustaining Superior Performance*, Collier Macmillan, London, 1985; new edn, Free Press, New York and London, 2004

Stalk, G., "Time: The Next Source of Competitive Advantage", *Harvard Business Review*, July–August 1988

Convergence

Convergence refers to the way in which the requirements to enter different industries have become so similar that firms can just as easily take part in one as in another. One area where convergence has been particularly evident is in banking and insurance. So common is the phenomenon of banks getting into the insurance business that the practice has been given a name: "bankassurance".

In utilities, too, convergence has become commonplace. In 1998, Accenture (then called Andersen Consulting) reckoned that 14 of the 30 largest gas and electricity firms in the United States had made convergence-related acquisitions or mergers in the two years from 1996 to 1998. Consumers found themselves buying their electricity from a gas company and their gas from an electricity company. In general, this had the effect of increasing competition.

As the utility industries (electricity, gas, telephone, water) were deregulated in the 1980s and 1990s, firms found that they required a hard core of competencies to run any one of them. These included sophisticated metering and billing services, a tightly controlled fleet of maintenance vans, and call centres that could deal with a high volume of orders and customer queries. This made firms that sold gas to retail customers feel competent to offer them electricity (bought wholesale from a deregulated manufacturer). Power generators went into electricity distribution, and water companies seemed to flow everywhere.

Convergence has been most controversial in the IT and media industries. The organisations that deliver information or entertainment content frequently feel that it must make sense for them to move into the industries which produce that content. Thus Japanese consumer electronics businesses Sony and Matsushita flirted for a while with Hollywood studios that made the movies they showed on their machines. AOL, an internet service provider, famously and disastrously bought Time Warner, a producer of movies and magazines.

There are two main reasons for convergence:

■ When companies find that their own markets are too crowded. IT and deregulation have enabled impudent new entrants to do things that would have been unthinkable 20 years ago. This has been particularly evident in banking. In a number of countries the degree of concentration in the industry was such that firms had few domestic takeover options that would not have incurred the wrath of the antitrust authorities. In effect, they were forced to vegetate or to do something different. For utilities providers, deregulation and privatisation allowed individual operators to entertain the idea of being a conglomerate.

◪ As firms become more customer-focused, they realise that customers who trust them to supply one type of product or service are inclined to trust them to supply many more. In utilities, for example, big customers in the United States increasingly turn to companies that can supply them with all their energy needs. Many of them prefer the convenience of a single supplier.

In the backlash against deregulation following the banking and economic crisis of 2008, convergence became less popular. In the banking industry in particular, governments became suspicious of do-it-all behemoths. The UK forced its banks to split their retail activity from their investment banking business – a split that had been enshrined in law in the United States before the 1980s, and in practice in the UK at the same time.

Further reading

Dollar, D. and Wolff, E.N., *Competitiveness, Convergence and International Specialisation*, MIT Press, 1993

Whitley, R. and Kristensen, P.H. (eds), *The Changing European Firm: Limits to Convergence*, Routledge, 1996

Core competence

The idea of core competence was introduced into management literature in 1990 by C.K. Prahalad (see page 297) and Gary Hamel (see page 245). The two business academics wrote:

> Core competencies are the collective learning in the organisation, especially how to co-ordinate diverse production skills and integrate multiple streams of technologies ... core competence is communication, involvement and a deep commitment to working across organisational boundaries ... core competence does not diminish with use. Unlike physical assets, which do deteriorate over time, competencies are enhanced as they are applied and shared.

Prahalad and Hamel went on to outline three tests to be applied in order to determine whether something is a core competence:

- First, a core competence provides potential access to a wide variety of markets.
- Second, a core competence makes a significant contribution to the perceived customer benefits of the end product.
- Third, a core competence is difficult for competitors to imitate because it is a complex harmonisation of individual technologies and production skills.

The two academics painted a picture of the corporation as a tree whose roots are its particular competencies. Out of these roots grow the organisation's "core products" which, in turn, nourish a number of separate business units. Lastly, out of these business units come "end products".

It was Prahalad and Hamel's contention that if a company could "maintain world manufacturing dominance in core products", it would "reserve the power to shape the evolution of end products". Many of the examples on which they based their theories were large, successful Japanese companies. Before the end of the century, however, the performance of many of these companies had become distinctly less exemplary.

The core competence idea was useful to managers not only for focusing them on the essentials, but also for identifying those things that were not "at the core". Why, management might ask, were these non-essential things being allowed to consume valuable resources?

Prahalad and Hamel succeeded in persuading managers to look at strategy as something fluid and imprecise. Their writing is spattered with references to things like "strategic intent", "strategy as stretch and leverage", "competitive space" and "expeditionary markets". It was a switch from the more modular approach of Michael Porter (see page 295) and of the tradition of scientific management (see page 159). Porter had turned strategic thinking back in the direction of Frederick Taylor (see page 309); Prahalad and Hamel changed that direction by several degrees.

The drive to identify core competencies moved in line with the growing popularity of outsourcing (see page 143). When companies were suddenly able to outsource almost any process that came under their corporate umbrella, they needed to know what lay in the hard core of activities that they were uniquely well qualified to carry out, the activities that it made no sense for them to hand over to a third party. In some cases the answer was very little.

As it has grown in popularity, the idea has spread from core competencies to core everything – core processes, core businesses – everything that constitutes the essence of what a company is and does. Management consultants encouraged companies to focus on their core as a source of untapped potential in a time of rapid change and unpredictability.

Chris Zook, a strategy consultant, has written a trilogy around the idea of getting more growth from core businesses. His second book, *Beyond the Core*, was subtitled *Expand Your Market Without Abandoning Your Roots*.

Further reading

Goddard, J., "The Architecture of Core Competence", *Business Strategy Review*, Vol. 1, 1997

Prahalad, C.K. and Hamel, G., "The Core Competence of the Corporation", *Harvard Business Review*, May–June 1990

Hamel, G. and Prahalad, C.K., *Competing for the Future*, Harvard Business School Press, 1994

Zook, C., *Beyond the Core: Expand Your Market Without Abandoning Your Roots*, Harvard Business School Press, 2004

Zook, C., "Finding Your Next Core Business", *Harvard Business Review*, April 2007

Corporate governance

The debate over how companies are best governed is at least as old as companies themselves. That there is no one best system of governing them is suggested by the fact that the world's greatest companies have grown up under a number of very different regimes. Consider only Toyota in Japan, Johnson & Johnson in the United States, Daimler-Benz in Germany and Marks & Spencer in the UK.

The differences between the regimes fall into four main categories:

1 **Accounting.** Drawing up a company's accounts and getting an outside auditor to verify them is essential. It enables investors to find out what managers are doing with their money. However, accounts prepared under different countries' rules can produce very different results. Using British or American rules (which might be expected to be reasonably similar) can make a difference of as much as 50% to a company's net profit. Even within a single country's set of rules there is plenty of room for interpretation (and exaggeration). Any one accountant is unlikely to come up with exactly the same figure for a company's profit as any other. So essential is auditing to the health of the capitalist system that there are (relatively) free-market economists who believe that this imprecision (and scope for private enterprise) argues for handing over the auditing function to government or, at least, to a government-supervised agency.

2 **Company boards.** The biggest distinction here is between Germany and the rest of the world. The German system has two boards – a supervisory board and a management board – their different roles explained largely by their names. Other countries have only one. But that one can still vary greatly in its composition and its powers. American boards are often stuffed with cronies of the CEO. French boards generally include someone who is or was a senior politician. German management boards, by law, must include workers' representatives.

3 **Company bosses.** "A fish", as the old proverb has it, "rots from the head." Good governance depends crucially on the attitude of the company's boss. "Manifestations of lax corporate governance, in my judgment, are largely a symptom of a failed CEO," said Alan Greenspan, when chairman of America's Federal Reserve Board. "Once you

as CEO go over the line, then people think it's okay to go over the line themselves," said Lawrence Weinbach, chairman of Unisys, a big American computer-software firm.

Different countries put different controls on CEOs. In the United States, they are given a free rein to run things much as they like. In the UK, public companies often separate the role of chairman and chief executive, giving (in theory) a heavy counterweight to the CEO's otherwise unbridled ambition. In Germany, CEOs are watched carefully by the supervisory board. In France, they tend to be watched by the government.

4 **The rewards.** In Europe and Japan, managers' rewards consist largely of salary and bonuses. Until recently, this was the case in America too. But then the idea arose that if managers were rewarded a bit like shareholders they would behave in ways that were more advantageous to those shareholders.

Giving senior managers shares and share options in their companies was the main way that this was achieved. But it has given rise to some gross excesses. The American top executive takes home about 350 times the pay of an average worker.

After the corruption at companies like WorldCom, Enron and Tyco, America tried to tighten up on governance with the introduction of the Sarbanes-Oxley Act, which imposed onerous new reporting requirements. But the jury is still out as to whether governance in the United States is improving. Are the accounts and the rewards more fair? Are bosses and boards better controlled? Sarbanes-Oxley failed to prevent the financial crisis of 2008.

Further reading

Handy, C., "What is a company for?", *Corporate Governance – an international review*, Vol. 1, No. 1, January 1993

Marks, R. and Minow, N., *Corporate Governance*, Wiley, 2011

OECD Principles of Corporate Governance, 2004

Pozen, R.C., "The Big Idea: The Case for Professional Boards", *Harvard Business Review*, December 2010

Tricker, B., *Corporate Governance*, OUP, 2009

Corporate social responsibility

The idea that corporations bear a responsibility that stretches beyond their shareholders is not new. Many companies in the 19th century built special housing for their employees in the belief that a well-housed employee was more productive than one living in a dump. In the early years of the 20th century, Theodore Roosevelt, then president of the United States, said:

> Corporations are indispensable instruments of our modern civilisation; but I believe that they should be so supervised and so regulated that they shall act for the interests of the community as a whole.

He introduced antitrust legislation and rules on health and safety, and on working hours.

In 1987, Adrian Cadbury, head of the eponymous chocolate firm, wrote in *Harvard Business Review*:

> The possibility that ethical and commercial considerations will conflict has always faced those who run companies. It is not a new problem. The difference now is that a more widespread and critical interest is being taken in our decisions and in the ethical judgments which lie behind them.

The debate then focused on how much of Roosevelt's supervision and regulation was needed to make sure that corporations act sufficiently in the interests of the wider community. Extreme free-marketers say all that is required to ensure the responsible behaviour of corporations is transparency about their affairs. Corporations will then behave responsibly towards the wider community without any coercion because it is in their own best interests. "Being good", said Anita Roddick, founder of an "ethical" cosmetics firm, The Body Shop, "is good business."

In the United States, the Better Business Bureau goes further and argues that unethical business is bad for business as a whole, not just for individual firms:

Unethical business practices create ill-will among customers and the community, not only toward a particular business firm, but toward business as a whole.

In recent years, the debate about corporate social responsibility (CSR) has focused on three main areas:

- **The environment.** This has stretched way beyond the simple demand that companies stop belching smoke out of factory chimneys to a demand that they control their appetite for natural resources – for bits of Brazilian rain forest, for example, or for the skins of rare animals. The organised hostility to such behaviour has forced companies to change. For example, suppliers frightened by the venom of the anti-fur lobby felt compelled to boast: "Make no mistake; all our furs are fake."
- **Exploitation.** The second strand is the exploitation of workers, especially of women in the developed world and of children in the developing world. There is a feeling that globalisation has increased the power of multinationals to exploit the poor and underpaid, at the same time as it has weakened the influence of trade unions and other organisations designed to protect them.
- **Bribery and corruption.** The third strand focuses on corruption, in particular on the question of what constitutes a bribe (when does generous corporate hospitality step over the line?), and what protections should be given to whistleblowers (employees or other insiders who report corporate misdeeds). Here there is a strong cultural element to confuse the issue. What constitutes bribery in Western countries, for example, may not be considered such in regions such as the Middle East.

Further reading

Hertz, N., *The Silent Takeover: Global Capitalism and the Death of Democracy*, Free Press, 2001

Karnani, A., "CSR stuck in a logical trap", *California Management Review*, Winter 2011

Porter, M.E. and Kramer, M.R., "Strategy and Society: The Link Between Competitive Advantage and Corporate Social Responsibility", *Harvard Business Review*, December 2006

Cost-benefit analysis

Cost-benefit analysis is a weighing-scale approach to making business decisions: all the pluses (the benefits) are put on one side of the balance and all the minuses (the costs) are put on the other. Whichever weighs the heavier wins. A company considering whether to buy new computer systems, for example, might put on the cost side things like:

- the price of the computers themselves;
- the cost of hiring people to install them;
- the cost of training staff to use them.

On the benefits side would be things like:

- greater speed in carrying out the company's operations;
- greater efficiency in organising data;
- a boost to staff morale from using the latest equipment.

All of us do intuitive cost-benefit analyses every day of our lives, at such times as when we ask, "Shall I take a taxi to my next meeting or will I not save enough time for it to be worth my while?"

Benjamin Franklin, inventor of the lightning conductor and co-author of the American Declaration of Independence, was an early practitioner. In 1772, he wrote:

> When difficult cases occur, they are difficult chiefly because while we have them under consideration, all the reasons pro and con are not present to the mind at the same time ... To get over this, my way is to divide half a sheet of paper by a line into two columns; writing over the one "Pro", and the other "Con". Then ... I put down under the different heads short hints of the different motives ... for and against the measure ... I endeavour to estimate their respective weights; where I find one on each side that seem equal, I strike them both out. If I find a reason pro equal to two reasons con, I strike out three ... and thus proceeding I find at length where the balance lies ... And, though the weight of reasons cannot be taken with the precision of algebraic

quantities, yet when each is thus considered, separately and comparatively, and the whole lies before me, I think I can judge better, and am less liable to take a rash step.

Franklin hints that this comparatively simple idea has complicated ramifications. The pluses and minuses are not all immediately obvious, and many of them are not easily measurable in monetary terms. How, for instance, do you quantify an increase in staff morale?

Moreover, decisions cannot be made in isolation. There are usually several competing options: if you do not invest in a new plant in west Africa you can increase capacity at your existing plant, or you can take over a new business, or you can just leave the money in the bank. An analysis has to be done for each of the options.

In recent years, cost-benefit analysis has been widely used for analysing public-sector projects, as a tool to help answer questions such as: "Should we subsidise the sale of things like unleaded petrol and solar panels?" or "Shall we turn this busy urban street into a pedestrian zone?" In these examples, the social costs are the most important ones. What are the benefits to human health of reducing the levels of lead in the atmosphere? And can you measure this – in terms, for example, of the medical facilities that will not be required as a result of the better health of the population?

Further reading

Boardman, A., Greenberg, D., Vining, A. and Weimer, D., *Cost-Benefit Analysis: Concepts and Practice*, Prentice Hall, 4th edn, 2010

Layard, R. and Glaister, S., *Cost-Benefit Analysis*, 2nd edn, Cambridge University Press, 1994

Roy, A., *Cost-Benefit Analysis: Theory and Application*, Johns Hopkins University Press, 1984

Crisis management

The Institute for Crisis Management (ICM), an American consulting firm that specialises in developing communications strategies for crisis-struck businesses, defines a crisis as "a significant business disruption which stimulates extensive news media coverage. The resulting public scrutiny will affect the organisation's normal operations and also could have a political, legal, financial and governmental impact on its business".

The idea that businesses face moments of crisis that require special skills not called upon in the normal course of commercial events is widely accepted. Allied to this is the idea that there are people who are especially good at handling crises, and that there are crisis-management skills that can be learned. Special training courses on the subject can be found in many countries.

Crises are commonplace. The ICM puts their causes into four categories, with over 60% of them falling into the last category (management decisions):

- ◪ Acts of God (storms, earthquakes, etc).
- ◪ Mechanical problems (metal fatigue, etc).
- ◪ Human errors (the wrong valve opened, miscommunication, etc).
- ◪ Management decisions/indecision (underestimating a problem, assuming nobody will find out).

In recent years, certain industries have been more prone to crises than others. The petroleum, shipbuilding and automobile industries headed the ICM's list for 2010. But tobacco companies have been in an almost permanent state of crisis as the medical evidence against them has unfolded over the years.

One of the worst environmental accidents so far, at the Union Carbide factory in India where thousands of people were killed by a leak of poisonous gas in 1984, made companies everywhere think again about how to manage crises on such a scale. Then the Exxon Valdez oil spill of 1989, generally regarded as one of the worst-managed crises of all time, showed how it should not be done. It took two weeks for Lawrence Rawl, Exxon's chief executive at the time, to visit the scene and make any kind of substantive statement about the tragedy.

There are several elements to good crisis management:

- **Be well prepared in advance.** Potential members of a crisis management "team" should rehearse how they would manage the impact of an incident. It is a bit like learning the safety instructions on a plane before take-off: you hope you will never need them, but you know it would be unwise to miss the lesson. The team should include the chief executive and a representative of the press office. Thereafter, all external enquiries relating to a crisis should be answered by the team.
- **Move fast.** It is the first few hours that count, the period when news of the crisis first breaks. One of the most difficult things is handling the ambiguity in those first hours and days. There are sure to be gaps and inconsistencies in the information available.
- **Get outside help and advice.** Because a crisis is often brought on by employees of the firm, it can be difficult for insiders to view the issue objectively.
- **Be honest.** Accurate and correct information is crucial. Misinformation invariably backfires. But if a company has a naturally secretive culture this is a difficult policy to pursue.
- **Look to the long term.** Do not seek just to contain short-term losses. A contaminated product may require the withdrawal of massive stocks to reassure customers over the longer term that the product is safe for consumption.

Further reading

Dezenhall, E. and Weber, J., *Damage Control: Why Everything You Know About Crisis Management is Wrong*, Portfolio Hardcover, 2007

Regester, M. and Larkin, J., *Risk Issues and Crisis Management: A Casebook of Best Practice*, Kogan Page, 2002

Watkins, M.D. and Bazerman, M.H., "Predictable Surprises: The Disasters You Should Have Seen Coming", *Harvard Business Review*, March 2003

Cross-selling

Cross-selling is an idea that became popular in the late 20th century. *The Economist* described it as "the synergistic notion that buyers of one of a firm's services would become customers for another".

Cross-selling involves selling an additional product and service on top of the one that a customer has already agreed to buy (or has already bought). Its close cousin is up-selling, the idea of upgrading the product that a customer is purchasing to something with extra features or extra services (and extra profit to the seller). The internet and the popularity of online shopping have made cross-selling both more easy and more popular.

One website lays down ten rules for cross-selling and up-selling:

1 **Sell first; tell later.** Do not attempt to up-sell or cross-sell until you have fulfilled the first order. Trying to sell additional items too early can endanger the original sale.
2 **The rule of 25.** The value of any additional sale should not increase the overall order by more than 25%.
3 **Make a profit.** The extra items sold must make enough profit at least to cover the cost of the additional time spent in selling them. But this should not be calculated over a short time frame. Frederick Reichheld, a marketing expert at management consultants Bain & Company, said that most cross-selling fails because companies think only of the next bottom line. They cannot resist trying to sell the highest-margin product rather than the most appropriate one.
4 **Don't dump junk.** Resist the urge to use cross-selling to move unwanted stocks.
5 **Limit and relate.** Limit the add-on items to those that clearly relate to the original purchase. If a customer is buying a blazer from a catalogue, suggesting a shirt and tie makes sense; suggesting a garden hose does not. Much cross-selling of financial services fails because firms try to sell inappropriate products at inappropriate times.
6 **Familiarity breeds success.** The more familiar customers are with the add-on item, the more likely they are to buy it. Cross-selling is not the occasion to introduce a brand new product. Misdirected marketing at such times can turn clients away in droves.

7 **Plan, plan, plan and plan again.** Decide in advance, for instance, which products each additional item can be related to.

8 **Train to avoid pain.** Make sure that the salesman thoroughly understands the products or services being offered.

9 **Test with the best, then roll with the rest.** Test cross-selling first with the best salespeople. They have the drive and initiative to smooth out any of the kinks.

10 **E = MC².** A cross-selling effort (E) is directly dependent on how motivated (M) the salesmen are. Compensation (C) is always a critical factor in selling, as is another word beginning with C – control.

Cross-selling got a bad name when Cendant, a firm that Wall Street had labelled "the growth stock of the universe", fell to earth with a bang in 1998. An accounting fraud of "historic proportions" undermined a company that was built on the skilful cross-selling of a bundle of franchises. These ranged from the Avis car-rental business to the Ramada hotel chain.

Carlson Companies, a huge marketing and travel group, is more successful at cross-selling. When Carlson's marketing arm arranges an event for a client (to celebrate an anniversary, say), the group's Carlson Wagonlit travel agents make the necessary bookings for those invited to the event. Many of them then stay in Carlson's Radisson hotels; others take a trip on one of Carlson's luxury cruise ships or eat at one of its TGI Friday restaurants.

Such integrated cross-selling is rare. But it can be hugely profitable.

Further reading

Harding, F., *Cross-selling Success: A Rainmaker's Guide to Professional Account Development*, Adams Media Corporation, 2002

Ritter, D.S., *The Cross-selling Toolkit: The Complete Guide to Cross-Selling your Bank's Products & Services*, Probus, 1994

Culture

A company's culture is the environment created by the priorities it sets. Sometimes those priorities are made explicit: in a company's formal mission statement, for example, or in the structure of the organisation and the power given to different departments and functions. Sometimes they are implicit: what the *Financial Times* once called "the large number of unspoken assumptions and beliefs which managers in the organisation share about 'the way we do things around here'".

Tom Tierney, a consultant and author of *Aligning the Stars*, says: "A corporation's culture is what determines how people behave when they are not being watched."

Several things shape a corporation's culture:

- **Its employees' behaviour.** New recruits in any business usually do what they see, not what they are told. This can range from dress codes to such things as respect for technology and for standard working hours. It can also include the importance given to symbols; for example, to exclusive parking spaces, or to the way that senior managers are addressed.
- **The employee selection process.** The type of person recruited by an organisation reflects and reinforces its culture. Some companies recruit people of a particular kind because they believe that kind is best for the job. Charles Handy (see page 249) once recounted the unusual selection process of the Brooke family, who effectively ran Sarawak for many years. They wanted:
  > [Men who] had been educated at any of the public schools in the West Country – west, that is, of the town of Oxford. This was the background of the Brooke family and therefore provided a kind of tribal bonding. Secondly, they must be over six feet tall (the Dyaks, the native people, were small and would it was thought, be impressed by taller rulers).
- **The nature of the business.** Certain industries, such as the movies or banking, foster a particular culture. New high-technology firms also foster their own (often Silicon-Valley-influenced) culture. Computer maker Hewlett-Packard, for instance,

has for a long time been conscious of its culture (The HP Way) and has worked hard to maintain it over the years.

◪ **The external environment.** Companies need to take into account the culture of the society in which they are operating. American multinationals, for instance, cannot transpose the methods of Milwaukee straight into downtown Mombasa and expect to have a harmonious operation.

One of the few areas of management study that has been dominated by Europeans rather than Americans is cross-cultural management. Europeans have a natural advantage. Fons Trompenaars, an authority in the field, once wrote that his Dutch father and his French mother gave him "an understanding of the fact that if something works in one culture, there is little chance that it will work in another".

As long ago as 1527, the unusually perceptive Niccolo Machiavelli had something to say about mixing cultures:

> When a conqueror acquires states in a province which is different from his own in language, customs and institutions, great difficulties arise, and excellent fortune and great skill are needed to retain them.

Machiavelli hit upon two things that brought about the 1990s revival of interest in the subject:

◪ **Globalisation.** The princes of the business world have been spreading their affairs more widely than ever before.
◪ **Mergers and acquisitions.** The princes have also been devouring new businesses at a rate that made Machiavelli's masters, the Borgia family, look anorexic.

Further reading

Ghemawat, P., "The Cosmopolitan Corporation", *Harvard Business Review*, May 2011
Hofstede, G., *Cultures and Organisations: Software of the Mind*, Profile Books, London, 1994; 2nd edn, McGraw-Hill, New York, 2005
Schein, E., *The Corporate Culture Survival Guide*, Jossey-Bass, 1999
Trompenaars, F. and Hampden-Turner, C., *Riding the Waves of Culture: Understanding Cultural Diversity in Business*, Nicholas Brealey, London, 1993; 2nd edn, McGraw-Hill, 1998

Customer relationship management

Customer relationship management, commonly known as CRM, is a way of designing an organisation's structures and systems so that they are focused on providing consumers with what they want, rather than on what the company wants them to want. It usually involves a restructuring of the company's IT systems and a reorganisation of its staff.

CRM is heavily dependent on a technique called data warehousing, a way of integrating disparate information about customers from different parts of the organisation and putting it together in one huge IT "warehouse". Dale Renner, once the boss of a data-mining business, said that CRM is something that encompasses "identifying, attracting and retaining the most valuable customers to sustain profitable growth".

This is contrary to the product-oriented way in which most firms grew up, when divisions and business units were built around products and product groups. It was not then unusual for each group to have its own accounts department, its own IT unit and its own marketing team. People who worked for these vertically integrated silos were often competing as much against other silos within the same organisation as against outside rivals in the marketplace. Their loyalty to their silo frequently blinded them to the wider interests of the company as a whole.

CRM is about putting structures and systems in place that cut across the vertical lines of the traditional firm and focus on individual customers. Without it, customers might be approached by the same firm in several different product guises over a short period. No one bit of the firm would know what any other bit was doing at any particular time.

The phrase "the customer is king" was first coined long before it was true. Only towards the end of the 20th century, when advances in technology and widespread market deregulation put enormous new power into the hands of consumers, did the phrase begin to stop sounding hollow.

Two things in particular brought home to companies the need to take better care of their customers. First, some terrible mistakes were made because of the blinkers imposed by the old product-silo approach. For example, market share was the main goal and yardstick of such structures. Yet when IBM was king of the mainframe computer market, it came to understand just in time that 100% of a market that was rapidly shrinking would soon be 100% of nothing. What its customers really wanted was not mainframe computers as such, but rather the power to process information electronically. Academics have described this different concept as "a market space". Children's playtime is a market space. A doll is a product.

The second thing that drove companies to focus more closely on their customers was a growing awareness that building up profits by aggregating narrow margins from the sale of individual products might not be the best way of ensuring the long-term health of the organisation. Companies that did this would always be vulnerable either to cherry-pickers (see page 33) or to nimble newcomers that were built on a different cost base, made possible by deregulation or by changing distribution channels.

More companies want to regard their customers as customers for life and not just as the one-off purchasers of a product – it is far less expensive to retain an existing customer than it is to acquire a new one. It then becomes important to measure a customer's lifetime value, and to think about cross-subsidising different periods in their lives. Banks make little or no money out of their student customers, for example, in the hope that they will become more valuable in later years.

This strategy was questioned by Werner Reinartz and V. Kumar, professors at INSEAD, a leading European business school in Fontainebleau, France, in an article in *Harvard Business Review*. Their research found no relationship between customer loyalty and profits. Not all loyal customers, it seems, are profitable, and not all profitable customers are loyal.

Further reading

Cross, R. and Thomas, R., "A Smarter Way To Network", *Harvard Business Review*, July/August 2011

Kotler, P., *Managing Customer Relationships: Lessons from the Leaders*, The Economist Intelligence Unit, 1998

Peppers D. and Rogers, M., *Managing customer relationships: A Strategic Framework*, John Wiley & Sons, 2004

Reinartz, W. and Kumar, V., "The Mismanagement of Customer Loyalty", *Harvard Business Review*, July 2002

Silverstein, M. and Butman, J., *Treasure Hunt: Inside the Mind of the New Consumer*, Portfolio, 2006

Decentralisation

Decentralisation is the process of distributing power away from the centre of an organisation. In the case of a corporation this usually means divesting authority away from the head office and out to operators in the field. Debate centres on which is the more efficient structure for an organisation that has a number of far-flung arms, especially a multinational with operations in several different countries: one where decision-making is concentrated at the centre, or one where it is diffused around the organisation?

Decentralisation has had its supporters for centuries. In the 1700s, the East India Company was a highly decentralised organisation. Its factors ran its factories in remote parts of the world. There was no telegraph, telephone or telex. They had to make decisions for themselves on the spot.

Decentralisation remained the dominant model for most of the 19th century. The Morgans, father and son, ran their banks in isolated independence in London and New York, and the various arms of the Rothschild family ran their operations independently in a number of European countries. Carrier pigeon was the fastest form of communication that they could hope for.

With the invention of the telephone and the telex, the centralised head office came into its own. Throughout most of the 20th century centralisation was the dominant philosophy, a shift brought about largely by the invention of Alexander Graham Bell.

There were some notable exceptions. DuPont, an American chemicals company, enthusiastically embraced the idea of decentralisation in the mid-1920s when its senior executives developed a multidivisional structure to cope with its diversification. Likewise, Alfred Sloan (see page 307) split General Motors into divisions, and each division was run as a company within a company. Sloan said the company was "co-ordinated in policy and decentralised in administration". It was a move that helped him to claw back some of the enormous advantage that Ford had gained from its introduction a decade earlier of mass production and the assembly line.

In his famous-for-its-title book *Small is Beautiful*, E.F. Schumacher (see page 301) argued that centralisation and decentralisation should not be considered as mutually exclusive:

Once a large organisation has come into being, it normally goes through alternating phases of centralising and decentralising, like swings of a pendulum. Whenever one encounters such opposites, each of them with persuasive arguments in its favour, it is worth looking into the depth of the problem for something more than compromise, more than a half-and-half solution. Maybe what we really need is not either/or but "the one and the other at the same time". This very familiar problem pervades the whole of real life.

In their bestseller, *In Search of Excellence*, Tom Peters (see page 293) and Robert Waterman took a similar line: "Excellent companies," they said, "are both centralised and decentralised." Alfred Chandler (see page 225) said much the same in *Strategy and Structure*, arguing that strategy and responsibility for head office should be centralised, while day-to-day operations should be left to decentralised units.

In the 1990s, the growth and rapid development of information technology began to turn the tables. The internet and other electronic information systems made the distribution of information ubiquitous and cheap. Power was once again diffused outwards to workers in the field. In an article in *Harvard Business Review* in 1998, C.K. Prahalad (see page 297) and Kenneth Lieberthal argued that this diffusion of power would have a particularly strong impact on multinationals. The old imperialist assumption that all innovation comes from the centre would no longer be valid.

In the mid-1990s Peters and Waterman were each asked separately to list the big challenges facing business. Peters subsequently wrote:

The lists bore little resemblance to one another – except for the first item. Both of us put ... decentralisation at the top of our lists ... after 50 (combined) years of watching organisations thrive and shrivel, we held to one, and only one, basic belief: to loosen the reins, to allow a thousand flowers to bloom and a hundred schools to contend, is the best way to sustain vigour in perilous gyrating times.

Further reading

Chandler, A., *Strategy and Structure*, MIT Press, 1969; reprint, 1990
Garvin, D.A. and Levesque, L.C., "The Multiunit Enterprise", *Harvard Business Review*, June 2008
Prahalad, C.K. and Lieberthal, K., "The End of Corporate Imperialism", *Harvard Business Review*, July–August 1998
Sloan, A.P., *My Years with General Motors*, Doubleday, 1964; rev., 1990

Delayering

Delayering is a reduction in the number of levels in an organisation's hierarchy. Classically, it referred to the trimming of the dozen or so layers of management that were typical of the large corporation in the 1950s down to the five or so that by the end of the 20th century were deemed to be the maximum with which any large organisation could function effectively.

Delayering does not necessarily involve stripping out jobs and cutting overheads. But it does usually mean increasing the average span of control (see page 169) of senior managers within the organisation. This can, in effect, chop the number of layers without removing a single name from the payroll.

It involves a radical redesign of an organisation's structure to take account of late 20th-century developments in information technology, education and consumer demand. Essentially, there is a flattening of the organisation from a giant pyramid into something more horizontal. It is not an anarchic denial of the need for structure.

Frank Ostroff's book *The Horizontal Organisation* reflected late 20th-century thinking about organisational structure. In it he wrote:

> Structure is still critical to designing an efficient organisation for the 21st or any other century, and certain essential points must be considered: Who goes where? What do they do? What are the positions and how are they grouped? What is the reporting sequence? What is each person accountable for? In other words, how does the authority flow?

In yet other words, how do the organisation's layers lie?

Among the benefits claimed for the delayered organisation are the following:

- It needs fewer managers.
- It is less bureaucratic.
- It can take decisions more quickly.
- It encourages innovation.

◾ It brings managers into closer contact with the organisation's customers.
◾ It produces cross-functional employees.

This is not easy to achieve, and delayering efforts often stumble. A common cause is failure to include a sufficiently sensitive reappraisal of the changed rewards that must go with redesigned jobs.

Further reading

Ashkenas, R. *et al.*, *The Boundaryless Organization: Breaking the Chains of Organizational Structure*, Jossey-Bass, 1995; revised 2002
Austin, N., "Flattening the Pyramid", *Incentive*, December 1993
Littler, C.R., Wiesner, R. and Dunford, R., "The Dynamics of Delayering: Changing Management Structures in Three Countries", *Journal of Management Studies*, 2003
Ostroff, F., *The Horizontal Organisation*, Oxford University Press, 1999

Differentiation

In Michael Porter's ground-breaking work on the competition of the firm (see page 295) he argued that there are only two ways for firms to compete: by charging a lower price, or by differentiating their products or services from those of their rivals. This differentiation can take real forms (soluble aspirin as against non-soluble aspirin, for example) or imaginary forms (by advertising that suggests one perfume makes you more attractive to the opposite sex than another).

The value of differentiation increases the more that products come to resemble each other. For example, different brands of airline flight or latte vary less and less as time goes by. So it becomes a bigger and bigger challenge to differentiate one from another.

Once a clear distinction has been established, however, it can be reaffirmed for years and years. Porsche, for example, differentiates itself as a fast-moving sports car for fast-moving high-fliers, and has done so at least since James Dean, an iconic film star, happened to die in one in 1956.

In consumer-goods industries it is common for a large number of differentiated products to be produced by a small number of firms. For example, most of the seemingly wide array of soaps and detergents available in the United States are produced by just two firms, Unilever and Procter & Gamble. In commodity markets, such as oil and coal, there is little or no scope for differentiation. Such industries generally have low returns on investment. The ability to differentiate improves the return.

Branding is one way of differentiating products and services. It is used with great effect in the garment and tobacco industries, for example, whose products often have little else to distinguish them from each other. Branding helps to retain customer loyalty, which is arguably a third way of differentiating products and services, on top of Porter's two.

Marketers maintain that most products can be differentiated in one way or another. Philip Kotler (see page 261) gives the example of the brick industry, which is about as close to being a commodity business as is possible. Yet one company in the industry was able to differentiate itself by altering its method of delivering bricks. Instead of dumping them on the ground (and breaking several), it stacked them together on pallets and used a small crane to lift them off their truck. So successful was the firm with this method that before long it became standard industry practice. The firm then, of course, had to look for new ways of differentiating itself.

Further reading

Beath, J. and Katsoulacos, Y., *The Economic Theory of Product Differentiation*, Cambridge University Press, 1991

Kotler, P. *et al.*, *Principles of Marketing*, Prentice Hall, 1996; 12th edn, 2008

Ries, A. and Trout, J., *Positioning: the Battle for your Mind*, McGraw-Hill, 1981; London, 2001

Trout, J., *Differentiate or Die: Survival in Our Era of Killer Competition*, John Wiley & Sons, 2000

Disruptive technology/innovation

In his book *The Innovator's Dilemma*, Clayton Christensen (see page 227) made a distinction between two different types of technology that affect business, a distinction that has since become accepted wisdom. On the one hand he described what he called "sustaining technologies", technological developments that help organisations to make marginal improvements in what they are doing. These require only gradual change and pretty much retain the status quo.

On the other hand, there are what Christensen termed disruptive technologies. These are wild and unexpected technological breakthroughs that require corporations to radically rethink their very existence. At first they seem of limited interest, but eventually they completely overturn existing products and markets. Christensen quotes the examples of the mobile phone (which took the wind out of the sails of fixed-line operators), digital photography (which sent sales of camera film plummeting and caused Kodak to change its whole business model) and online retailing (which continues to bruise many a traditional shop).

One problem with disruptive technologies is that they do not always hit the market with a bang. They are often born prematurely, so that those firms which pioneer them see their performance deteriorate at first.

Another problem is that disruptive technologies often come at the world from unlikely directions. They rarely emerge from big established organisations, for which they do not initially seem to represent a worthwhile opportunity. Large companies are designed to be comfortable with sustaining technologies. They know their markets and want to capitalise on the value of that knowledge. They don't want to be distracted by risky "maybes".

In his follow-up book, *The Innovator's Solution*, Christensen changed the term from "disruptive technology" to "disruptive innovation", arguing that it was rarely the technology per se that was disruptive (or sustaining) but the use that companies made of it, the innovation that it enabled them to undertake.

Christensen's distinction between the disruptive and the sustaining reflects a long-recognised dilemma of corporate strategists – whether to go for the big bang change or whether to shuffle along with business more or less as usual. For a while in the 1990s the slow shuffle was in favour, backed by concepts such as *kaizen* (see page 109), the Japanese idea of gradual improvement, and BPR or business process re-engineering (see page 25). But by the late 1990s, along with a disruptive innovation called the internet, a certain impatience had crept in.

More and more companies began to look for "breakthrough opportunities", developments that would enable them to leapfrog ahead of their opponents. This they needed because more and more of them came to believe (along with GE's legendary leader, Jack Welch) that they had to be number one or two in their markets, or not in them at all. For those at the back, there was only one way to jump into those positions – by a big dramatic change. Business as usual was just not going to make it.

Christensen believes that the best way for big organisations to harness the potential of disruptive innovations is to set up (or buy) separate "spin-off organisations" that can behave as if they are small and buzzy. Such spin-offs, however, need to have a very different culture from their parents. They need to get excited about small markets, for instance, and they have to have a much higher tolerance of failure.

Further reading

Bower, J. and Christensen, C., "Disruptive Technologies: Catching the Wave", *Harvard Business Review*, January–February 1995

Christensen, C., *The Innovator's Dilemma: When New Technologies Cause Great Firms to Fail*, Harvard Business School Press, 1997

Christensen, C. and Raynor, M., *The Innovator's Solution*, Harvard Business School Press, 2003

Snow, D.C., "Beware of Old Technologies' Last Gasps", *Harvard Business Review*, January 2008

Diversification

From time to time companies that are primarily in a single line of business become nervous about putting all their commercial eggs into one basket. Their heads are turned by the portfolio theory of investment, in which exposure to risk is reduced through the ownership of a wide range of shares. So they set out to do the same – to reduce the risk from being in too few businesses by getting into more of them. They do this either by buying businesses or by starting them up internally from scratch, the former being the more common method used.

Companies that follow a strategy of diversification are called conglomerates. Conglomerates shift the job of spreading risk from individual shareholders into the hands of professional managers. Shareholders can choose to buy either a diversified portfolio of shares, or a share with a diversified portfolio.

The idea of diversification was given a big boost by a book called *Portfolio Selection*, first published in the late 1950s. It urged investors (individual and corporate) to spread their risks by spreading their investments. In 1952 a company called Royal Little had shown the way, acquiring companies in unrelated industries while maintaining steady growth.

Enthusiasm for diversification increased in the 1960s and early 1970s. Between 1960 and 1980, the percentage of *Fortune* 500 companies that could be described as conglomerates rose from 50 to 80. The prototype was ITT. Under Harold Geneen, an Englishman who headed the American company for many years, ITT simultaneously owned bakeries, telephone companies, hotels and a forest-products business. In the early 1970s it had over 400 separate subsidiaries operating in over 70 different countries. The British equivalent was a company called Hanson Trust. In the early 1960s it was a small family haulage business based in Yorkshire. By the early 1990s it was the UK's fourth largest manufacturer, making batteries, typewriters, bricks, HP sauce and Jacuzzi whirlpool baths after a riot of acquisitions in both the UK and the United States.

Diversification went out of fashion in the 1980s and 1990s, however, when companies began to see again the virtues of "sticking to their knitting". Many shed businesses that they had bought only a few years earlier in their headlong rush to be a conglomerate. Exxon rapidly withdrew from the electronics business, for example, and BP retreated from coal. CBS, an American broadcaster, is reckoned to have sold off more than 80% of its portfolio of businesses. British companies such as Hanson and BTR were among the conglomerates that were unbundled in the 1990s. At the beginning of that decade, Hanson had been worth $13.4 billion; by 1997 its value had fallen to $4.9 billion.

Diversification proved a highly successful strategy for some large companies. Constantinos Markides, a professor at London Business School, says that the rewards and risks can be extraordinary. He quotes success stories such as General Electric, Disney and 3M, but also mentions notorious failures, such as Quaker Oats's doomed entry into the fruit juice business through a company called Snapple, and Blue Circle, a British cement producer, which diversified into making lawn mowers on no firmer grounds, according to one former executive of the company, than that "your garden is next to your [cement] house".

A role model for the late 20th-century conglomerate is Bombardier, a Canadian firm. Founded in 1942 as a manufacturer of snow-going equipment, it grew rapidly in the last quarter of the 20th century to become a diversified manufacturer of products ranging from mass-transit systems to personal watercraft. In 1997 the company's chief executive described its strategy:

> Bombardier never diversified at breakneck speed. The first move, entering the mass-transit equipment industry, occurred in 1974; the second step, acquiring Canadair, was taken 12 years later. After each initial foray into a new industry, we made a series of acquisitions within it to strengthen our position. [Moreover,] each new sector we entered shares certain fundamental similarities in terms of key manufacturing processes, procurement, engineering design, and product development.

Further reading

Geneen, H. (with Moscow, A.), *Managing*, Doubleday, 1984

Kenny, G., *Diversification Strategy*, Kogan Page, 2009

Markowitz, H.M., *Portfolio Selection: Efficient Diversification of Investments*, Yale University Press, 1970; 2nd edn, Blackwell, Oxford, 1991

Markides, C., *Diversification, Refocusing and Economic Performance*, MIT Press, 1995

Downsizing

Downsizing is a process whereby a corporation makes itself smaller in response to changed market circumstances. Although downsizing implies a reduction in assets, it is not (as its critics often maintain) merely a reduction in human assets.

Other terms have been used to distance the concept from its association with ruthless job-slashing – for example, rightsizing and restructuring. In the first IBM annual report after his appointment as chief executive of the huge consulting company Lou Gerstner said: "Shortly after I joined, I set as my highest priority to rightsize the company as quickly as we could."

Downsizing was at its most intense in the late 1980s and early 1990s. In the United States alone, some 3.5m workers lost their jobs to downsizing in the decade after 1987. The losses had much to do with getting rid of layers of middle managers – a move enforced by increasing competition and the growth of information technology which reduced the need for human ciphers.

Some saw this as a return to organisational structures of times gone by. In a 1988 article, Peter Drucker (see page 235) wrote that one of the best examples of a large and successful information-based organisation that had no layers of middle managers was the British civil administration in India. It never had more than 1,000 members, most of whom were under 30 years of age. Each political secretary (a senior rank) had at least 100 people reporting directly to him, "many times what the doctrine of the span of control [see page 169] would allow". It worked, added Drucker, "in large part because it was designed to ensure that each of its members had the information he needed to do his job".

By the late 1990s there was a sharp reaction against downsizing. Companies started asking themselves whether it had gone too far. By then they knew that there was a considerable downside to downsizing. First, it left organisations shell-shocked and demoralised. Those who had job options resigned, and their employer was then frequently forced to rehire in what has been described as a process of "binge and purge". The short-term benefits to the bottom line from downsizing could be offset by the long-term damage to the loyalty, morale and (possibly) the productivity of those employees who did stay.

In 1995, the American Management Association (AMA) surveyed 1,000 companies on the effects of downsizing. Only 48% of those that had cut jobs since 1990 said that their profits had gone up afterwards. The AMA survey also found that downsizing failed to improve product quality at most of these companies.

In a special report on the changing structure of the workplace published in October 1994, *Business Week* magazine warned that the great risk of downsizing was that it simply resulted in fewer people working harder. It did little to change the way that work was done within the corporation. A middle manager at a high-tech company recounted his experience:

> This year, I had to downsize my area by 25%. Nothing changed in terms of the workload. It's very emotionally draining. I find myself not wanting to go in to work, because I'm going to have to push people to do more, and I look at their eyes and they're sinking into the back of their heads. But they're not going to complain, because they don't want to be the next 25%.

Another apparent downside to downsizing is the loss of a company's innovative ability. In "The Effects of Organisational Downsizing on Product Innovation", an article published in *California Management Review* in 1995, Deborah Dougherty and Edward Bowman said that downsized firms lose the ability to carry out a crucial final stage in the process of bringing a new product to market. Downsizing interferes with the network of informal relationships which innovators use to gain support for new product development. Innovative activities no longer connect with the rest of the firm.

The caring company's alternative to downsizing is reallocation. If jobs have to go, it does not mean that employees have to go as well. 3M's policy, for example, is to find similar jobs for excess workers in other divisions. During the 1990s it reassigned 3,500 workers in this way rather than make them redundant. It was able to do this because it is constantly creating new products and new divisions to which people can be relocated.

Further reading

Burke, R. and Cooper, C., *The Organisation in Crisis: Downsizing, Restructuring and Privatisation*, Blackwell, 2000

Drucker, P., "The Coming of The New Organisation", *Harvard Business Review*, Vol. 66, No. 1, 1988

Mishra, A.K. *et al.*, "Downsizing the Company without Downsizing Morale", *Sloan Management Review*, Spring 2009

E-commerce

The term e-commerce embraces all the ways of trans   business via electronic data. But it is most closely identified with commercial transactions over the internet, and it is the internet that put e-commerce near the top of the corporate agenda in the first decade of the 21st century.

E-commerce is merely an elision of electronic commerce, but it embodies a revolutionary idea: that electronic commerce is qualitatively different from ordinary time-worn commerce, that (in the jargon) there is a paradigm shift in the way that business is conducted in the world of e-commerce. Doing business via the internet is not only much quicker and much cheaper than other methods, it is also thought to overturn old rules about time, space and price. There is the much-vaunted death of distance: a customer 10,000 miles away becomes as accessible as one around the corner. And e-commerce has created the phenomenon of the long tail (see page 119).

Furthermore, economies of scale (see page 71) are undermined. In its report "Making Open Finance Pay", Forrester Research, an American research company, gave examples of the way in which the internet had altered the pricing structure of a number of industries, particularly those with high information content. Before the advent of the internet it cost $100 to make an equity market order. Afterwards it cost just $15, an 85% fall in price, far more than could ever have been gleaned from traditional economies of scale. This was a revolution for organisations whose structures and strategies had built-in assumptions about relationships between price and volume.

Electronic commerce has grown rapidly. Online sales in the United States are reckoned to have grown by some 12% in 2011, to reach almost $200 billion. The country's five largest online retailers (often called e-tailers) are Amazon, Staples, Apple, Dell and Office Depot. Dell became a market leader in computers through early use of the internet to sell goods and services direct to consumers, and to buy components from suppliers.

Financial-services offerings over the internet have also sprouted like mushrooms, although security issues have imposed some restraint on the industry. At Charles Schwab, an American retail brokerage firm, it took just three years for online dealing to account for more than half of all its securities trading.

or banks, the economic logic of e-commerce is compelling. It has been estimated that a banking transaction over the telephone costs the bank half as much as the same transaction conducted over a counter in a traditional branch, and that an ATM transaction costs a quarter as much. But a banking transaction over the internet costs a mere 1% of an over-the-counter transaction at a branch.

E-commerce also allows unknown firms to establish new businesses cheaply and rapidly, and to compete with old-timers. This they do not only by cutting prices and offering wider choices, but also by allowing consumers to make real-time price comparisons and to switch rapidly (and frequently) to the cheapest provider. This control that consumers have over prices has led some analysts to predict that e-commerce can at best only ever be a low-margin business, and at worst a no-margin business.

"The future of e-commerce", wrote *The Economist* in November 2011, "is Chinese." It cited a report by the Boston Consulting Group that predicted by 2015 China will have over 250m online shoppers, each of them spending about $1,000 a year, roughly what America's 170m online purchasers were spending in 2011.

Further reading

Chaffey, D., *E-business and E-commerce Management: Strategy, Implementation, and Practice*, Financial Times/Prentice Hall, 2002; 4th edn, 2011

Landon, K.C., *E-Commerce 2010*, Pearson Education, 2009

Ostrofsky, M., *Get Rich Click*, Razor Media Group, 2011

Rayport, J.F. and Jaworski, B.J., *Introduction to E-commerce*, Irwin/ McGraw-Hill, 2002; 2nd international edn, 2003

Economies of scale and scope

Economies of scale

Economies of scale cause the average cost of producing something to fall as the volume of its output increases. While it might cost $3,000 to produce 100 copies of a magazine, it may take only $4,000 to produce 1,000 copies. The average cost has fallen from $30 to $4 a copy because the main elements of cost in producing a magazine (editorial and design) are unrelated to the number of magazines produced.

Economies of scale were the main drivers of corporate gigantism in the 20th century. They were fundamental to Henry Ford's revolutionary assembly line (see Mass production, page 127), and they continue to be the spur to many mergers and acquisitions today.

There are two types of economies of scale:

- **Internal.** These are cost savings that accrue to a firm regardless of the industry, market or environment in which it operates.
- **External.** These are economies that benefit a firm because of the way in which its industry is organised.

Internal economies of scale arise in a number of ways. For example, it is easier for large firms to carry the overheads of sophisticated research and development (R&D). In the pharmaceuticals industry R&D is crucial. Yet the cost of discovering the next blockbuster drug is enormous and increasing. Several of the mergers between pharmaceuticals companies in recent years have been driven by the companies' desire to spread their R&D expenditure across a greater volume of sales.

Economies of scale, however, have a dark side, called diseconomies of scale. The larger an organisation becomes in order to reap economies of scale, the more complex it has to be to manage and run such scale. This complexity incurs a cost, and eventually this cost may come to outweigh the savings gained from greater scale. In other words, economies of scale cannot be gleaned for ever.

Frederick Herzberg, a distinguished professor of management, suggested a reason why companies should not aim blindly for economies of scale:

Numbers numb our feelings for what is being counted and lead

71

to adoration of the economies of scale. Passion is in feeling the quality of experience, not in trying to measure it.

T. Boone Pickens, a geologist turned oil magnate turned corporate raider, wrote about diseconomies of scale in his 1987 autobiography:

It's unusual to find a large corporation that's efficient. I know about economies of scale and all the other advantages that are supposed to come with size. But when you get an inside look, it's easy to see how inefficient big business really is. Most corporate bureaucracies have more people than they have work.

Economies of scope

First cousins to economies of scale are economies of scope, factors that make it cheaper to produce a range of products together than to produce each one of them on its own. Such economies can come from businesses sharing centralised functions, such as finance or marketing. Or they can come from interrelationships elsewhere in the business process, such as cross-selling (see page 51) one product alongside another, or using the outputs of one business as the inputs of another.

Just as the theory of economies of scale has been the underpinning for all sorts of corporate behaviour, from mass production to mergers and acquisitions, so the idea of economies of scope has been the underpinning for other sorts of corporate behaviour, particularly diversification (see page 65).

The desire to garner economies of scope was the driving force behind the vast international conglomerates built up in the 1970s and 1980s, including BTR and Hanson in the UK and ITT in the United States. The logic behind these amalgamations lay mostly in the scope for the companies to leverage their financial skills across a diversified range of industries.

A number of conglomerates put together in the 1990s relied on cross-selling, thus reaping economies of scope by using the same people and systems to market many different products. The combination of Travelers Group and Citicorp in 1998, for instance, was based on the logic of selling the financial products of the one by using the sales teams of the other.

Further reading

Sloan, A.P., *My Years with General Motors*, Doubleday, 1964; revised, 1990
Smith, A., *The Wealth of Nations*, 1776

Empowerment

Empowerment is the idea that an organisation is most productive when all its employees are empowered to make and take decisions on their own, when authority is devolved down to all levels of the organisation. It is a feel-good idea that seems to prove what all sensitive, liberal folk believe should be the case.

The idea was most closely associated with Rosabeth Moss Kanter (see page 257), a Harvard Business School professor who also edited *Harvard Business Review*. It was central to her influential book *When Giants Learn to Dance* where she argued that large companies need to liberate their employees from stultifying hierarchies if they are going to be able to "dance" in the flexible, fast-changing future. Too many employees, she believed, still needed "the crutch" of hierarchy. These "powerless" people, said Kanter, "live in a different world ... they may turn instead to the ultimate weapon of those who lack productive power – oppressive power". She felt that women were particularly in need of empowerment because traditionally they had been allocated low-status jobs.

The idea harks back to Douglas McGregor's Theory X and Theory Y (see page 187), but gives McGregor's framework a new spin by adding information technology. IT has the ability to put into the hands of Theory Yers (self-motivating individuals) the raw material (knowledge, or power) that they need in order to act responsibly and to take decisions for themselves.

Ten years after Kanter's book was published, another Harvard Business School professor, Chris Argyris, wrote an article in *Harvard Business Review* entitled "Empowerment: The Emperor's New Clothes". In it he said, more or less, "Nice idea; shame about the results". Everyone is talking about empowerment, said Argyris, but it is not working. Chief executives subtly undermine it, despite Kanter's assertion that "by empowering others, a leader does not decrease his power". Employees are often unprepared or unwilling to assume the new responsibilities that it entails.

To understand why it was not working, Argyris set empowerment in the context of commitment, an individual's commitment to his or her place of work. He said that there are two types of commitment:

■ External commitment, or contractual compliance. This is the sort of commitment that employees display under the command-and-control type of structure, when they have little control over their own destiny and little idea of how to change things.

■ Internal commitment. This is something that occurs when employees are committed to a particular project or person for their own individual reasons. Internal commitment, said Argyris, is closely allied with empowerment.

Argyris argued that the problem with many corporate programmes designed to encourage empowerment was that they created more external than internal commitment. One reason was that the programmes were riddled with contradictions and sent out mixed messages, such as "do your own thing – but do it the way we tell you". The result was that employees felt little responsibility for the programme, and people throughout the organisation felt less empowered.

Argyris suggested that companies should recognise that empowerment has its limits. It should not be a goal in itself; it is only a means to the ultimate goal of superior performance. Organisations should then set out to establish working conditions that will encourage their employees' internal commitment, clearly recognising how this differs from the external variety.

Further reading

Argyris, C., "Empowerment: The Emperor's New Clothes", *Harvard Business Review*, May–June 1998

Gershon, D. and Straub, G., *Empowerment: the Art of Creating Your Life as you Want It*, Sterling Ethos, 2011

Kanter, R.M., "Power Failures in Management Circuits", *Harvard Business Review*, July–August 1979

Kanter, R.M., *When Giants Learn to Dance: Mastering the Challenge of Strategy, Management, and Careers in the 1990s*, Simon & Schuster, 1989; Unwin, 1990

Enterprise resource planning

Enterprise resource planning (ERP) is the setting up of electronic information systems throughout an organisation in such a way that disparate parts of the organisation are brought together, parts that may rarely in the past have had access to information about each other – manufacturing, for instance, and customer relationship management (CRM – see page 55).

ERP software, designed to implement this, acts as a sort of central nervous system for the corporation. It gathers information about the state and activity of different parts of the body corporate and conveys this information to parts elsewhere that can make fruitful use of it. The information is updated in real time by the users and is accessible to all those on the network at all times.

Just as the central nervous system's capacity can at times seem to transcend the collective capacity of its individual parts (a phenomenon that we call consciousness), so too can that of ERP systems. They (as it were) make the corporation self-aware. In particular, ERP systems link together information about finance, human resources, production and distribution. They embrace stock-control systems, customer databases, order-tracking systems, accounts payable, and so on. They also interface when and where necessary with suppliers and customers.

The interlinking of ERP systems can be extraordinarily complex. Firms usually start with a pilot project before implementing a group-wide scheme.

The history of ERP is the history of SAP (System Analyse und Programmentwicklung), a German software company that in the 1990s established an extraordinary dominance in the market for ERP systems. SAP was set up by three engineers in Mannheim in 1972. Their aim was to help companies link their different business processes by correlating information from various functions and using it to run the whole business more smoothly.

SAP's software was designed to be modular so that a company's systems could be rapidly adapted to take account of growth and change. It was so successful in recognising and meeting business's IT needs that by the late 1990s SAP's share of the market for ERP systems was greater than that of its five nearest rivals put together. Its systems were reckoned to be running in at least half of the world's 500 largest companies. By

2005 two firms, SAP and Oracle, were reckoned to have over half the ERP market.

Its extraordinarily rapid growth (at one time an annual average rate of increase in sales of over 40%) was backed by a marketing strategy that encouraged management consultants to implement SAP systems within client firms. Many consultants set up specialist SAP departments for the purpose. Without this support in implementation, there might have been a crippling bottleneck in the growth of SAP's business.

The ERP systems market itself grew rapidly as firms saw the benefits to be gained from consolidating information about their geographically and functionally dispersed bits and pieces. ERP systems enabled them to have a view of their organisation as a whole that they had never previously enjoyed. It was a bit like seeing the early colour photographs of earth taken from outer space.

These systems were initially most popular with large multinationals:

◪ they had the advanced IT infrastructures on which they could run the systems;
◪ they were keen to standardise their diverse range of business processes;
◪ they had the staff necessary to manage the systems once they were up and running.

As this big-company market became saturated, ERP systems providers began to look at how they might adapt their products to suit smaller organisations.

Further reading

James, D. and Wolf, M.L., "A Second Wind for ERP", *McKinsey Quarterly*, No. 2, 2000

Wagner, B. and Monk, E., *Enterprise Resource Planning*, Course Technology, 3rd edn, 2008

Entrepreneurship

Jean-Baptiste Say, a French economist who first coined the word entrepreneur in about 1800, said: "The entrepreneur shifts economic resources out of an area of lower and into an area of higher productivity and greater yield." One dictionary says an entrepreneur is "one who undertakes an enterprise, especially a contractor acting as the intermediary between capital and labour".

Entrepreneurship is the special collection of skills possessed by an entrepreneur. They include a propensity to take risks over and above the normal, and a desire to create wealth. Entrepreneurs are people who find ways round business difficulties; they persevere with a business plan at times when others run for the shelter of full-time employment.

They are also opportunistic, sometimes ruthless to a fault. Abraham Zaleznik, a Harvard Business School professor, once said, "I think if we want to understand the entrepreneur, we should look at the juvenile delinquent".

Until recently, there was a general feeling that entrepreneurs were born not made. The skills they required were, it was thought, either learned at the dinner table when young, or they were instinctive, a "seat of the pants" thing. *The Economist* once wrote, "Entrepreneurs – the most successful, though not the only, practitioners of innovation [see page 105] – rarely stop to examine how they do it."

The main constraint on entrepreneurs has traditionally been a shortage of finance, not of ideas. The old picture was of the entrepreneur, brimming with bright ideas, beating a path to the closed doors of one bank after another. In recent years, however, a whole industry has grown up – the venture-capital industry – to meet the financial needs of entrepreneurs and to share in the fruits of their endeavour.

Those fruits are usually gathered through a listing on a quoted stock exchange. A number of small exchanges have been set up especially to encourage small entrepreneurial firms to follow this route.

Some management writers have tried to take the idea of entrepreneurship into big organisations, encouraging full-time employees (on monthly salaries and the promise of a pension) to think like entrepreneurs. The idea has been dubbed "intrapreneurship". One definition says that intrapreneurship is "the introduction and implementation of a significant innovation for the firm by one or more employees working within an established organisation".

The selling of the Post-It note (see Champion, page 29) by Spence Silver, an employee of 3M, is one of the classic and most quoted examples of intrapreneurship. 3M has been particularly successful at encouraging intrapreneurs. It maintains that the first thing you have to do is to create a corporate culture which permits ideas to blossom. "You have to kiss a lot of frogs to find the prince," the company told *The Economist*. "But remember, one prince can pay for a lot of frogs."

Entrepreneurs tend to flourish when regular jobs decline. The numbers rose by some 20% in mature economies in 2011.

The Global Entrepreneurship Monitor (GEM), a university-backed organisation based in San Francisco, reckoned there were nearly 400m entrepreneurs active in 2011 in the 54 different countries it monitors.

Further reading

Block, Z. and MacMillan, I.C., *Corporate Venturing: Creating New Businesses within the Firm*, Harvard Business School Press, 1993

Byrne, J.A., *World Changers: 25 Entrepreneurs Who Changed Business As We Know It*, Portfolio Hardcover, 2011

Drucker, P., *Innovation and Entrepreneurship: Practice and Principles*, Harper & Row, New York, 1985; revised edn, Butterworth-Heinemann, Oxford, 1999

Jennings, R., Cox, C. and Cooper, C., *Business Elites: the Psychology of Entrepreneurs and Intrapreneurs*, Routledge, 1994

The experience curve

The experience curve is an idea developed by the Boston Consulting Group (BCG) in the mid-1960s. Working with a leading manufacturer of semiconductors, the consultants noticed that the company's unit cost of manufacturing fell by about 25% for each doubling of the volume that it produced. This relationship they called the experience curve: the more experience a firm has in producing a particular product, the lower are its costs. Bruce Henderson, the founder of BCG, put it as follows:

> Costs characteristically decline by 20–30% in real terms each
> time accumulated experience doubles. This means that when
> inflation is factored out, costs should always decline. The decline
> is fast if growth is fast and slow if growth is slow.

There is no fundamental economic law that can predict the existence of the experience curve, even though it has been shown to apply to industries across the board. Its truth has been proven inductively, not deductively. And if it is true in service industries such as investment banking or legal advice, the lower costs are clearly not passed on to customers.

By itself, the curve is not particularly earth shattering. Even when BCG first expounded the relationship, it had been known since the second world war that it applied to direct labour costs. Less labour was needed for a given output depending on the experience of that labour. In aircraft production, for instance, labour input decreased by some 10–15% for every doubling of that labour's experience.

The strategic implications of the experience curve came closer to shattering earth. For if costs fell (fairly predictably) with experience, and if experience was closely related to market share (as it seemed it must be), then the competitor with the biggest market share was going to have a big cost advantage over its rivals. QED: being market leader is a valuable strategic asset that a firm relinquishes at its peril.

This was the logical underpinning of the idea of the growth share matrix (see page 95). The experience curve justified allocating financial resources to those businesses (out of a firm's portfolio of businesses) that were (or were going to be) market leaders in their particular sectors. This, of course, implied starvation for those businesses that were not and never would be market leaders.

Over time, managers came to find the experience curve too imprecise to help them much with specific business plans. Inconveniently, different products had curves of a different slope and different sources of cost reduction. They did not, for instance, all have the same downward gradient as the semiconductor industry, where BCG had first identified the phenomenon. A study by the Rand Corporation found that "a doubling in the number of [nuclear] reactors [built by an architect–engineer] results in a 5% reduction in both construction time and capital cost".

Part of the explanation for this discrepancy was that different products provided different opportunities to gain experience. Large products (such as nuclear reactors) are inherently bound to be produced in smaller volumes than small products (such as semiconductors). It is not easy for a firm to double the volume of production of something that it takes over five years to build, and whose total market may never be more than a few hundred units.

In theory, the experience curve should make it difficult for new entrants to challenge firms with a substantial market share. In practice, new firms enter old industries all the time, and before long many of them become major players in their markets. This is often because they have found ways of bypassing what might seem like the remorseless inevitability of the curve and its slope. For example, experience can be gained not only first-hand, by actually doing the production and finding out for yourself, but also second-hand, by reading about it and by being trained by people who have first-hand experience. Furthermore, firms can leapfrog over the experience curve by means of innovation and invention. All the experience in the world in making black and white television sets is worthless if everyone wants to buy colour ones.

Further reading

De Bono, E., *Practical Thinking*, Cape, 1971; Penguin, 1976

Ghemawat, P., "Building Strategy on the Experience Curve", *Harvard Business Review*, March–April 1985

Gottfredson, M. and Schaubert, S., *The Breakthrough Imperative*, HarperCollins, 2008

Henderson, B.D., *The Logic of Business Strategy*, Ballinger Publishing, 1984

Sallenare, J.P., "The Uses and Abuses of Experience Curves", *Long Range Planning*, Vol. 18, No. 1, 1985

Stern, C.W. and Stalk, G. Jr (eds), *Perspectives on Strategy: From the Boston Consulting Group*, John Wiley & Sons, 1998

Flexibility

In a business context, flexibility can refer to a number of different ideas. Its most common usage is in the workplace where it refers to such things as flexi-time, variable hours and extended periods of leave. But the word has a longer pedigree in the area of strategy, where it generally refers to a firm's ability to respond to changes in its environment both rapidly and at low cost. In the (limited) sense that strategy is an unchanging commitment to something, it is the antithesis of flexibility.

A firm's strategic flexibility depends partly on its liquidity, since its ability to respond speedily is inevitably determined by its access to funds. But more importantly it depends on its organisational structure, on the way in which its various units work with each other, and the freedom they have to take decisions on their own initiative.

The trade-off between flexibility and firmness has been a long-running subject of management discussion. Julian Birkinshaw, a professor at London Business School and author of *The Flexible Firm*, wrote an article in the summer 2004 edition of the *Sloan Management Review* called "Building Ambidexterity Into an Organisation". In it he says:

> *For a company to succeed over the long term it needs to master both adaptability and alignment – an attribute that is sometimes referred to as ambidexterity.*

For adaptability, read flexibility; and for alignment, read firmness. The balance between the two, ambidexterity, is a term which Birkinshaw claims was first used in this sense in 1976.

Sumantra Ghoshal (see page 241) put the dilemma slightly differently. In an article in the *Sloan Management Review* in autumn 2002 he wrote:

> *One of the most fundamental and enduring tensions in all but very small companies is between sub-unit autonomy and empowerment on the one hand, and overall organisational integration and cohesion on the other.*

Autonomy and cohesion; adaptability and alignment; flexibility and firmness. The words are different though the dilemma remains the same.

For most of the past century, firmness has had the upper hand in corporate strategy. Companies have set themselves on a particular course, and it has taken a huge effort to divert them. A big company, wrote one author at the end of the 1990s, "is a bit like an oil tanker. There is no way it can turn on a sixpence".

In the 21st century companies have come to value flexibility more and more, and have looked for ways in which they could, indeed, turn on a sixpence. Peter Brabeck, when head of Nestlé, set out at the turn of the 21st century to transform the company from being run "like a super-tanker" into being more like an "agile fleet" of vessels, a fleet that called into action different business units to seize different market opportunities as and when they arose.

Some, however, felt that the enthusiasm for flexibility went too far. A senior executive at Yahoo! was reported by the *Wall Street Journal* in December 2006 as having written an internal memo bewailing the fact that:

> We lack a focused cohesive vision for our company. We want to do everything and be everything to everyone...We are scared to be left out. We are reactive instead of charting an unwavering course. We need to boldly and definitively declare what we are and what we are not.

In his book *Does IT Matter*, Nicholas G. Carr, an editor at *Harvard Business Review*, found a compromise. Writing of the future, he said:

> Successful companies will therefore work to establish and protect distinctive strategic positions even as they use more temporary competitive advantages as stepping stones to new advantages. They will be, so to speak, flexibly inflexible.

Further reading

Birkinshaw, J. and Hagström, P. (eds), *The Flexible Firm: Capability Management in Network Organizations*, Oxford University Press, 2000
Birkinshaw, J., "Building Ambidexterity Into an Organisation", *Sloan Management Review*, 2004
Carr, N.G., *Does IT Matter? Information Technology and the Corrosion of Competitive Advantage*, Harvard Business School Press, 2004

Flexible working

The idea that employees should have the freedom (within limits) to work at times which suit them caught on in the last decades of the 20th century. The "9 to 5" mentality, that employees worked only between those eight hours of the day, with one hour off for lunch, was still prevalent in the early 1980s when a popular film was made with that title. The office-based staff in the film clocked in and out of work much as assembly-line workers had done in pre-war car factories. The working practices of the three main actresses in the film look as out of date today as the clothes that they wear.

Three things in particular changed that practice:

- A shift from manufacturing to service industries (at least in developed economies). While production-line workers have to be physically present at one spot at more or less the same time, service workers are much less constrained. An insurance clerk, for example, can process claims at almost any hour of the day, and many creative types (in advertising, say, or graphic design) would claim to work better between the hours of 9pm and 5am than between 9am and 5pm. As services came to account for a larger and larger percentage of economic activity, so the opportunities to work more flexibly increased. This took pressure off the fabled urban rush-hour. Rush-hours did not disappear altogether, but they did become less intense and more extended.
- The growing number of women in the workforce forced employers to be more flexible. Women need time off to collect children from school, to take family members for hospital visits, and to do all the other tasks that had been expected of them before they entered the workforce in bulk. They did not expect to work fewer hours than men; they merely expected them to be less rigidly predetermined. They also wanted to take longer periods of leave – to give birth or to care for elderly relatives. If employers wanted to benefit from women's skills (and the generally lower price of their labour), they would have to accommodate these requirements.
- While workers wanted more flexibility, technology enabled them to have it. The PC, cheaper telecommunications and broadband

internet enabled the creation of near-virtual firms whose employees were flexible in both the time and the place that they worked. Some of them worked at home, but others worked out of the back of a van or the company car, keeping themselves in touch with their office via wireless internet access and mobile telecommunications. Another chunk of service workers – consultants and the like – spent much of their time in offices provided by their clients. A company as big as IBM could say that only 60% of its employees actually worked on company premises. The other 40% were elsewhere.

For some, this flexibility was a source of freedom, but for others it was, perversely, a burden. Several surveys found that flexible working could mean working all hours of the day. Afraid that their bosses would assume (as surprisingly many still do) that absence meant skiving, employees felt under pressure to work ever harder and to overcompensate. What's more, they feared that being out of sight meant they were out of mind when it was time to be considered for promotion.

Further reading

Harvard Business Review on Work and Life Balance, Harvard Business School Press, 2000

Franchising

Franchising is a system of marketing that enables firms to increase their turnover without increasing their assets. Almost every type of business has been franchised at some time or other, from Big Apple Bagels to DreamMaker Baths & Kitchens. One of the best known franchises is the McDonald's chain of hamburger restaurants. Approximately 80% of McDonald's restaurant businesses around the world are owned and operated by franchisees.

Franchising involves two parties, the franchiser and the franchisee. The franchiser owns a trademark or brand, which he (or she) agrees to allow the franchisee to use for a fee (often an original purchase price plus a percentage of sales). The franchiser provides the franchisee with assistance (financial, choice of site, and so on) in setting up their operation, and then maintains continuing control over various aspects of the franchisee's business; for example, via the supply of products, discussion of marketing plans and/or centralised staff training.

The franchisee buys into a proven business plan and considerable expertise. Other advantages to the franchisee include cost savings from the bulk-buying capacity of a large operation, and the marketing benefits of central advertising and promotion of the business.

Many franchisees sign a franchise agreement believing it to be less risky than setting up a business on their own. But things can go badly wrong, even with well-known and well-established operations. Some franchisers have antagonised their franchisees by selling new franchises on sites close to existing operations. Many contracts now stipulate that franchises cannot be sold less than a certain distance apart, and in some American states there is legislation controlling their sale.

McDonald's has said that its system is successful because:

> [it is] built on the premise that the corporation should only make money from its franchisees' food sales, which avoids the potential conflicts of interest that exist in so many franchising operations [where fees are not tied so closely to sales]. All our franchisees are independent, full-time franchisees rather than conglomerates or passive investors.

McDonald's also says that it "remains committed to franchising as a predominant way of doing business".

Elements of the idea of franchising have been in use for centuries. An article in *McKinsey Quarterly* (No. 1, 1998) says:

> *The 18th-century North West Company featured decentralised decision-making, a franchise-like structure, and strong incentive systems, features that enabled it to overtake the entrenched Hudson's Bay Company despite its overwhelming structural advantages.*

The growth in franchising in the 1990s was fast. In 1999 the International Franchise Association reckoned that "more than 540,000 franchise businesses dot the American landscape, generating more than $800 billion in sales". A decade later it was estimated that there were over 825,000 franchise businesses across the United States, generating over $2.1 trillion in sales and creating around 18m jobs.

Franchises can bring great wealth to both parties; but they can also be a disaster for both parties. A restaurant franchise in the UK called Pierre Victoire was started in 1987 by Pierre Levicky, a Frenchman living in Edinburgh. By 1996 there were over 100 Pierre Victoire outlets in the UK and Levicky was planning to float his business on the London stockmarket with a tentative valuation of £14m. But a number of problems (not least a lack of control over the franchise quality) led the receivers to be called in in 1998. Some of the franchisees took over the business; others had to abandon their restaurant's name. Levicky himself ended up as a chef in one of his former franchisee's restaurants.

Further reading

Norman, J., *What No One Ever Tells You About Franchising*, Kaplan Business, 2006

Shook, C., Shook, R.L. and Cherkasky, W.B., *Franchising: The Business Strategy That Changed the World*, Prentice Hall, 1993

Game theory

The idea of business as a game, in the sense that a move by one player sparks off moves by others, runs through much strategic thinking. It is borrowed from a branch of economics (game theory) in which no economic agent (individual or corporate) is an island, living and acting independently of others.

In sectors where firms compete fiercely for market share and customer loyalty, this stylised progression of moves closely parallels actual behaviour. Few firms nowadays think about strategy without adding a bit of game theory. John von Neumann and Oskar Morgenstern, the two economists who developed the idea, said that strategy was "a complete plan: a plan which specifies what choices [the player] will make in every possible situation".

Seeing business life as a never-ending series of games, each of which has a winner and a loser, can be a handicap. In business negotiations, for example, with external suppliers or customers, or with trade unions or colleagues, it can be unhelpful if participants see it only in terms of a victory or a loss. That way one party has to walk away feeling bad about the outcome. In some non-Western cultures the aim is different. The negotiation process is steered towards a win-win outcome, one with which both parties can be reasonably content.

The language of business is scattered with references to games. Regulators try to make sure that companies operate on a "level playing field", and competition is, according to at least one dictionary, "a series of games". Business games that have enjoyed (sometimes brief) popularity include the following:

- **The end game.** This is a strategy for a product that seems to be on its last legs. Should the company bleed it for all it is worth before it dies? Or should it introduce an aggressive pricing policy aimed at forcing its competitors out of business and allowing it to continue in a much reduced niche market (see page 135)? In her book *Managing Maturing Businesses*, Kathryn Harrigan, a professor at Columbia Business School, argued that end games can be highly profitable. She wrote: "The last surviving player makes money serving the last bit of demand, when the competitors drop away."

- ◪ **The croquet game.** In *The Change Masters*, Rosabeth Moss Kanter (see page 257) wrote:

  I think the game that best describes most businesses today is the croquet game in Alice in Wonderland. *In that game nothing remains stable for very long. Everything is changing around the players. Alice goes to hit a ball, but her mallet is a flamingo. Just as she's about to hit the ball, the flamingo lifts its head and looks in another direction. That's just like technology and the tools that we use.*

- ◪ **The win-win game.** This is a game where both parties end up as winners; for example, a merger between two companies where synergy (see page 183) genuinely allows them to become more than the sum of their parts.

- ◪ **The zero-sum game.** This is shorthand for the idea that in every game, whether in business or on the sports field, the value of the winner's gains and the loser's losses are equal. In such games there is no incentive to co-operate with opponents because every inch given to them is an inch lost. The idea of the zero-sum game is modified by the introduction of the possibility of change in the nature of the game while it is being played. Hence, for instance, companies that are fighting for market share are playing a zero-sum game if they see that market as fixed. But if the market is continually expanding (or if the companies redefine it so that it is), the players are playing a game in which they can have a declining share of a bigger cake and still see their business grow.

Further reading

Berne, E., *Games People Play: The Psychology of Human Relationships*, Grove Press, New York, 1964; Penguin, 1968

Friedman, S.D., Christensen, P. and DeGroot, J., "Work and Life: the End of the Zero-Sum Game", *Harvard Business Review*, November–December 1998

McDonald, J., *Strategy in Poker, Business and War*, W.W. Norton, 1st edn, 1950; 1996

Shubik, M., *Games for Society, Business and War: Towards a Theory of Gaming*, Elsevier, 1975

Sun Tzu, *The Art of War*, 500 BC (Oxford University Press, 1963)

Von Neumann, J. and Morgenstern, O., *Theory of Games and Economic Behavior*, Princeton University Press, 1944; 60th anniversary edn, 2004

Genchi genbutsu

This is a Japanese phrase meaning "go and see for yourself". It is a central pillar of the Toyota Way, the famous management system adopted by the Japanese car company. *Genchi genbutsu* is sometimes referred to as "get your boots on", which has a similar cadence and meaning. It is not dissimilar to the idea behind management by walking about (MBWA – see page 123), an all-too-briefly popular American version of the same principle.

Both MBWA and *genchi genbutsu* are more a frame of mind than a plan of action. They acknowledge that when information is passed around within organisations it is inevitably simplified and generalised. The only real way to understand a problem is to go and see it on the ground.

In at least one important respect *genchi genbutsu* represents a fundamental difference between Western and Japanese management styles. Whereas in the West knowledge is gleaned and digested in the office or the boardroom, in Japan it is gleaned on the factory floor. When asked to resolve a problem, Japanese managers go to see the place where it has arisen. American managers generally make their diagnosis from a distance.

Another Japanese word, *gemba*, is allied to the same concept. *Gemba* means "place", the place (as it were) where the action happens. *Genchi genbutsu* involves going to the *gemba* to check on the *genbutsu* (the relevant objects). Masaaki Imai, a Japanese management writer who introduced the West to the idea of *kaizen* (see page 109), wrote a book called *Gemba Kaizen*. This combined the concept of gradual improvement (*kaizen*) with an on-the-spot presence (*gemba*) – being there in order to spot every small opportunity for improvement.

Imai says there are five golden rules of what he calls *gemba* management:

- When a problem arises, go to the *gemba* first – don't try to make a diagnosis on the phone.
- Check the *genbutsu* – the relevant objects – because "seeing is believing".
- Take temporary counter-measures on the spot to resolve the problem.

■ Then find the root cause of the problem.
■ Lastly, standardise procedures to avoid a recurrence.

Toyota is the most devoted exponent of *genchi genbutsu*. An article in 2004 in the *Chicago Sun-Times* gave a vivid example of the principle in action inside the company. Yuji Yokoya, a Toyota engineer, was given responsibility for re-engineering a new generation of the Toyota Sienna minivan for the North American market. So he drove the van more than 53,000 miles across America, from Anchorage to the Mexican border and from Florida to California. As the paper described it:

> *Crossing the Mississippi River by bridge, he [Yokoya] noted that the Sienna's crosswind stability needed improvement. He observed excessive steering drift while traversing gravel roads in Alaska, and the need for a tighter turning radius along the crowded streets in Santa Fe. Driving through Glacier National Park, he decided the handling needed to be crisper. He also made an all-wheel-drive option a priority, along with more interior space and cargo flexibility.*
>
> *Finally, he decided that the new Sienna would have to be a minivan that families, and especially kids, could live in for extended periods of time. Upgrading seat quality became a priority, along with "kid friendly" features such as a roll-down window for second-row passengers, an optional DVD entertainment centre and a conversation mirror so parents could monitor what was going on in the back seat.*

Further reading

Imai, M., *Gemba Kaizen: A Commonsense Low-Cost Approach to Management*, McGraw-Hill, 1997

The glass ceiling

The expression "the glass ceiling" first appeared in the *Wall Street Journal* in 1986 and was then used in the title of an academic article by A.M. Morrison and others published in 1987. Entitled "Breaking the Glass Ceiling: Can Women Reach the Top of America's Largest Corporations?", it looked at the persistent failure of women to climb as far up the corporate ladder as might be expected from their representation in the working population as a whole. The idea behind the expression was that a transparent barrier, a glass ceiling, blocked them. Invisible from the bottom when women started their careers, it was steely strong in stopping them attaining equality with men later on. It helped explain the fact that in large corporations in Europe and North America women have rarely come to account for more than 10% of senior executives and 4% of CEOs and chairmen.

A secondary issue is that of women's pay. There is evidence that even when women do reach the highest levels of corporate management, they do not receive the same pay as men for the same job; a figure of 75% is often quoted. And, rather than getting better over time, the position may be deteriorating. One survey found that women executives in the United States were earning an even lower percentage of their male counterparts' remuneration in 2000 than they were in 1995.

So worried was the American government about the issue that in 1991 it set up something called the Glass Ceiling Commission, a 21-member body appointed by the president and Congress and chaired by the labour secretary. The commission focused on barriers in three areas:

- the filling of management and decision-making positions;
- skills-enhancing activities; and
- compensation and reward systems.

The Glass Ceiling Commission "completed its mandate" in 1996 and was disbanded. Needless to say, the problem did not disappear with it. One of the first women to head a major Japanese company, when asked in 2005 what had changed least in Japanese business in the previous 20 years, said: "The mindset of Japanese gentlemen."

Several theories have been presented to explain the glass ceiling:

- **The time factor.** One theory is that the cohorts of first-class female graduates have not yet had time to work through the pipeline and reach the top of the corporate hierarchy. Qualifications for a senior management post usually include a graduate degree and 25 years of continuous work experience. In the early 1970s, when today's senior managers were graduating, fewer than 5% of law and MBA degrees were being awarded to women. Nowadays, women gain over 40% of all law degrees in the United States and 35% of MBAS.
- **Motherhood.** Sometimes the blame for the glass ceiling is laid at the door of motherhood. Women are distracted from their career path by the need to stay at home and rear children. They are unable to undertake the tasks required to reach the top; for example, extended trips abroad, wearing air miles like battle medals, long evenings "entertaining" clients, and changing plans at short notice.
- **Lack of role models.** In her 1977 book *Men and Women of the Corporation*, Rosabeth Moss Kanter (see page 257) suggested that because managerial women are so often a token female in their work environment they stand out from the rest. This makes them (and their failures) much more visible, and exaggerates the differences between them and the dominant male culture.

Some authors have gone so far as to challenge the metaphor of the glass ceiling, arguing that it presents the image of a one-off blockage somewhere high up the career ladder, whereas in reality there is a whole series of obstacles along the way that hold women back.

Further reading

Eagly, A.H. and Carli, L.L., "Women and the Labyrinth of Leadership", *Harvard Business Review*, September 2007

Kanter, R.M., *Men and Women of the Corporation*, 1st edn, Basic Books, 1977; 1993

"Women in Business", *The Economist*, 23rd July 2005

www.ilr.cornell.edu – copies of the Glass Ceiling Commission's fact-finding report, *Good for Business: Making Full Use of the Nation's Human Capital*, and the recommendations report, *A Solid Investment: Making Full Use of the Nation's Human Capital*

Globalisation

Globalisation is the more or less simultaneous marketing and sale of identical goods and services around the world. So widespread has the phenomenon become over the past two decades that no one is surprised any more to find Coca-Cola in rural Vietnam, Accenture in Tashkent and Nike shoes in Nigeria. The statistic that perhaps best reflects the growth of globalisation is the value of cross-border world trade expressed as a percentage of total global GDP: it was around 15% in 1990, 20% in 2005, and expected by McKinsey & Company, a consulting firm, to rise to 30% by 2015.

Use of the word in its business context is alleged to go back at least as far as 1944. But its first very visible appearance was in the writings of Theodore Levitt (see page 263), a professor of marketing whose article published by *Harvard Business Review* in 1983 was entitled "The Globalisation of Markets". In it he foresaw "the emergence of global markets for standardised products on a previously unimagined scale of magnitude".

In "Can We Sustain Globalisation?", a report published in 2007 by SustainAbility, a consulting firm, the authors wrote:

> *Frustratingly Levitt did not provide a compelling definition of globalisation in his article – and the void has subsequently encouraged a dizzying proliferation of competing definitions.*

The report claims to have come across more than 5,000 of them. SustainAbility's favourite is one provided by two *Economist* journalists. Globalisation, they wrote, "is the freer movement of goods, services, ideas and people around the world".

The concept was popularised by an American author, Thomas Friedman, in his book *The World is Flat*. Published in 2005, the book reached the top of several bestseller lists with its headline message that the world is now just one big integrated market.

Globalisation has been encouraged by:

- the growing liberalisation of markets around the world, giving Western multinationals access to customers they never thought they would reach;

■ easy internet access and cheap international telecommunications, the most obvious manifestation of which is call centres in India that are servicing customers and corporations in Europe and the United States;

■ the rapid growth of large developing countries such as China, India and Brazil, and their growing demand not only for Western consumer goods and technologies but also for goods and services from other developing countries. Trade between China and Africa, for instance, rose from $3 billion in 1995 to over $32 billion in 2005.

Companies have approached globalisation in two distinct ways. On the one hand are those such as Gillette and Heineken that have made little concession to local tastes. They manufacture their goods in a few centralised production facilities that follow strictly uniform standards. "The product must be the same everywhere," wrote one Heineken chairman. "To ensure quality, every 14 days our breweries send samples to professional tasters in the Netherlands."

On the other hand are companies that tailor their products or services for each local market. Among them are Japanese carmakers such as Toyota, which now has plants in several countries producing for local markets, and Coca-Cola, which never tastes quite the same from one country to the next. A former chief executive of Coca-Cola admitted that the company had once upon a time changed its globalisation strategy. "We used to be an American company with a large international business," he said. "Now we're a large international company with a sizeable American business."

Further reading

Alexander, M. and Korine, H., "When You Shouldn't Go Global",
    Harvard Business Review, December 2008
Bartlett, C.A. and Ghoshal, S., "Going Global: Lessons from Late
    Movers", *Harvard Business Review*, March 2000
Friedman, T., *The World is Flat: A Brief History of the Globalized World in
    the Twenty-first Century*, Allen Lane, 2005; Penguin 2006
Ghemawat, P., *Redefining Global Strategy: Crossing Borders in a World
    Where Differences Still Matter*, Harvard Business School Press, 2007
Levitt, T., "The Globalisation of Markets", *Harvard Business Review*,
    May–June 1983

Growth share matrix

The growth share matrix is a framework developed by the Boston Consulting Group (BCG) in the 1960s to help companies think about the priority (and resources) that they should give to their different businesses. Also known as the Boston matrix, it puts each of a firm's businesses into one of four categories. The categories were all given memorable names – cash cow, star, dog and question mark – which helped to push them into the collective consciousness of managers all over the world.

The two axes of the matrix are relative market share (or the ability to generate cash) and growth (or the need for cash).

- **Cash cows** are businesses that have a high market share (and are therefore generating lots of cash) but low growth prospects (and therefore a low need for cash). They are often in mature industries that are about to fall into decline.
- **Stars** have high growth prospects and a high market share.
- **Question marks** have high growth prospects but a comparatively low market share (and have also been known as wild cats).
- **Dogs**, by deduction, are low on both growth prospects and market share.

Such an analysis should lead companies to transfer the surplus cash from their cash cows to the stars and the question marks, and to close down or sell off the dogs. In the end, question marks reveal themselves as either dogs or stars, and cash cows become so drained of finance that they inevitably turn into dogs.

The trouble with this colourful schema is that classifying businesses in this way can be self-fulfilling. Knowing that you are working for a dog is not particularly motivating, whereas working for an acknowledged star usually is. Moreover, some companies misjudge when industries are mature. This may lead them to decide that businesses are to be treated as cash cows when they are in fact stars. One such industry was consumer electronics. Considered by many to be mature in the 1970s, it rebounded in the 1980s with the invention of the CD and the VCR. Not, however, before some companies had consigned their electronics businesses to the fate of the cash cow.

The growth share matrix has been blamed for persuading companies to focus obsessively on market share. In a world where markets are increasingly fluid, it is argued, this can blind them to the bigger picture. If Lego, for example, considered its market to be mechanical toys, it would miss the fact that it also competes with companies such as Nintendo for a share of young boys' attention.

The growth share matrix started a fashion for matrices among management consultants. For a while no self-respecting report or theory was complete without one.

Like many leading figures in the world of management theory, Bruce Doolin Henderson, the American founder of the Boston Consulting Group (and the man most responsible for the Boston matrix), was an engineer. One of his favourite quotations was a saying of Archimedes: "Give me a lever and a place to stand, and I'll move the world." He believed that "while most people understand first-order effects, few deal well with second- and third-order effects. Unfortunately, virtually everything interesting in business lies in fourth-order effects and beyond".

Henderson worked for Westinghouse before joining the Arthur D. Little management consultancy. He left ADL in 1963 to set up the Boston Consulting Group, which rapidly established a reputation as the prime strategic consultancy. On his death in 1992, the *Financial Times* said: "Few people have had as much impact on international business in the second half of the 20th century."

Henderson and the firm he created were pioneers in thinking about corporate strategy and competition. BCG was responsible for other enduring ideas besides the growth share matrix. These included the experience curve (the idea that unit costs decline as production increases through the acquisition of experience – see page 79); the significance of being market leader; and time-based competition.

Further reading

Henderson, B., *Henderson on Corporate Strategy*, Abt Books, 1979
Stern, C.W. and Stalk, G. Jr (eds), *Perspectives on Strategy: From the Boston Consulting Group*, John Wiley & Sons, 1998; 2nd edn, The Boston Consulting Group on strategy, 2006

The halo effect

The so-called halo effect is the phenomenon whereby we assume that because people are good at doing A they will be good at doing B, C and D (or the reverse – because they are bad at doing A they will be bad at doing B, C and D). The phrase was first coined by Edward Thorndike, a psychologist who used it in a study published in 1920 to describe the way that commanding officers rated their soldiers. He found that officers usually judged their men as being either good right across the board or bad. There was little mixing of traits; few people were said to be good in one respect but bad in another.

Later work on the halo effect suggested that it is highly influenced by first impressions. If we see a person first in a good light, it is difficult subsequently to darken that light. The old adage that "first impressions count" seems to be true. This is used by advertisers who pay heroic actors and beautiful actresses to promote products about which they have absolutely no expertise. We think positively about the actor because he played a hero, or the actress because she was made to look incredibly beautiful, and assume that they therefore have deep knowledge about car engines or anti-wrinkle cream.

Recognition that the halo effect has a powerful influence on business has been relatively recent. Two consultants, Melvin Scorcher and James Brant, wrote in *Harvard Business Review* in 2002:

> In our experience, CEOs, presidents, executive VPs and other top-level people often fall into the trap of making decisions about candidates based on lopsided or distorted information ... Frequently they fall prey to the halo effect: overvaluing certain attributes while undervaluing others.

This is to consider the halo effect in the context of recruitment. But the effect also influences other areas of business. Car companies, for instance, will roll out what they call a halo vehicle, a particular model with special features that helps to sell all the other models in the range.

In his prize-winning book *The Halo Effect*, published in 2007, Phil Rosenzweig, an academic at IMD, a business school near Lausanne in Switzerland, argued:

Much of our thinking about company performance is shaped by the halo effect ... when a company is growing and profitable, we tend to infer that it has a brilliant strategy, a visionary CEO, motivated people, and a vibrant culture. When performance falters, we're quick to say the strategy was misguided, the CEO became arrogant, the people were complacent, and the culture stodgy ... At first, all of this may seem like harmless journalistic hyperbole, but when researchers gather data that are contaminated by the halo effect – including not only press accounts but interviews with managers – the findings are suspect. That is the principal flaw in the research of Jim Collins's Good to Great, *Collins and Porras's* Built to Last, *and many other studies going back to Peters and Waterman's* In Search of Excellence. *They claim to have identified the drivers of company performance, but they have mainly shown the way that high performers are described.*

Further reading

Rosenzweig, P., *The Halo Effect ... and the Eight Other Business Delusions that Deceive Managers*, Free Press, 2007

Scorcher, M. and Brant, J., "Are You Picking the Right Leaders?", *Harvard Business Review*, February 2002

The Hawthorne effect

The Hawthorne effect is named after what was one of the most famous experiments (or, more accurately, series of experiments) in industrial history. It marked a sea change in thinking about work and productivity. Previous studies, in particular Frederick Taylor's influential ideas (see Scientific management, page 159), had focused on the individual and on ways in which an individual's performance could be improved. Hawthorne set the individual in a social context, establishing that the performance of employees is influenced by their surroundings and by the people that they are working with as much as by their own innate abilities.

The experiments took place at Western Electric's factory at Hawthorne, a suburb of Chicago, in the late 1920s and early 1930s. They were conducted for the most part under the supervision of Elton Mayo (see page 271), an Australian-born sociologist who eventually became a professor of industrial research at Harvard.

The original purpose of the experiments was to study the effects of physical conditions on productivity. Two groups of workers in the Hawthorne factory were used as guinea pigs. One day the lighting in the work area for one group was improved dramatically while the other group's lighting remained unchanged. The researchers were surprised to find that the productivity of the more highly illuminated workers increased much more than that of the control group.

The employees' working conditions were changed in other ways too (their working hours, rest breaks and so on), and in all cases their productivity improved when a change was made. Indeed, their productivity even improved when the lights were dimmed again. By the time everything had been returned to the way it was before the changes had begun, productivity at the factory was at its highest level ever. Absenteeism had plummeted.

The experimenters concluded that it was not the changes in physical conditions that were affecting the workers' productivity. Rather, it was the fact that someone was actually concerned about their working conditions, and the opportunities this gave them to discuss changes before they took place.

A crucial element in Mayo's findings was the effect that working in groups had on the individual. At one time he wrote:

The desire to stand well with one's fellows, the so-called human instinct of association, easily outweighs the merely individual interest and the logic of reasoning upon which so many spurious principles of management are based.

Later in life he added:

The working group as a whole actually determined the output of individual workers by reference to a standard that represented the group conception (rather than management's) of a fair day's work. This standard was rarely, if ever, in accord with the standards of the efficiency engineers.

Fritz Roethlisberger, a leading member of the research team, later wrote:

The Hawthorne researchers became more and more interested in the informal employee groups, which tend to form within the formal organisation of the company, and which are not likely to be represented in the organisation chart. They became interested in the beliefs and creeds which have the effect of making each individual feel an integral part of the group.

Further reading

Gillespie, G., *Manufacturing Knowledge, A History of the Hawthorne Experiments*, Cambridge University Press, 1991

Mayo, E., *The Human Problems of an Industrial Civilization*, Macmillan, 1933; 2nd edn Harvard University, 1946

Mayo, E., *The Social Problems of an Industrial Civilization*, Routledge and Kegan Paul, 1949; later edn with appendix, 1975

Roethlisberger, F.J. and Dickson, W.J., *Management and the Worker: An Account of a Research Program Conducted by the Western Electric Company, Hawthorne Works, Chicago*, Harvard University Press, 1939

Hierarchy of needs

The hierarchy of needs is an idea associated with one man, Abraham Maslow (see page 267), the most influential anthropologist ever to have worked in industry. It is a theory about the way in which people are motivated. First presented in a paper ("A Theory of Human Motivation") published in the *Psychological Review* in 1943, it postulated that human needs fall into five different categories. Needs in the lower categories have to be satisfied before needs in the higher ones can act as motivators. Thus a violinist who is starving cannot be motivated to play Mozart, and a shop worker without a lunch break is less productive in the afternoon than one who has had a break.

The theory arose out of a sense that classic economics was not giving managers much help because it failed to take into account the complexity of human motivation. Maslow divided needs into five:

- **Physiological needs:** hunger, thirst, sex and sleep. Food and drinks manufacturers operate to satisfy needs in this area, as do prostitutes and tobacco growers.
- **Safety needs:** job security, protection from harm and the avoidance of risk. At this level an individual's thoughts turn to insurance, burglar alarms and savings deposits.
- **Social needs:** the affection of family and friendship. These are satisfied by such things as weddings, sophisticated restaurants and telecommunications.
- **Esteem needs** (also called ego needs), divided into internal needs, such as self-respect and sense of achievement, and external needs, such as status and recognition. Industries focused on this level include the sports industry and activity holidays.
- **Self-actualisation**, famously described by Maslow: "A musician must make music, an artist must paint, a poet must write, if he is to be ultimately happy. What a man can be, he must be. This need we may call self-actualisation." This involves doing things such as going to art galleries, climbing mountains and writing novels. The theatre, cinema and music industries are all focused on this level. Self-actualisation is different from the other levels of need in at least one important respect. It is never finished, never fully

satisfied. It is, as Shakespeare put it, "as if increase of appetite grows by what it feeds on".

An individual's position in the hierarchy is constantly shifting and any single act may satisfy needs at different levels. Thus having a drink at a bar with a friend may be satisfying both a thirst and a need for friendship (levels one and three). Single industries can be aimed at satisfying needs at different levels. For example, a hotel may provide food to satisfy level one, a nearby restaurant to satisfy level three, and special weekend tours of interesting sites to satisfy level five.

The hierarchy is not absolute. It is affected by the general environment in which the individual lives. The extent to which social needs are met in the workplace, for instance, varies according to culture. In Japan the corporate organisation is an important source of a man's sense of belonging (although not of a woman's); in the West it is much less so.

Peter Drucker (see page 235) took issue with the hierarchy of needs. He wrote:

> What Maslow did not see is that a want changes in the act of being satisfied ... as a want approaches satiety, its capacity to reward, and with it its power as an incentive, diminishes fast. But its capacity to deter, to create dissatisfaction, to act as a disincentive, rapidly increases.

One of Maslow's early disciples was a Californian company called NLS (Non-Linear Systems). In the early 1960s it dismantled its assembly line and replaced it with production teams of six or seven workers in order to increase their motivation. Each team was responsible for the entire production process, and they worked in areas that they decorated according to their own taste. A host of other innovations (such as dispensing with time cards) revolutionised the company. Profits and productivity soared, but Maslow remained sceptical. He worried that his ideas were being too easily "taken as gospel truth, without any real examination of their reliability".

Further reading

Hoffman, E., *The Right to be Human: a Biography of Abraham Maslow*, McGraw-Hill, 1999

Kaplan, A. (ed.), *Maslow on Management*, John Wiley & Sons, 1998

Maslow, A., "A Theory of Human Motivation", *Psychological Review*, Vol. 50, 1943

Maslow, A., *Motivation and Personality*, 3rd edn, Harper & Row, 1987

Human resources transformation

Human resources transformation refers to the massive restructuring of corporate human resources (HR) departments that took place in the decade or so after 1995. Before that, the staff in HR departments had generally been seen as administrators, not as people to be involved in high-level strategic discussions. HR staff saw themselves as lifetime career specialists with little need for knowledge or experience of what the rest of the business was about.

But with the growing appreciation of the value of a company's human assets, and a need to ensure that the talent (see page 185) that an organisation requires is not just on board but also properly motivated, the role of HR has more and more come to be seen as strategic. The old-style HR that dealt with strikes, bonuses and gripes was rarely suited to this task.

So companies began to look at ways to revamp their HR departments. They were heavily influenced by the ideas of Dave Ulrich (see page 315), a professor of business at the Ross School of Business at the University of Michigan and author of a 1997 bestseller, *Human Resource Champions*, the book that more than any other set the HR transformation ball rolling. Ulrich's idea was that the HR function should be divided into three:

- what are normally called shared service centres (SSCs), groups that deliver the traditional HR services (and do jobs that can often be easily outsourced);
- something described as centres of expertise (COEs), which house the designers of remuneration packages that ensure an organisation can attract the people that it needs;
- business partners, HR people whose job it is to do high falutin' strategic thinking.

The role of business partners has been subject to a wide range of interpretations. Some companies have chosen to appoint hundreds of them; others have appointed just a few. One large organisation with 60,000 employees had 350; another, with some 50,000 employees, had just two. A 2004 study of 20 large American companies by PricewaterhouseCoopers's Saratoga Institute found a median ratio of one HR business partner for every 1,000 employees.

HR transformation became very popular. A 2005 survey of American companies by Mercer, a consulting firm, found half of them "currently in the midst of a transformation process", while another 23% had recently completed an HR transformation. A further 10% were planning to start one within the next 12 months.

The consequences of HR transformation have been dramatic, and in some cases painful. On average, it has been reckoned that around 25–30% of HR staff lose their jobs in the transformation process, with another 20% or so following them over the next few years. A study by IBM's Institute for Business Value estimated that some transformations eliminated up to 70% or more of the workload of the traditional HR generalist.

The great expectations that HR transformation aroused, however, were largely frustrated. After a decade, fewer than 5% of executives said they thought that their organisation's management of people was not in need of improvement. Part of the problem lay in making traditional HR people think strategically. "Don't kid yourself", said one senior executive, "that people who have never been strategic are suddenly going to become so."

For some companies the answer was to look outside their own organisation. Companies such as Microsoft and BT hired HR directors from outside the HR discipline, and others built in the expectation that fast-stream recruits destined for the top should spend time in HR as a matter of course along their career path. In "A Dearth of HR Talent", a report published in *McKinsey Quarterly*, the authors wrote:

> *The troubling gulf between the needs of the business and the ability of HR to respond will force many companies to rethink their approach to the recruitment, training and development of HR employees.*

Further reading

DeLong, T. and DeLong, S., "The Paradox of Excellence", *Harvard Business Review*, June 2011

Losey, M., Ulrich, D. and Meisinger, S., *The Future of Human Resource Management: 64 Thought Leaders Explore the Critical HR Issues of Today and Tomorrow*, John Wiley & Sons, 2005

Ulrich, D., *Human Resource Champions: The Next Agenda for Adding Value and Delivering Results*, Harvard Business School Press, 1997

"A Dearth of HR Talent", *McKinsey Quarterly*, May 2005

Innovation

Innovation is "a creative idea that has been made to work", wrote David Hussey in his book *The Innovation Challenge*. "It can be as basic as a procedural change in a distribution system or as complex as entry into a whole new market." Innovation has been a subject of fascination for centuries. At the end of the 1500s Sir Francis Bacon wrote: "He that will not apply new remedies must expect new evils: for time is the greatest innovator." John Jewkes, author of *The Sources of Invention*, reviewing the history of the subject, wrote:

> There seems to be no subject in which traditional and uncritical stories, casual rumours, sweeping generalisations, myths and conflicting records more widely abound, in which every man seems to be interested and in which, perhaps because miracles seem to be the natural order, scepticism is at a discount.

Peter Drucker (see page 235) suggested seven areas where companies should look for opportunities to be innovative. The first four are internal to the company; the last three are external:

1 The unexpected success that is rarely dissected to see how it has occurred.
2 Any incongruity between what actually happens and what was expected to happen.
3 Any inadequacy in a business process that is taken for granted.
4 A change in industry or market structure that takes everybody by surprise.
5 Demographic changes caused by things like wars, migrations or medical developments (such as the birth-control pill).
6 Changes in perception and fashion brought about by changes in the economy.
7 Changes in awareness caused by new knowledge.

Drucker maintained that creativity was rarely a limiting factor: "There are more ideas in any organisation, including business, than can possibly be put to use," he wrote. The issue is how to manage innovation so that it creates economic value.

Everybody recognises companies that do it well. In lists of them the same names come up again and again – Virgin, Apple, 3M, Toyota – companies where continual innovation has produced exceptionally high returns. 3M's progressive policy on innovation used to commit it to earning 30% of its revenue from products that had been brought to market within the previous four years. Others have since copied its idea.

In the 1990s the emphasis switched from the pure invention of new products to the invention of new processes, shifting from the things companies make to the way that they make them. In 1999, James Brian Quinn, a professor at Tuck School of Business at Dartmouth and co-author of a classic textbook, *The Strategy Process*, wrote: "Most of today's innovation is not in products, but in services and software."

Several commentators have divided innovation into two parts: invention and implementation. The old idea was that invention and implementation followed each other in an unhurried sequence. Alfred Marshall, an economist who lived early in the 20th century, once wrote:

> The full importance of an epoch-making idea is often not
> perceived in the generation in which it is made ... a new
> discovery is seldom fully effective for practical purposes till
> many minor improvements and subsidiary discoveries have
> gathered themselves around it.

Although this may have been true in Marshall's time, it is far less so today. In the online business world, things happen at such a speed that the "minor improvements and subsidiary discoveries" take place almost at the same time as the epoch-making idea itself.

Further reading

Christensen, C., Dyer, J. and Gregersen, H., "The Innovator's DNA",
    Harvard Business Review, December 2009

Drucker, P., *Innovation and Entrepreneurship: Practice and Principles*,
    Harper & Row, 1985; revised edn, Butterworth-Heinemann, 2007

Jewkes, J.,Sawers, D. and Stillerman, R. *The Sources of Invention*,
    Macmillan, London, 1960; 2nd edn, W.W. Norton, New York,1969

Quinn, J.B., "Managing Innovation: Controlled Chaos", *Harvard Business
    Review*, May–June 1985

Just-in-time

When first developed in Japan in the 1970s, the idea of just-in-time (JIT) marked a radical new approach to the manufacturing process. It cut waste by supplying parts only as and when the process required them. The old system became known (by contrast) as just-in-case; inventory was held for every possible eventuality, just in case it came about.

JIT eliminated the need for each stage in the production process to hold buffer stocks, which resulted in huge savings. JIT has other advantages too. It involves the workforce much more directly in controlling their own inventory needs, and it allows a variety of models to be produced on the same assembly line simultaneously. Before its introduction, assembly lines had been able to cope with only one model at a time. To produce another model required closure of the line and expensive retooling.

At the heart of JIT lies the *kanban*, the Japanese word for card. In this context it refers to the card that is sent to reorder a standard quantity of parts as and when they have been used up in the manufacturing process. Before JIT, batches of, say, X + Y parts would be ordered at a time, and the *kanban* would be sent for a replacement order when only Y parts were left. Y was precisely the quantity needed to carry on until the new parts arrived. With JIT only Y parts were ordered, and the *kanban* was sent off as soon as the new order arrived. It thus eliminated, in effect, the need to hold X parts in permanent storage.

Over the years, JIT gathered around it the trappings of an almost mystical philosophy. In their book *Operations Management*, Roberta Russell and Bernard Taylor described how it evolved:

> *If you produce only what you need when you need it, then there is no room for error. For JIT to work, many fundamental elements must be in place – steady production, flexible resources, extremely high quality, no machine breakdowns, reliable suppliers, quick machine set-ups, and lots of discipline to maintain the other elements. Just-in-time is both a philosophy and an integrated system for production management that evolved slowly through a trial-and-error process over a span of more than 15 years. There was no masterplan or blueprint for JIT.*

107

Taiichi Ohno (see page 283), a Toyota employee, is credited with adopting the first JIT manufacturing method at one of the Japanese car company's plants in the early 1970s. However, some say that the idea predates the Toyota experience, and that it began in the 1950s when Japanese shipbuilders were able to take advantage of overcapacity in the steel industry to demand delivery of steel as and when they required it. Some shipbuilders became so skilled at this that they were able to cut their inventories from 30 days' worth to three days' worth.

The system was soon being widely copied, both inside and outside Japan. There was some initial scepticism in the United States, however, until companies like Hewlett-Packard (where it became known as "stockless production") began to demonstrate that the system could be transplanted successfully into other cultures. One study found that American firms that introduced JIT gained over the following five years (on average) a 70% reduction in inventory, a 50% reduction in labour costs and an 80% reduction in space requirements.

Further reading

Cheng, T.C.E. and Podolsky, S., *Just-in-Time Manufacturing*, Chapman & Hall, 1993; 2nd edn, 1996

Russell, R.S. and Taylor, B.W., *Operations Management*, 4th edn, Prentice Hall, 2003

Womack, J., Jones, D. and Roos, D., *The Machine that Changed the World*, Rawson Associates, New York, and Maxwell Macmillan International, Oxford, 1990

Kaizen

Kaizen is a Japanese word meaning, roughly, continuous improvement. It is one of a batch of oriental ideas seized upon by Western companies in the 1980s when it was thought that Japan was the source of most wisdom about management.

"When applied to the workplace," said Masaaki Imai, an author whose 1986 book on *kaizen* sparked much of the Western interest, "*kaizen* means continuous improvement involving everyone, managers and workers alike." Imai subsequently became chairman of the Kaizen Institute, a network of consultants around the world dedicated to helping clients to "sustain continual improvement in all aspects of their enterprises".

Kaizen has also been translated as "refinement", the process by which a rough diamond gradually gets smoothed into a high-quality gemstone. In Japanese culture, the idea of refinement has a particular significance. It is not, for example, considered to be copying to take someone else's idea and then to refine it for yourself. It is considered more like a celebration of your environment.

Like several other Japanese business concepts of the time, *kaizen* begins with the letter K – like *keiretsu* (see page 111), *kanban* (see Just-in-time, page 107) and *kakushin* (revolutionary change).

Kaizen has three underlying principles:

- that human resources are a company's most important asset;
- that processes must evolve by gradual improvement rather than by radical change;
- that improvement must be based on a quantitative evaluation of the performance of different processes. (See also Total quality management, page 191. TQM is a system designed for implementing *kaizen*.)

Kaizen lost some of its shine with the slowdown of the Japanese industrial bulldozer. Even Toyota, one of its most devoted exponents, came to acknowledge that *kaizen* had to be mixed with more radical reforms. In an interview in 2007, the company's boss, Katsuaki Watanabe, said:

Fifteen years ago I would have said that as long as we had enough people Toyota could achieve its goals through kaizen. In today's world, however, change ... may also need to be brought about by kakushin.

However, Watanabe also acknowledged that "when 70 years of very small improvements accumulate, they become a revolution".

Influential in the decline of the idea was the new-found emphasis on the speed of change and on the need for firms to "morph" in double-quick time to seize the opportunities presented by e-commerce (see page 69) and other developments in information technology. It was hard to fit the steady deliberation of *kaizen* into such an environment. *Kaizen*'s gradualism no longer seemed to suit the mood of the times.

Further reading

Imai, M., *Kaizen: the Key to Japan's Competitive Success*, Random House, 1988

Imai, M., *Gemba Kaizen: A Commonsense Low-Cost Approach to Management*, McGraw-Hill, 1997

Lewis, K.C., *Kaizen: The Right Approach to Continuous Improvement*, ifs International, 1995

Keiretsu

*K*eiretsu is a Japanese word which, translated literally, means headless combine. It is the name given to a form of corporate structure in which a number of organisations link together, usually by taking small stakes in each other and usually as a result of having a close business relationship, often as suppliers to each other. The structure, frequently likened to a spider's web, was much admired in the 1990s as a way to defuse the traditionally adversarial relationship between buyer and supplier. If you own a bit of your supplier, reinforced sometimes by your supplier owning a bit of you, the theory says that you are more likely to reach a way of working that is of mutual benefit to you both than if your relationship is at arm's length.

American trade officials, however, disliked Japan's *keiretsu* because they saw them as a restraint of trade. Jeffrey Garten, once under-secretary of commerce in charge of international trade and then dean of Yale School of Management, said that a *keiretsu* restrains trade "because there is a very strong preference to do business only with someone in that family".

Despite its government's disapproval, corporate America liked the idea. Jeffrey Dyer wrote in *Harvard Business Review* in 1996 that Chrysler had created "an American *keiretsu*". The company's relationship with its suppliers, which were reduced in number from 2,500 in 1989 to 1,140 in 1996, had improved to such an extent, claimed Dyer, that "the two sides now strive together to find ways to lower the costs of making cars and to share the savings".

At about the same time Richard Branson, founder of the UK's Virgin group, wrote in *The Economist*: "At the centre of our *keiretsu* brand will be a global airline and city-centre megastores acting like flagships for the brand around the world." In *The New Yorker* in 1997, Ken Auletta mapped out the intricate *keiretsu* that he claimed was being woven by six of the world's mightiest media, entertainment and software giants: Microsoft, Disney, Time Warner, News Corporation, TCI and GE/NBC. Meanwhile, closer to the original home of the *keiretsu*, the South Korean economic miracle was being fired by that country's *chaebol*, industrial groupings that had been modelled closely on the *keiretsu*.

The American variety, however, was fundamentally different from the Japanese model. In Japan the *keiretsu* were regulated by specific laws, and they were structured in such a way that co-operation between them was almost compulsory. But outside Japan, the word *keiretsu* came to mean any loose network of alliances between more than two organisations.

Moreover, American companies' reasons for linking together were slightly different from those of traditional Japanese groups such as Mitsubishi or Sumitomo. The Americans were joining forces, wrote Auletta, "to create a safety net of sorts, because technology is changing so rapidly that no one can be sure which technology or which business will be ascendant". In the process, he predicted that the *keiretsu* would become "the next corporate order". (See also Strategic alliance, page 171.)

Further reading

Auletta, K., "American Keiretsu", *The New Yorker*, October 1997

Dyer, J.H., "How Chrysler Created an American Keiretsu", *Harvard Business Review*, July–August 1996

Miwa, Y. and Ramseyer, J.M., *The Fable of the Keiretsu: Urban Legends of the Japanese Economy*, University of Chicago Press, 2006

Miyashita, K. and Russell, D., *Keiretsu: Inside the Hidden Japanese Conglomerates*, McGraw-Hill, 1994

Cunostible Management

Knowledge management

In 1988 Peter Drucker (see page 235) wrote:

> *The typical business [of the future] will be knowledge-based,*
> *an organisation composed largely of specialists who direct*
> *and discipline their own performance through feedback from*
> *colleagues, customers and headquarters. For this reason it will be*
> *what I call an information-based organisation.*

In such an organisation, the management of knowledge and information becomes a key to gaining competitive advantage.

"Business today", echoed Charles Handy (see page 249) in 1992, "depends largely on intellectual property, which resides inalienably in the hearts and heads of individuals." Both writers were reflecting a growing awareness that companies had moved far from Victorian times, when they were (as Handy put it) "properties with tangible assets worked by hands whose time owners bought". They had become properties whose most valuable asset was intangible – the knowledge which exists in the heads and hearts of employees or in formal databases, patents, copyrights and so on.

Knowledge was seen as the key to the creation not only of business wealth but also of national wealth. In the British government's 1998 White Paper on the competitiveness of the nation, it said:

> *Our success depends on how well we exploit our most valuable*
> *assets: our knowledge, skills and creativity ... they are at the heart*
> *of a modern knowledge-driven economy.*

Lester Thurow, an American management professor, went so far as to suggest in a 1997 article in *Harvard Business Review* that intellectual property rights had become more important than manufacturing products or dealing in commodities. Once companies realised this they became aware of the need to find out how to manage that knowledge, how best to use it to create extra value. This was not an issue they had addressed systematically in the past.

Information technology helped in their efforts to introduce good knowledge-management practices. Developments in IT advanced the science immeasurably. Data warehousing (the centralising of information in vast electronic databases) enabled companies to be more sophisticated and customer-oriented in their business. At last the left hand knew what the right hand was doing; the marketing department knew who was already a customer of the company, and for what product or service.

Knowledge management has been considered as four separate activities:

- **Capturing information.** Companies need to ensure that they are not suddenly bereft of vital information when an important individual employee moves to another employer.
- **Generating ideas.** All employees should be encouraged to come up with new ideas, through ideas boxes or by being rewarded for ideas that make or save money for the company.
- **Storing information.** Data warehouses have to be structured so that the information in them can be accessed by everybody who needs it.
- **Distributing information.** Organisations must encourage the spread of information to others. The hoarding of information has historically been seen as a source of power.

Further reading

Davenport, T.H. and Glaser, J., "JIT Comes to Knowledge Management", *Harvard Business Review*, July 2002

Hansen, M.T., Nohria, N. and Tierney, T., "What's Your Strategy for Managing Knowledge?", *Harvard Business Review*, February 2000

"Managing the Knowledge Manager", *McKinsey Quarterly*, No. 3, 2001

Nonaka, I. and Takeuchi, H., *The Knowledge-Creating Company*, Oxford University Press, 1995

Stewart, T., *The Wealth of Knowledge: Intellectual Capital and the Twenty-first Century Organization*, Currency/Doubleday, New York, and Nicholas Brealey, London, 2001

Leadership

Leadership is "one of the most observed and least understood phenomena on earth", wrote one man in a position to know. In business, interest has focused on three aspects of the phenomenon:

- the nature and behaviour of leaders;
- the nature and behaviour of those who are led;
- the structure of the organisation in which the leading takes place.

Most is written about the first of these. There is a visceral fascination with leaders and their character, and with the great issue that surrounds them: can they be made or are they only ever born?

There is no general agreement about the qualities of a leader. Field Marshal Montgomery thought that a leader "must have infectious optimism, and the determination to persevere in the face of difficulties. He must also radiate confidence, even when he himself is not too certain of the outcome". Henri Fayol (see page 237), an early French writer on management, said that the leader's task is "thinking out a plan and ensuring its success". It is, he added, "one of the keenest satisfactions for an intelligent man to experience".

David Ogilvy, founder of an advertising agency, Ogilvy & Mather, and himself a leader of quality, said:

> Great leaders almost always exude self-confidence. They are never petty. They are never buck-passers. They pick themselves up after defeat ... They do not suffer from the crippling need to be universally loved ... The great leaders I have known have been curiously complicated men.

This view of the leader as complicated is supported by the personality of some undeniably great leaders, such as Napoleon and Winston Churchill. It may also lie behind the fact that up to 60% of past presidents of the United States and prime ministers of the UK had lost their fathers before they were 14.

The leadership of people like Alfred P. Sloan, the legendary boss of General Motors, however, owed more to the structure and systems that they put in place in their organisations than it did on the individual's personality. Henry Ford II's success in revitalising his family's firm after the second world war depended largely on his reorganisation of the company. The man himself was a jet-setting playboy who rarely met David Ogilvy's standards of a great leader.

The leading management thinker on leadership in recent years has been Warren Bennis (see page 217), a professor at the University of Southern California. He has said that successful leaders follow an almost universal principle of management "as true for orchestra conductors, army generals, football coaches, and school superintendents as for corporate executives". When they came to head an organisation, successful leaders "paid attention to what was going on, determined what part of the events at hand would be important for the future of the organisation, set a new direction, and concentrated the attention of everyone in the organisation on it". He also found that the vast majority of successful leaders were white males who remained married to the same person all their lives.

Abraham Zaleznik, in an influential article in *Harvard Business Review*, argued that "because leaders and managers are basically different, the conditions favourable to one may be inimical to the growth of the other". In other words, a long career as a manager may not be the best training for a leader. Yet this is the training that most business leaders get.

The nature of leadership has been discussed since time immemorial. In perhaps the most famous book on the subject, *The Prince*, written in Florence in the 1520s, Niccolò Machiavelli set out his ideas about what a prince must do to survive and prosper, surrounded as he inevitably will be by general human malevolence. Dedicated to Lorenzo de Medici, the book draws on examples from history, of Alexander the Great and of the German city states, to teach its readers some eternal lessons. Many a corporate chief has a copy near his bedside.

Further reading

Bennis, W. and Nanus, B., *Leaders: The Strategies for Taking Charge*, Harper & Row, 1985; 2nd edn, HarperBusiness, 1997

Kotter, J.P., *The Leadership Factor*, Free Press, 1988

McAlpine, A., *The New Machiavelli*, John Wiley & Sons, 1998

Senior, C. et al., "How Earlobes Can Signify Leadership Potential", *Harvard Business Review*, November 2011

Zaleznik, A., "Managers and Leaders: Are they Different?", *Harvard Business Review*, May–June, 1977

Lean production

Lean production is the name given to a group of highly efficient manufacturing techniques developed (mainly by large Japanese companies) in the 1980s and early 1990s. Lean production was seen as the third step in an historical progression which took industry from the age of the craftsman through the methods of mass production (see page 127) and into an era that combined the best of both. It has been described as "the most fundamental change to occur since mass production was brought to full development by Henry Ford early in the 20th century".

The methods of lean production aim to combine the flexibility and quality of craftsmanship with the low costs of mass production. In lean-production systems a manufacturer's employees are organised in teams. Within each team a worker is expected to be able to do all the tasks required of the team. These tasks are less narrowly specialised than those demanded of the worker in a mass-production system, and this variety enables the worker to escape from the soul-destroying repetition of the pure assembly line.

With lean production, components are delivered to each team's work station just-in-time (see page 107), and every worker is encouraged to stop production when a fault is discovered. This is a critical distinction from the classic assembly-line process, where stoppages are expensive and to be avoided at all costs. Faulty products are put to one side to be dealt with later, and a large stock of spares is kept on hand so faulty components can be replaced immediately without causing hold-ups. With such a system, workers on the assembly line learn nothing and the faults persist.

When a lean-production system is first introduced, stoppages generally increase while problems are ironed out. Gradually, however, there are fewer stoppages and fewer problems. In the end, a mature lean-production line stops much less frequently than a mature mass-production assembly line.

Lean production gains in another way too. In typical assembly-line operations, design is farmed out to specialist outsiders or to a separate team of insiders. Gaining feedback from both the production-line workers and the component suppliers is a long and awkward process. With lean production, designers work hand-in-hand with production workers and suppliers. There is a continuous two-way interchange. Snags can be ironed out immediately and machine tools adapted on the hoof. With the assembly-line model, the communication is linear.

Lean-production methods have been introduced by many companies without sacrificing economies of scale (see page 71). Japanese car manufacturers have achieved unit costs of production well below those of more traditionally organised European and American manufacturers with twice their volume. These same Japanese companies have also been leaders in the speed and efficiency of new product design, a crucial skill in a world where time to market is an important competitive lever.

According to Michael Cusumano, who wrote a book on the Japanese car industry, the high productivity achieved by the lean-production methods of Japan's car manufacturers depends not as some have maintained on a peculiarity of Japanese culture or of Japanese workers, but on technology and management. He wrote:

> The methods challenged fundamental assumptions about mass production. These consisted of revisions in American and European equipment, production techniques, and labour and supplier policies introduced primarily in the 1950s and 1960s when total Japanese manufacturing volumes and volumes per model were extremely low by US or European standards.

Criticism of the idea has centred on the feeling that it is possible to be too lean. Beyond a certain point, a sort of corporate anorexia sets in. The total absence of surplus stock or labour can become a serious liability when there is even the slightest disturbance in normal processes or procedures.

Further reading

Cusumano, M., "Manufacturing innovation: lessons from the Japanese auto industry", *Sloan Management Review*, Vol. 30, 1988

Ruffa, S.A., *Going Lean*, AMACOM, 2008

Womack, J., Jones, D. and Roos, D., *The Machine that Changed the World*, Rawson Associates, New York, and Maxwell Macmillan International, Oxford, 1990

The long tail

Companies have always had a strong incentive to come up with new products and services. They may be hoping to incorporate some new technical innovation that their competitors have not yet got hold of, or they may be hoping to penetrate some market segment that has hitherto remained beyond them. The rate of introduction of new products and services, however, has accelerated rapidly in recent years. One American telecoms company, offering a wide range of packages for different consumer groups, was reckoned to have 377m different possible combinations of its services, many of which, of course, were never requested.

This growth has led people to suggest that, in future, companies will be producing for a market of one (see Mass customisation, page 125). Some car manufacturers already claim that no two vehicles that they sell are ever identical, so profuse are the options open to consumers, from the colour of the dashboard to the in-car music system.

Another expression used to refer to this phenomenon is the "long tail" – derived from the fact that when the sales of a company's many products are plotted along an axis they come to look like a long tail, with the most popular at the thickest end and the many not-so-popular ones stretching the tail out to its length.

The phenomenon was given a big boost by e-commerce (see page 69) and internet shopping. Whereas new products used to have to compete for physical shelf space with existing products and literally catch the consumer's eye, with the internet that was not necessary. It became much easier to reach the small markets that exist for products that companies previously would have withdrawn because they couldn't persuade stores to stock them. For example, the internet has helped make it possible for publishers to keep a much larger range of books in print, and it has also transformed the market for antiquarian and out-of-print books, making it possible to search for a particular title across numerous book dealers.

The expression was popularised by Chris Anderson, a former journalist at *The Economist* and editor-in-chief of *Wired* magazine, in his book *The Long Tail: Why the Future of Business is Selling Less of More*. Anderson's theory is that even though the products near the end of the tail do not, individually, sell well, when taken together "all the niches add up".

The idea that it is sound strategy for companies to have a long tail has been criticised on the grounds that it still in many cases does not make economic sense. Since it is virtually costless for iTunes to store music, it can keep stocks of an almost infinite variety of songs. But carmakers cannot offer their customers great variety without huge cost in terms of inventory and ever more complex production processes. The more successful Japanese carmakers, notably, do not offer a wide range of models or options.

In their book *The Breakthrough Imperative*, Mark Gottfredson and Steve Schaubert quote research findings showing that less complex companies grow 80–100% faster than the most complex companies. They say that "the great advantage of modern information technology is not that it allows products and services to proliferate. The real advantage is that IT can help simplify processes."

Further reading

Anderson, C., *The Long Tail: Why the Future of Business is Selling Less of More*, Hyperion, 2006

Gottfredson, M. and Schaubert, S., *The Breakthrough Imperative*, HarperCollins, 2008

Management by objectives

The idea of management by objectives (MBO), first outlined by Peter Drucker (see page 235) and then developed by George Odiorne, his student, was popular in the 1960s and 1970s. In his book *The Practice of Management*, published in 1954, Drucker outlined a number of priorities for the manager of the future. Top of the list was that he or she "must manage by objectives". John Tarrant, Drucker's biographer, reported in 1976 that Drucker once said he had first heard the term MBO used by Alfred Sloan (see page 307), author of the influential *My Years with General Motors*.

With the benefit of hindsight, it may seem obvious that managers must have somewhere to go when they set out on a journey. But Drucker pointed out that managers often lose sight of their objectives because of something he called "the activity trap". They get so involved in their current activities that they forget their original purpose. In some cases it may be that they become engrossed in this activity as a means of avoiding the uncomfortable truth about their organisation's condition.

MBO received a boost when it was declared to be an integral part of "The H-P Way", the widely acclaimed management style of Hewlett-Packard, a computer company. At every level within Hewlett-Packard, managers had to develop objectives and integrate them with those of other managers and of the company as a whole. This was done by producing written plans showing what people needed to achieve if they were to reach those objectives. The plans were then shared with others in the corporation and co-ordinated.

Bill Packard, one of the two founders of HP, said of MBO:

> No operating policy has contributed more to Hewlett-Packard's success ... MBO ... is the antithesis of management by control. The latter refers to a tightly controlled system of management of the military type ... Management by objectives, on the other hand, refers to a system in which overall objectives are clearly stated and agreed upon, and which gives people the flexibility to work toward those goals in ways they determine best for their own areas of responsibility.

MBO urged that the planning process, traditionally done by a handful of high-level managers, should be delegated to all members of the organisation. The plan, when it finally emerged, would then have the commitment of all of them. As the plan is implemented, MBO demands that the organisation monitor a range of performance measures, designed to help it stay on the right path towards its objectives. The plan must be modified when this monitoring suggests that it is no longer leading to the desired ends.

One critic claimed that MBO encouraged organisations to tamper with their plans all the time, as and when they no longer seemed to be heading towards their latest objective. Many firms came to prefer the vague overall objectives of a mission statement (see page 133) to the firm, rigid ones demanded by MBO.

After a while, Drucker himself downplayed the significance of MBO. He said:

> MBO is just another tool. It is not the great cure for management inefficiency ... Management by objectives works if you know the objectives: 90% of the time you don't.

Management by objectives is now largely ignored. Its once widely used abbreviation, MBO, has been taken over by management buy-out, the purchasing of a company by a group of its managers with the aim of making as much money for themselves as possible.

Further reading

Drucker, P., *The Practice of Management*, Harper, New York, 1954; Heinemann, London, 1955; revised edn, Butterworth-Heinemann, 2007

Levinson, H., "Management by Whose Objectives?", *Harvard Business Review*, July–August 1970

Odiorne, G.S., *Management by Objectives: a System of Managerial Leadership*, Pitman Publishing, 1965

Management by walking about

This is a style of management commonly referred to as MBWA. It is variously lengthened to management by wandering about or management by walking around. MBWA usually involves the following:

- Managers consistently reserving time to walk through their departments and/or to be available for impromptu discussions. (MBWA frequently goes together with an open-door management policy.)
- Individuals forming networks of acquaintances throughout their organisations.
- Lots of opportunities for chatting over coffee or lunch, or in the corridors.
- Managers getting away from their desks and starting to talk to individual employees. The idea is that they should learn about problems and concerns at first hand. At the same time they should teach employees new methods to manage particular problems. The communication should go both ways.

One of the main benefits of MBWA was recognised by W. Edwards Deming (see page 233), who once wrote:

If you wait for people to come to you, you'll only get small problems. You must go and find them. The big problems are where people don't realise they have one in the first place.

The difficulty with MBWA is that (certainly at first) employees suspect it is an excuse for managers to spy and interfere unnecessarily. This suspicion usually falls away if the walkabouts occur regularly, and if everyone can see their benefits.

MBWA has been found to be particularly helpful when an organisation is under exceptional stress; for instance, after a significant corporate reorganisation has been announced or when a takeover is about to take place. It is no good practising MBWA for the first time on such occasions, however. It has to have become a regular practice before the stress arises.

By the turn of the century it did not seem extraordinary that managers should manage by walking about. The technologies of mobile communications made it so much easier for them to both walk about and stay in touch at the same time. But in the 1950s many white-collar managers turned their offices into fortresses from which they rarely emerged. Edicts were sent out to the blue-collar workforce whom they rarely met face-to-face. The outside world filtered through via a secretary who, traditionally, sat like a guard dog in front of their (usually closed) office door. Even in the 1980s such practices were not uncommon, as demonstrated in the film 9 to 5.

MBWA was popularised by becoming an important part of "The H-P Way", the open style of management pioneered by Bill Hewlett and Bill Packard, the two founders of the eponymous computer company. Many of the practices of The H-P Way became widely copied by corporations throughout the United States in the late 1980s and early 1990s.

The idea received a further boost when Tom Peters (see page 293) and Robert Waterman wrote that top managers in their "excellent" companies believed in management by walking about. In his second book, *A Passion for Excellence*, Peters said that he saw "managing by wandering about" as the basis of leadership and excellence. Peters called MBWA the "technology of the obvious". As leaders and managers wander about, he said that at least three things should be going on:

- They should be listening to what people are saying.
- They should be using the opportunity to transmit the company's values face to face.
- They should be prepared and able to give people on-the-spot help.

Further reading
Peters, T. and Austin, N., *A Passion for Excellence: The Leadership Difference*, Grand Central Publishing, 1989

Mass customisation

Mass customisation is a production process that combines elements of mass production with those of bespoke tailoring. Products are adapted to meet a customer's individual needs, so no two items are the same.

Mass customisation uses some of the techniques of mass production; for example, its output is based on a small number of platforms, core components that underlie the product. In the case of a watch, the internal mechanism is a platform to which can be added a wide variety of personalised options at later stages of production. Thus the purchaser of a Swatch has thousands of different options in terms of colour, straps, fascia, and so on. Yet all are based on only a few time-keeping mechanisms. The same is increasingly true of cars. Even a traditional mass production manufacturer like BMW boasts that no two cars rolling along its assembly lines on any given day are identical.

Mass customisation is made possible by the use of information technology. Levi Strauss, which pioneered the idea in 1994 with its Original Spin jeans for women, measured customers in its stores and sent their details electronically to its factory. The customised jeans were then cut electronically and mailed to the customer.

The internet greatly increased the possibilities for mass customisation. For example, Dell, a computer company, established its leadership of the PC market by allowing customers more or less to assemble their own PCs online. The company put together the components as requested at the last minute before delivery. Ford likewise allows its customers to build a vehicle from a palette of online options.

Companies that have difficulties introducing mass customisation tend to have them for two reasons:

◪ They fail to define clearly the dimensions along which they are prepared to allow their customers to individualise their purchase. This leads to unnecessary cost and complexity. Dell and Swatch do not offer consumers infinite choice. They are not trying to be all things to all customers. In any case, consumers generally prefer to be told what their limits are, and then to be allowed free rein within them. Successful mass customisers first find out what limits their customers are happy to live within, and then organise their operations accordingly.

◪ They fail to shift their production satisfactorily from a system based on a series of tightly integrated processes, as demanded by mass production, to a system of loosely linked autonomous units that can be configured as and when the consumer wishes. As Joseph Pine, an early writer on the subject, put it: "Mass customisation organisations never know what customers will ask for next. All they can do is strive to be ever more prepared to meet the next request."

There is a danger that mass customisation becomes so popular that it detracts customers from more profitable sales. A company in California, for instance, offered booths in record shops where customers could put together cassette tapes from the recordings of a wide range of artists. It soon found that the service was such a hit that it was cannibalising sales of traditional cassettes and CDs.

Joseph Pine pushed the idea a step further. In *The Experience Economy: Work is Theatre and Every Business a Stage*, he proposed that we are on the threshold of what he called "the experience economy", a new economic era in which businesses will have to orchestrate memorable events for their customers. It will not be enough merely to flog products and services, no matter how individualised they are. Examples of early movers into the experience economy include Starbucks coffee shops. The nature of the overall Starbucks experience allows the chain to charge a premium price for its products.

Further reading

Gardner, D.J. and Piller, F., *Mass Customization*, Happy About, 2009
Pine, B.J. II and Gilmore, J.H., "The Four Faces of Mass Customisation", *Harvard Business Review*, January–February 1997
Pine, B.J. II, *Mass Customization: The New Frontier in Business Competition*, Harvard Business School Press, 1993
Pine, B.J. II and Gilmore, J.H., *The Experience Economy: Work is Theatre and Every Business a Stage*, Harvard Business School Press, 1999

Mass production

Mass production is a way of manufacturing things en masse (and for the masses) that takes the initiative for choosing products out of the hands of the consumer and puts it into the hands of the manufacturer. Before mass-production methods were introduced, producers made things to order. They did not, by and large, manufacture things in the vague hope of selling them at some later date. They made things when they knew they had a customer.

In Elizabethan times, shops were not stuffed with goods waiting for buyers. They were full of craftsmen waiting to fulfil orders. With mass-production methods, manufacturers produce things in large quantities without having orders for them in advance. They worry about selling them later – the price they pay for enjoying economies of scale (see page 71) in the manufacturing process.

Mass production is based on the principles of specialisation and division of labour as first described by Adam Smith in *The Wealth of Nations* in 1776, and as first practised in places like Eli Whitney's gun factory in America in the 1790s. Mass-production methods use highly skilled labour to design products and to set up production systems, and highly unskilled labour to produce standardised components and assemble them (with the help of specialised machinery). The early businesses that used such methods were able to take workers directly out of agricultural labour on the land and on to the factory floor. No significant retraining was required.

The parts used in mass production are often manufactured elsewhere and then put together on a moving production facility known as an assembly line. The result is a standardised product made in a fairly small number of varieties, produced at low cost and of mediocre quality. The work is repetitive, and the workers are regarded as a variable cost to be taken on or laid off as demand dictates. In factories that are designed on the principles of mass production, stopping an assembly line to correct a problem at any one point stops work at all points.

The seminal event in the history of mass production was the appearance of the Model T automobile which, to quote its manufacturer, the Ford Motor Company, "chugged into history on October 1st 1908". Henry Ford himself called it the "universal car", and it became so popular that, by the end of 1913, Ford was making half of all the cars produced in the United States.

To keep up with demand, says Ford's official record of events:

> [The company] initiated mass production in the factory. Mr Ford reasoned that with each worker remaining in one assigned place, with one specific task to do, the automobile would take shape more quickly as it moved from section to section and countless man-hours would be saved. To test the theory, a chassis was dragged by rope and windlass along the floor of the Highland Park, Michigan, plant in the summer of 1913. Modern mass production was born! Eventually, Model T's were rolling off the assembly lines at the rate of one every 10 seconds of each working day.

The moving assembly line was the start of an industrial revolution. In the 19 years that the Model T was in production, over 15m cars were produced and sold in the United States alone. Ford became an industrial complex that was the envy of every industrialist in the world.

In *Innovation in Marketing*, Theodore Levitt (see page 263) gave an alternative view of the Ford saga:

> [Henry Ford's real genius] was marketing. We think he was able to cut his selling price and therefore sell millions of $500 cars because his invention of the assembly line had reduced the costs. Actually he invented the assembly line because he had concluded that at $500 he could sell millions of cars. Mass production was the result, not the cause of his low prices.

Not until the Japanese introduced techniques such as just-in-time (see page 107) did manufacturing industry again experience such a dramatic change. And not until the late 20th century did the development of the internet make it seem possible that the initiative in the buyer/seller relationship would shift back, out of the hands of manufacturers and into the hands of consumers.

Further reading
Ford, H., *My Life and Work*, Doubleday, Page & Co, 1922; Arno Press, 1973
Levitt, T., *Innovation in Marketing*, McGraw-Hill, 1962
Smith, A., *The Wealth of Nations*, 1776

Matrix management

Matrix management is a structure for running those companies that have both a diversity of products and a diversity of markets. In a matrix structure, responsibility for the products goes up and down one dimension and responsibility for the markets goes up and down another. This leaves most managers with a dual reporting line: to the head of their product division on the one hand, and to the head of their geographical market on the other.

Despite the potential confusion that this duality creates, matrix management was enormously popular in the 1970s and 1980s. Leading the fashion was Philips, a Dutch multinational electronics company, which first set up a matrix structure after the second world war. It had national organisations (NOs) and product divisions (PDs), and for a while they operated successfully as a network. The network was held together by a number of co-ordinating committees, which resolved any conflict between the two.

The crux came with the profit and loss account. Who was to be held accountable for it? At first, the answer was both the NOs and the PDs. But this was unsatisfactory, and the NOs eventually got the upper hand. Philips's PDs did not like that, and they fought back. In the 1990s, when the company was not doing so well, its organisational structure was completely overhauled. A few powerful PDs were given worldwide responsibility for the profit and loss account, and the NOs became subservient to them.

In an article in *Harvard Business Review* in 1990, Christopher Bartlett and Sumantra Ghoshal (see page 241) suggested that the problem (especially for multinationals) was that:

> *Dual reporting led to conflict and confusion; the proliferation of channels created informational log-jams as a proliferation of committees and reports bogged down the organisation; and overlapping responsibilities produced turf battles and a loss of accountability. Separated by barriers of distance, language, time and culture, managers found it virtually impossible to clarify the confusion and resolve the conflicts.*

The authors maintained that matrix management had been part of an attempt by companies to create complicated structures that matched their increasingly complicated strategies. But it focused only on the anatomy of the organisation. It ignored the physiology (the systems that allow information to flow in and around the organisation) and the psychology (the "shared norms, values and beliefs" of the organisation's managers).

Organisations could implement matrix management successfully, Bartlett and Ghoshal claimed, if they started at the other end. Their first objective should be "to alter the organisational psychology … only later do they consolidate and confirm their progress by realigning organisational anatomy through changes in the formal structure".

Nigel Nicholson of London Business School says that the matrix structure is "one of the most difficult and least successful organisational forms". Evolutionists like him allege that matrix forms are inherently unstable because they have conflicting forces pulling towards too many different centres of gravity.

Matrix management still has its admirers, although most of them think that it works best in situations where there is a finite task involved and where everyone shares a similar sense of purpose. These include situations like launching a new product, or starting a new business, or putting on a Broadway show, or getting a man to the moon.

Further reading

Bartlett, C. and Ghoshal, S., "Matrix Management: Not a Structure, a Frame of Mind", *Harvard Business Review*, July–August 1990

Nicholson, N., "How Hardwired is Human Behaviour?", *Harvard Business Review*, July–August 1998.

Mentoring

Mentoring is a relationship between two people in which one of them offers advice and guidance to help the other develop in a particular area. This has occurred for centuries in the arts: musicians and painters have traditionally sat at the feet of a master, their mentor, to learn from him. Today, sports stars often have a personal trainer, an individual who looks after not only their physical fitness but also their mental preparedness.

Business executives have become the latest group to subscribe to the benefits of mentoring. Sometimes their mentor is another person inside their own organisation, but more often than not it is an outsider. Mentors differ from executive coaches in that they need to have an overall appreciation of the job of the person that they are mentoring. Coaches are only attempting to pass on specific skills.

Business's enthusiasm for mentoring has been aroused by several things:

- An awareness that the pace of change itself is accelerating, and that to be successful they have to improve their understanding of its implications. Mentoring (by an outsider in particular) is seen as one way of helping them to view the wider context of change in which their businesses are operating.
- A shift in focus back to the importance of the individual. Business has bred its own stars, just like tennis or athletics (think of people like Sir Richard Branson, Steve Jobs or Meg Whitman), and stars need others to help them retain their sparkle. Attending conferences and seminars is not enough for their development and training. They need to work one-on-one (individual to individual) with someone they can trust. These individuals do not have to be brilliant managers themselves, any more than a tennis star's coach needs to be a brilliant tennis player. But they do need a certain level of knowledge and skill in order to have a proper appreciation of the technical and psychological issues facing the person they are mentoring.
- The awareness (or, more correctly, the expression of an awareness) that it is lonely at the top. It has become acceptable to admit that

senior executives are, by necessity, cut off and restricted in whom they can talk to and what they can say. A mentor from outside can set problems in a wider context and talk about them in a disinterested, non-confrontational way.

Managers can be both mentored and a mentor at the same time, in the same way that an athletics star can be a mentor for an up-and-coming young athlete, even while the older person is still competing in the sport and being mentored.

Mentoring does not, however, happen by accident. It has to be formalised to some extent. Meetings have to be scheduled at regular intervals. But in these meetings there should be no fixed agenda – just a mutual interest, good communication skills and some available spare time.

Mentoring is widespread in the United States, in both corporations and not-for-profit organisations. In other countries few companies have made extensive use of it, but its popularity is growing fast – so fast that some worry about the undesirable characters that the business is attracting. Steven Berglas, a psychotherapist and professional mentor, has written that some of "the former athletes, lawyers, business academics and consultants" who have become executive coaches "do more harm than good". They cannot, he says, "spot the difference between a problem executive and an executive with a problem". The former needs training; the latter needs help of a different kind.

Further reading

Berglas, S., "The Very Real Dangers of Executive Coaching", *Harvard Business Review*, June 2002

Johnson, W.B. and Ridley, C.R., *The Elements of Mentoring*, Palgrave Macmillan, revised edn, 2008

Lewis, G., *The Mentoring Manager: Strategies for Fostering Talent and Spreading Knowledge*, Pitman, 1996; Prentice Hall, 2000

Coaching and Mentoring, Harvard Business School Press, 2004

Mission statement

A mission statement is an organisation's vision (see page 209) translated into written form. It makes concrete (for all to see and read) a leader's view of the direction and purpose of an organisation. For many corporate leaders it is a vital part of their attempt to motivate employees and to set priorities.

The challenge is to distil this into a few short, pithy paragraphs that will be memorable to all those with an interest in the company. It is all too easy for a mission statement to become a bland idealistic blur, as in this (anonymous but real) example: "The mission of X is to maximise the company value by providing total quality services, empowering customer-oriented employees and growing through expansion, acquisition and new technology." Such jargon is not likely to fire imaginations struggling to establish an entirely new market.

Many companies buttress their mission statements with a catchy slogan, something that acts as a quick and easy guide to what the company is really about. The best of these can be taken at several different levels and suit many purposes – for example, Harley-Davidson's "It's not the destination, it's the journey"; Nike's "Just do it"; and IKEA's "To create a better everyday life for the people we aim to serve".

Three main benefits are attributed to mission statements:

- They help companies to focus their strategy by defining some boundaries within which to operate. Federal Express, for example, has said it is "dedicated to maximising financial returns by providing totally reliable, competitively superior, global air–ground transportation of high priority goods and documents that require rapid, time-certain delivery". It is not, evidently, going to enter the business of bulk shipping oil products or semiconductors.
- They define the dimensions along which an organisation's performance is to be measured and judged. The most common candidate (not surprisingly) is profit. DuPont, for example, said that it considered itself successful "only if we return to our shareholders a long-term financial reward comparable to the better performing large industrial companies". Corporations often acknowledge their responsibility to other stakeholders as

well, mentioning their attitude to employees ("to treat them with respect, promote teamwork, and encourage personal freedom and growth" – Dow Chemical), or to customers ("to continually exceed our customers' increasing expectations" – Johnson Controls).

◪ They suggest standards for individual ethical behaviour. For example, Body Shop in the UK had what it called "Our reasons for being". Among them were: "To passionately campaign for the protection of the environment, human and civil rights, and against animal testing within the cosmetics and toiletries industries."

Some companies' statements have an almost missionary zeal. One of the most extraordinary was that once drawn up by Marks & Spencer, a British retailer. Its mission, it said, was:

The subversion of the class structure of 19th century England by making available to the working and lower-middle classes, upper-class quality at prices the working and lower-middle classes could well afford.

Johnson & Johnson, one of the most admired companies in the United States, created what it called the J&J Credo. Written in 1943 by Robert W. Johnson Jr when he succeeded his father as chairman of what was then still essentially a family firm, the J&J Credo set priorities by stating that J&J's first responsibility was to its customers. Its second responsibility was to its employees, its third to its management, its fourth to the community, and its fifth and last to its shareholders.

Steve Jobs's mission statement for Apple, written in 1980, was: "To make a contribution to the world by making tools for the mind that advance humankind."

Mission statements got a big boost from the wide publicity given to that of the NASA moon mission articulated by President Kennedy in 1961: "Achieving the goal, before this decade is out, of landing a man on the moon and returning him safely to earth." That mission was achieved, just in time, in July 1969.

Further reading

Abrahams, J., *101 Mission Statements from Top Companies*, Ten Speed Press, 2007

Collins, J. and Porras, J., "Organisational Vision and Visionary Organisations", *California Management Review*, 1997

Niche market

A niche market is a small group of customers who share a characteristic that makes them receptive to a particular product or service. This characteristic may be no more complicated than the fact that they fancy a luxury chocolate every now and then.

Launching a product into a niche market is far cheaper than launching a mass-market product. Potential customers are easier to identify and to target. Niche markets often develop as a subset of mass markets (the market for invalid cars, for example, or for left-handed oven gloves), and mass-market manufacturers sometimes choose to launch niche products as well. Chrysler, for instance, manufactures the Dodge SRT Viper, a niche vehicle that sells in extremely limited quantities to hard-core motor enthusiasts. Fiat produces the Ferrari.

Conversely, what are expected to be niche markets sometimes develop into mass markets. When Apple introduced the PC in the early 1980s, for instance, it did not expect it to become a mass-market product. Out of the mass market for PCs there ultimately emerged some niches, such as the specialist market for architects and designers.

The trouble with niche markets that do not develop into mass markets is that they soon reach a limit. A niche, which can be helpful in getting a product off the ground, can soon become a straitjacket. Manufacturers have to find another niche product, or another market in which to sell their existing product. Specialist food suppliers in Scotland, for instance, soon need to spread south to England, and then to the rest of Europe. Or they need to add oatcakes to their range of smoked salmon and cock-a-leekie soup. And so on.

The internet has features that make it ideal for niche marketing. Through online networks it can gather electronically in one point of cyberspace precisely those groups of customers with similar interests that are a niche marketer's dream. There are online communities with an interest in doll collecting, car racing, cycling in the Himalayas – almost anything you care to mention.

Television too, with its proliferation of channels aimed at specific groups, has become more user-friendly for niche marketing.

Niche marketing has been seen as one phase in a 20th-century journey from mass marketing to one-to-one marketing. This journey was well described in *Maximarketing* by Stan Rapp and Tom Collins:

> *The 50s and 60s were the heyday of mass marketing. There was one kind of Coca-Cola soft drink for the thirsty ... one kind of Holiday Inn motel for the traveller. The 70s became a decade of segmentation and line extension. It was followed in the early 80s by intensified niche marketing that sliced markets into smaller and smaller groups of consumers ... by the mid-80s Robitussin was offering four kinds of medicine for four kinds of cough ... from mass marketing to segmented marketing to niche marketing to tomorrow's world of one-to-one marketing – the transformation will be complete by the end of the 80s.*

That was written in 1987, and the authors' crystal ball got a bit fuzzy at the edges. Two decades later, the internet promised to bring about the one-to-one marketing of goods and services – tailored for a single individual rather than a class of individuals – that the authors had foreseen as the next step after niche marketing. But even then it was still only a promise.

Further reading

Linneman, R.E. and Stanton, J.L., *Making Niche Marketing Work: How to Grow Bigger by Acting Smaller*, McGraw-Hill, 1991

Rapp, S. and Collins, T., *Maximarketing*, McGraw Hill, 1999

Sander, J.B. and Sander, P., *Niche and Grow Rich: Practical Ways to Turn Your Ideas into a Business*, Entrepreneur Press, 2003

Offshoring

Offshoring – the wholesale shifting of corporate functions and jobs (particularly those of back-office workers in IT and accounting-type roles) to overseas territories – is what gave outsourcing (see page 143) a bad name. It is important, however, to note a crucial distinction between the two:

- Outsourcing need not necessarily result in job losses in a particular territory or country. A job can simply be handed over to another organisation of the same nationality and geographical location where (the company handing it over hopes) it can be carried out more efficiently. Sometimes that other organisation may be in another country, but more often than not it is not.
- Offshoring, however, does involve shifting jobs to another country, but it may not involve transferring jobs to another organisation. For example, a company may simply decide to move its local customer services operation to one of its own subsidiaries abroad. That is offshoring, but it is not outsourcing.

Economists argue that offshoring is a win-win phenomenon: the country that sends the work abroad gains from lower costs, and the country that gains the work gets extra jobs. But countries sometimes panic about the scale of offshoring. When production jobs moved en masse to China and other cheap labour destinations, rich-world governments did not worry unduly because they thought that their workers could glide painlessly from manufacturing jobs to service jobs. Who, they thought, would begrudge giving up a lifetime on the factory floor for a lifetime in a clean, antiseptic office?

The real problem arose when the service jobs also started to go abroad, when every other service company's call centre suddenly seemed to be based in Bangalore, in the middle of India, not Indiana. What were Western workers going to move on to this time, once they had been priced out of the services sector?

At one stage, Americans became almost hysterical about the issue. A 2004 report by Forrester Research, a highly reputable firm, estimated that 3.3m American jobs would have gone offshore by 2015. This was immediately taken as a known fact. But the author of the report subsequently told the *Wall Street Journal* that his estimates were no more than "educated guesses". As one commentator said: "The public's intense desire to understand the scope of the problem has bred a reliance on statistics that even [Forrester] admits are based heavily on guesswork."

In practice, the hysteria died down, even as the benefits of offshoring were being questioned more and more. Managers found it increasingly difficult to manage far-flung service operations in cultures they did not understand, and firms began to bring some functions back to their home base – especially call centres, where customers often found it difficult to explain localised problems to someone working in a totally different climate in a totally different time zone. Indeed, in 2006 an Indian call-centre operator opened a new centre in Northern Ireland. The phenomenon became known as "re-shoring".

Closely allied to offshoring is the concept of nearshoring, a phenomenon whereby companies shift operations, often IT-related ones, to foreign countries that are close to their own, but where they can still gain a labour-cost advantage – from the United States, for example, where Spanish is the second language, to Mexico; or from Japan to the Chinese city of Dalian, which was occupied by the Japanese for many years and where there are Japanese-speakers. Nearby countries are more likely to speak the same language as the country of the corporation doing the offshoring; they are more easily accessible at short notice; and they are unlikely to leave the short-stay visitor with jet lag.

Further reading

Friedman, T., *The World is Flat*, Farrar, Strauss and Giroux, 2005
Kobayashi-Hillary, M. (ed.), *Building a Future with BRICs: The Next Decade for Offshoring*, Springer, 2008
"Exploding the Myths of Offshoring", *McKinsey Quarterly*, July 2004
"Offshoring: Is It a Win-Win Game?", McKinsey Global Institute, August 2003

Open-book management

This is the unconventional idea that firms are most effective if their accounts are left open for all their employees to see as and when they wish, at the same time as the employees are taught to understand better the full financial picture. Traditionally, only a handful of senior executives are made to feel responsible for whether a business makes money or not. Open-book management attempts to extend this feeling of responsibility to everybody in the organisation.

It is described by John Case, the man who claims to have invented the expression, as the idea "that companies do better when employees care not just about quality, efficiency or any other single performance variable, but about the same thing that senior managers are supposed to care about: the success of the business". It spread the burden of P&L responsibility – the responsibility for the profit and loss account of a business unit that is generally given as a reward to rising managers – to everyone in the organisation. With open-book management, the idea is that everyone has a certain amount of P&L responsibility.

Open-book management is based on the same sort of logic that persuades parents to leave household bills lying around in sight of their teenage children, in the (frequently vain) hope that the children will make different economic choices if they can see that their telephone bills are much the same as the price of a Caribbean vacation. A corporation's gain from open-book management comes from the extra motivation that employees may get from knowing its true situation, and from feeling that they are trusted not to abuse that information. The danger is that proprietary information will be spread to rivals, and that if business is bad, employees will be damagingly demotivated. Moreover, not every employee wants details of their salary to be widely bandied about.

Although John Case, once a journalist with *Inc.* magazine, claims credit for the invention of the expression, the idea of open-book management was pioneered by a company called Springfield ReManufacturing Corporation. It opened its books to its employees in 1983, and a book called *The Great Game of Business*, written by Jack Stack, the company's president, documented its experience. Every other Wednesday, 35–40 Springfield employees would sit around a U-shaped table and receive a financial presentation from the company's finance director. Departments would also report their results to the meeting. The exercise is said to have made the company's employees act more like business people and less like hired hands.

Several companies have used open-book management as part of an attempt to generate intrapreneurship (see page 77). They have also used it in line with compensation schemes related to the business's performance. In one company, the boss even quizzed employees on the company's profit and loss account and rewarded correct answers with $50 bonuses handed out on the spot.

When R.R. Donnelley, the world's largest printing firm, adopted open-book management it found that it failed to live up to expectations. Case, however, claimed to have found over 100 US-based companies that had raised profits by opening up their books in one form or another. But even he admitted that it takes up to four years to make the culture change that is necessary for open-book management to work.

Further reading

Case, J., *Open-book Management: The Coming Business Revolution*, HarperBusiness, 1995

Case, J., "Opening the Books (open-book management)", *Harvard Business Review*, March–April 1997

Davis, T.R.V., "Open-book management: its promise and pitfalls", *Organizational Dynamics*, Winter 1997

Stack, J., *The Great Game of Business*, Doubleday, 1992

Operations research

At the heart of operations research (OR) is the use of computer modelling and the simulation of business processes as a means of coming up with improvements in the way that things are done within an organisation. The tasks that OR examines are complex and involve many variables. They include things like designing an optimal telecommunications network in a situation where future demand is uncertain, or automating a paper-based bank clearing system.

According to the Operational Research Society:

> Operational Research (OR), also known as Operations Research or Management Science (OR/MS), looks at an organisation's operations and uses mathematical or computer models, or other analytical approaches, to find better ways of doing them.

The term "operational research" is generally used in the UK; the United States favours "operations research" or "management science". Information technology is central to the skill of an operational researcher. But OR also draws on mathematics, engineering, physics and economics.

The heyday of OR was the 1950s and 1960s when, as Russell Ackoff, an OR academic, once put it, "use of quantitative methods became an 'idea in good currency'". By the 1990s, though, Ackoff found that OR had been pushed into "the bowels of the organisation not the head. When it could no longer be pushed down, it was pushed out". This, he believed, was because OR had been "equated by managers to mathematical masturbation and to the absence of any substantive knowledge or understanding of organisations, institutions or their management". Ackoff also claimed that there was a more fundamental flaw to OR. It is, he said, designed to "prepare perfectly for an imperfectly predicted future", and it "helps us little and may harm us much".

Igor Ansoff (see page 215), author of the classic *Corporate Strategy*, was heavily influenced by the time he spent working on sophisticated operations research for the Rand Foundation in the early 1950s. Among other things, he analysed the extent of the exposure of NATO air forces to enemy attack.

OR had been given a big boost by the second world war when

researchers had applied the principles of physics and engineering to military operations. Among other things, it was credited with sharply improving the rate at which U-boats were hit by the simple expedient of changing the depth at which depth charges were triggered. After the war, military personnel took these practices with them to civvy street, and to the companies that they then went to work for. OR was often the entry point for engineers, like Ansoff, to come into general management. Many management gurus, including Frederick Taylor (see page 233), W. Edwards Deming (the founder of the quality movement – see page 155), Henry Mintzberg (see page 275) and Bruce Henderson (the man behind the experience curve – see page 79), were trained first as engineers.

Further reading

Ackoff, R.L., *Redesigning the Future: A Systems Approach to Societal Problems*, John Wiley & Sons, 1974

Kirby, M., *Operational Research in War and Peace: The British Experience from the 1930s to 1970*, Imperial College Press, 2003

Taha, H.A., *Operations Research: an Introduction*, 9th edn, Prentice Hall, 2010

Journal of the Operational Research Society

Outsourcing

Outsourcing is a term used to describe almost any corporate activity that is managed by an outside vendor, from the running of the company's cafeteria to the provision of courier services. It is most commonly used, however, to apply to the transfer of the management of an organisation's computer facilities to an outside agent. This transfer of management responsibility is frequently accompanied by a transfer (from the buyer of the outsourcing service to the vendor) of the specialist internal staff who are already carrying out the activity.

Outsourcing has three main advantages:

- The greater economies of scale (see page 71) that can be gained by a third party that is able to pool the activity of a large number of firms. It is thus frequently cheaper for a firm to outsource specialist activities (where it cannot hope to gain economies of scale on its own) than it is to carry them out itself. Some firms gain the economies of scale by taking on the activity of others, becoming an outsourcer themselves.
- The ability of a specialist outsourcing firm to keep abreast of the latest developments in its field. This has been a particularly significant factor in the area of information technology, where technological change has been so rapid that companies' in-house capabilities are hard pressed to keep up with it.
- The way that it enables small firms to do things for which they could not justify hiring full-time employees.

The most commonly cited disadvantage of outsourcing is the loss of control involved in derogating responsibility for particular processes to others.

Outsourcing is not a new phenomenon. Companies have outsourced their advertising, for instance, for almost as long as advertising has been in existence (and J. Walter Thompson has been in business since the 1880s). Financial services such as factoring and leasing, the outsourcing respectively of the accounts receivable function and of capital funding, have also been available from outside providers for many years.

But it has grown exceptionally fast. According to one estimate, in 1946 only 20% of a typical American manufacturing company's value-added in production and operations came from outside sources; 50 years later the proportion had tripled to 60%.

Much of the increase has come from the outsourcing of IT functions. This was bolstered later by the outsourcing of other functions (such as logistics) that were in areas that themselves had a high degree of IT content. Banks, for instance, began to outsource the IT-intensive processing of financial instruments such as loans or mortgage-backed securities.

The savings from such moves could be dramatic. By deciding to outsource the origination, packaging and servicing of all its personal loans, both old and new, one British bank cut the average cost of processing by over 75%. In the car industry in the 1990s, firms with the biggest profit per car, such as Toyota, Honda and Chrysler, were also the biggest outsourcers (sourcing around 70% to various suppliers). Those that outsourced the least (General Motors, for example, which outsourced only 30% of its value-added) were the least profitable.

The nature of outsourcing contracts has changed over time. What started off as a straightforward arm's-length agreement between a buyer and a supplier moved on to become structured more like a partnership agreement. In this, not only is any increase in the clients' volume of business reflected in the outsourcer's scale of charges, but both parties in some way share the risks and rewards of the outsourced activity.

Relationships like this vary over time and require firms to learn how to work together in entirely new ways. In the early 1990s, in a ground-breaking five-year outsourcing agreement with BP, Accenture (then called Andersen Consulting) took over responsibility for running the day-to-day operation of BP's accounting systems. BP retained control of accounting policy and the interpretation of data for business decision-making. In return, Accenture guaranteed BP that it would reduce the cost of running the service by 20%.

Some firms have been so taken with the idea of outsourcing that they have left themselves with little to do. An American company called Monorail Computers outsourced the manufacture of its computers as well as the ordering, delivery and the accounts receivable. Only the design was left to be handled in-house.

Further reading

Magretta, J., *What Management Is: How It Works and Why It's Everyone's Business*, Free Press, New York, 2002; Profile Books, London, 2003
Oshri, I., Kotlarsky, J. and Willcocks, L., *The Handbook of Global Outsourcing and Offshoring*, Palgrave Macmillan, 2009

Performance-related pay

Any system that relates the rewards of an individual employee to the performance of the organisation that he or she works for is called performance-related pay, or PRP. Such systems are designed to motivate employees and to align their effort more closely with the aims of the organisation. The pay is often financial, but it can also be non-financial, anything from $10 Wal-Mart vouchers to transatlantic flights. Payments under such schemes are usually made separately from regular salary payments. In this way the recipient appreciates that they are variable, separate and not guaranteed.

Sometimes the rise in an employee's annual basic salary is also performance related. This can be helpful in retaining employees who are at the top end of the pay scale for their job ranking, but whose performance is still outstanding. Such employees are more numerous in today's flatter organisations, where the opportunities for promotion to a higher rank are fewer than they were in the multi-layered organisations of 30 years ago.

PRP schemes are most commonly used for managers in private-sector organisations. Technical, clerical and manual employees are less often included, even though (ironically) their performance can be more easily measured. Such schemes are generally self-funding; the improvement in performance more than pays for the rewards.

Some critics argue that pay is not a major motivator in the workplace. They quote Frederick Herzberg's view that the job itself is the source of true motivation, backing up their claim with studies such as one in which staff cited pay as fifth on their list of top ten motivators. Others object to PRP on the grounds that it accentuates the difference between the highest-paid and lowest-paid employees in an organisation. CEO pay as a multiple of average pay has been rising steeply in recent years.

PRP schemes have drawbacks. It can be difficult to design an objective and fair measure of performance that does not emphasise the individual's effort at the expense of that of the team. It can also be difficult to base the rewards on the right time frame. If they are too short-term, they may not be in the best interests of the organisation as a whole; if they are too long-term, they may not be sufficiently motivating to the participants. Poorly designed PRP schemes can interfere with other improvement programmes. One company, for instance, found that its attempts to introduce a just-in-time (see page 107) system were hindered by the reluctance of staff to undertake the necessary training. The training interfered with their productivity in the short term, and hence with their take-home pay.

PRP schemes became increasingly popular in the 1980s and 1990s. One study found that in 1989 44% of American companies had PRP plans in place for employees other than senior management. By 1991 the figure had increased to 51%. A 1998 survey by the UK's Institute of Personnel and Development found that some 40% of a sample of British companies had PRP systems in operation at the time. Ten years later, half of all British companies had PRP schemes for at least some of their workforce. Overall, though, such schemes covered only about a quarter of all workers.

In their 1982 book *In Search of Excellence*, Tom Peters (see page 293) and Robert Waterman mentioned the great variety of non-monetary incentives used by the excellent companies that they studied. They said that excellent companies actively look for excuses to hand out rewards. At Hewlett-Packard, for instance, they found members of the marketing team who would anonymously send 1lb bags of pistachio nuts to salesmen who sold a new machine.

In the 1990s, shares and share options became a regular feature of performance-related pay, particularly in the United States. Behind them lay the idea that the ultimate purpose of companies is to add value for shareholders. And the best way to do that is to turn managers into shareholders by rewarding them with options.

Such schemes succeeded in turning a few senior managers into multimillionaires, as much because of the general bullishness of the stockmarket as of the performance of the managers or of their business. One side effect was that ruthless managers pursued the goal of increasing share value by any means possible, including lying, fiddling the accounts, bribing investment bankers and backdating their stock options so that they began on particularly favourable days.

Further reading

Ferracone, R.A., *Fair Pay, Fair Play*, Jossey-Bass, 2010

Herzberg, F., "One More Time: How do you Motivate your Employees?", *Harvard Business Review*, January–February 1968

Rappaport, A., "New Thinking on How to Link Executive Pay with Performance", *Harvard Business Review*, March–April 1999

Planned obsolescence

Planned obsolescence is a business strategy in which the obsolescence of a product (the process of becoming obsolete – that is, unfashionable or no longer usable) is planned and built into it from its conception. This is done so that in future the consumer feels a need to purchase new products and services that the manufacturer brings out as replacements for the old ones.

Consumers sometimes see planned obsolescence as a sinister plot by manufacturers to fleece them. But Philip Kotler, a marketing guru (see page 261), once said: "Much so-called planned obsolescence is the working of the competitive and technological forces in a free society – forces that lead to ever-improving goods and services."

A classic case of planned obsolescence was the nylon stocking. The inevitable "laddering" of stockings made consumers buy new ones and for years discouraged manufacturers from looking for a fibre that did not ladder. The garment industry in any case is not inclined to such innovation. Fashion of any sort is, by definition, deeply committed to built-in obsolescence. Last year's skirts are always designed to be replaced by this year's new models.

The strategy of planned obsolescence is common in the computer industry too. New software is often carefully calculated to reduce the value to consumers of the previous version. This is achieved by making programs upwardly compatible only; in other words, the new versions can read all the files of the old versions, but not the other way round. Someone holding the old version can communicate only with others using the old version. It is as if every generation of children came into the world speaking a completely different language from their parents. While they could understand their parents' language, their parents could not understand theirs.

The production processes required for such a strategy are illustrated by Intel. The American semiconductor firm works on the production of the next generation of PC chips before it has begun to market the last one.

A strategy of planned obsolescence can backfire. If a manufacturer produces new products to replace old ones too often, consumer resistance may set in. This has occurred at times in the computer industry when consumers have been unconvinced that a new wave of replacement products is giving sufficient extra value for switching to be worth their while.

As the life cycle of products has increased – largely because of their greater technical excellence – firms have found that they need to plan for those products' obsolescence more carefully. Take, for instance, the automobile. Its greater durability has made consumers reluctant to change their models as frequently as they used to. As the useful life of the car has been extended, manufacturers have focused on shortening its fashionable life. By adding styling and cosmetic changes to their vehicles, they have subtly attempted to make their older models look outdated, thus persuading consumers to trade them in for new ones.

Planned obsolescence is obviously not a strategy for the luxury car market. Marques such as Rolls-Royce rely on propagating the idea that they may (like antiques) one day be worth more than the price that was first paid for them; Patek Philippe advertised its watches as being something that the owner merely conserves for the next generation. At the same time as the useful life of consumer goods becomes shorter, consumers hanker after goods that endure.

Further reading

Slade, G., *Made to Break: Technology and Obsolescence in America,* Harvard University Press, 2006

Portfolio working

Portfolio working is a vision of the way people will work in the future. In her book *Portfolio Working*, Joanna Grigg defined it as working for "a group or cluster of different employers, or a job and a business, or whatever combination comes together best for us".

It involves expanding the concept of freelance work far beyond the traditional collection of self-employed professionals – individual accountants, lawyers or portrait photographers who work for themselves, selling their skills to a number of clients. The cost of such people's work is not just a function of time; it is a function of time plus, as the artist Whistler once famously put it, "a lifetime of experience".

Charles Handy (see page 249), who was largely responsible for popularising the idea, wrote in his book *The Empty Raincoat*:

> *Going portfolio means exchanging full-time employment for independence. The portfolio is a collection of different bits and pieces of work for different clients. The word "job" now means a client ... I told my children when they were leaving education that they would be well advised to look for customers not bosses ... They have "gone portfolio" out of choice, for a time. Others are forced into it, when they get pushed outside by their organisation. If they are lucky, their old organisation will be the first client in their new portfolio. The important difference is that the price-tag now goes on their produce, not their time.*

Portfolio workers are never unemployed. Like actors, they may be resting. But at that time they need to be marketing themselves, or they need to have a good agent doing it for them. Handy believes that the age of the portfolio worker will mark the return of the professional agent. A good agent, he says, will "help to organise your life so that there is some order in the necessary chaos of the independent's schedule".

Portfolio workers lack a lot of the things that full-time employees take for granted, ranging from secretarial assistance to office parties. They need to acquire a far wider range of competencies, such as computer skills, marketing, accounting and filling in tax returns. Moreover, unlike full-time employees, portfolio workers should not hope to find confirmation of a job well done (a crucial part of any worker's motivation) from within their own organisation. They have to find it outside, primarily from their clients. This, it can be argued, makes them intensely customer-centric, something that might be expected to serve them well in the 21st century.

Portfolio working has evolved from a growing belief that guarantees of permanent full-time employment cannot continue for much longer. Downsizing (see page 67) and delayering (see page 59) resulted in the shedding of many skilled employees who had little option but to become portfolio workers. The privatisation of state enterprises had a similar impact.

There has been demand–pull as well as supply–push operating in the market for portfolio workers. Many young people now prefer to work in this way. They see it as freeing them from the drudgery of the job-for-life and full-time employment contract that was frequently their parents' main ambition. Portfolio working offers them freedom to plan their days and a far more varied workload.

Nevertheless, portfolio working has not taken off to the extent that some people once expected. The comfort and allure of full-time employment remain compelling.

Further reading

Grigg, J., *Portfolio Working: A Practical Guide to Thriving in the Changing Workplace*, Kogan Page, 1997
Handy, C., *The Empty Raincoat*, Hutchinson, 1994

Private equity

Private equity refers to the money that is used to buy publicly quoted companies (or parts of them) and take them private. It is the antithesis of an IPO (an initial public offering). From next to nothing in the early 1990s, it has grown to be a multitrillion dollar business. It is also a global business, having played a role in developing the Indian mobile telecoms market and China's Shenzen Development Bank.

The private-equity market has been driven by both demand and supply factors. In a low-inflation environment there was a growing "supply" of money in search of higher returns than could be obtained in conventional investment markets. At the same time, there was a growing "demand" from company managers eager to work outside the quarterly results cycle of the public markets and what they saw as regulatory straitjackets such as the Sarbanes-Oxley Act.

Private-equity firms give ambitious managers the freedom and motivation to do well. They have managed to attract some of the best brains in business: Lou Gerstner, a former boss of IBM, and Jack Welch of GE joined private-equity firms on their retirement.

One of the first changes that any private-equity firm makes on buying a company is to align the incentives of its senior managers with the goals of the business. Private-equity firms (much like publicly quoted ones) often give their senior managers shares in the business as an incentive because the ultimate goal is, ironically, to return the business to the public markets via an IPO, whereby the private-equity investors hope to make a substantial capital gain.

Sealy Corporation, an old-established American maker of mattresses, was bought by a private-equity firm in 1997 and sold in 2004 for five times the purchase price. Frans Bonhomme, a French plumbing company, was bought and sold by private-equity firms four times in 11 years, with each seller making a profit on the deal. Most private-equity firms are looking to turn around their purchases in four or five years.

Over time, private equity moved into bigger and bigger businesses. What started as a means to squeeze what were little more than overgrown family firms developed into massive projects of corporate regeneration (such as that at Deutsche Telekom). Some private-equity firms have begun to look like old-style conglomerates such as Hanson or ITT, consisting of a small headquarters whose main task is to distribute capital and choose the right people to run the businesses in their portfolio. With both Hanson and ITT, that strategy soon ran out of steam.

The private-equity market ran out of steam when the credit crisis of 2008 cut it off from its lifeblood – borrowed money. Traditionally the market had relied on taking companies over with highly leveraged deals. Businesses backed by private equity generally had a high ratio of borrowed capital to equity than did publicly quoted companies. With credit in short supply, the number of deals was sharply reduced and several good businesses owned by private-equity firms were forced into bankruptcy.

Exacerbating the industry's problems was a strong determination on both sides of the Atlantic to ensure that the market was more tightly regulated in future than it had been in the past. American legislators tried to compel "private investment companies" (which included hedge funds and private-equity firms) to register with the Securities and Exchange Commission, their main capital-market watchdog. In Europe, the EU commission moved in a similar direction with proposals for legislation that would oblige firms to disclose data to regulators.

Further reading

Gadiesh, O. and MacGregor, H., *Lessons from Private Equity*, Harvard Business School Press, 2008

Lerner, J., Hardyman, F. and Leamon, A., *Venture Capital and Private Equity: a Casebook*, Wiley, 5th edn, 2012

Product life cycle

This is the idea that products, like people, have a birth, a life and a death, and that they should be financed and marketed with this in mind. Even as a new product is being launched, its manufacturer should be preparing for the day when it has to be killed off knowing that its sales and profits start at a low level, rise (it is hoped) to a high level and then decline again to a low level. This cycle is sometimes referred to simply as PLC.

Philip Kotler (see page 261) breaks the product life cycle into five distinct phases:

1 **Product development.** The phase when a company looks for a new product. New products do not have to be "out-of-the-blue" new (like the video-cassette recorder or the compact disc). They may be merely additions to existing product lines (the first cigarette with a filter tip, for instance) or improvements to existing products (a new whiter-than-white washing powder).
2 **Introduction.** The product's costs rise sharply as the heavy expense of advertising and marketing any new product begins to take its toll.
3 **Growth.** As the product begins to be accepted by the market, the company starts to recoup the costs of the first two phases.
4 **Maturity.** By now the product is widely accepted and growth slows down. Before long, however, a successful product in this phase will come under pressure from competitors. The producer will have to start spending again in order to defend the product's market position.
5 **Decline.** A company will no longer be able to fend off the competition, or a change in consumer tastes or lifestyle will render the product redundant. At this point the company has to decide how to bring the product's life to an end – what is the best end-game that it can play? (See Game theory, page 87.)

Even if managers know that a new product will follow this cycle, they cannot be sure when each phase will start and for how long it will last. Although some products appear to have been around for ever (Kellogg's corn flakes, for example, or Kleenex tissues) the products that bear these names today are vastly different from the ones that carried the same name

50 years ago. The continuity of the brand name helps to disguise the fact that the product itself has been through several life cycles.

Products of fashion, by definition, have a shorter life cycle, and they thus have a much shorter time in which to reap their reward. A distinction is sometimes made between fashion items, such as clothing, and pure fads, such as the notorious pet rocks. It is not always immediately obvious into which of these two categories a product falls. When they were first introduced in the early 1980s, in-line skates seemed as if they might be a brief fad. But 30 years later they were still selling strongly, firmly set in the mature stage of their life cycle. They may not be destined for the life cycle of the corn flake, but they have already outlived many seemingly more permanent products.

Further reading

Kotler, P., *Marketing Management: Analysis, Planning, Implementation and Control*, Prentice Hall, 1967; 12th edn, 2006

Levitt, T., "Exploit the Product Life Cycle", *Harvard Business Review*, March 2009

Treacy, M. and Wiersema, F., *The Discipline of Market Leaders*, Addison-Wesley, 1997

Quality circle

The idea of the quality circle was first introduced by a number of large Japanese firms in a systematic attempt to involve all their employees, at every level, in their organisation's drive for quality.

According to the *Quality Circles Handbook*:

> *A quality circle is a small group of between three and 12 people who do the same or similar work, voluntarily meeting together regularly for about one hour per week in paid time, usually under the leadership of their own supervisor, and trained to identify, analyse and solve some of the problems in their work, presenting solutions to management and, where possible, implementing solutions themselves.*

There are two main tasks assigned to quality circles: the identification of problems; and the suggestion of solutions. A further aim is to boost the morale of the group through attendance at the meetings and the formal opportunity to discuss work-related issues.

Meetings are held in an organised way. A chairman is appointed on a rotating basis and an agenda is prepared. Minutes are also taken. They serve as a useful means of following up proposals and their implementation. The success of quality circles has been found to depend crucially on the amount of support they get from senior management, and on the amount of training that the participants are given in the ways and aims of the circles.

Kaoru Ishikawa, a professor at Tokyo University who died in 1989, is attributed with much of the development of the idea of quality circles. They created great excitement in the West in the 1980s, at a time when every Japanese management technique was treated with great respect. Many firms in Europe and the United States set them up, including Westinghouse and Hewlett-Packard. It was claimed at one time in the 1980s that there were as many as 10m people participating in quality circles in Japanese industry alone.

However, the method also came in for a good deal of criticism. Even Joseph Juran (see page 255), one of the two American post-war germinators of the quality idea (the other was W. Edwards Deming, see page 233), considered that quality circles were pretty useless if the company's management was not trained in the more general principles of total quality management (see page 191).

Others criticised the way in which the idea was transferred from one culture to another without any attempt to tailor it to local traditions. It may, such critics suggested, be well suited to Japan's participative workforce, but in more individualistic Western societies it became a formalised hunt for people to blame for the problems that it identified. The original intention was for it to be a collective search for a solution to those problems.

Quality circles fell from grace as they were thought to be failing to live up to their promise. One study found that 80% of a sample of large companies in the West that had introduced quality circles in the early 1980s had abandoned them before the end of the decade. In his book *Quality: A Critical Introduction*, John Beckford quotes the example of a Western retailer that took almost every wrong step in the book. These included:

- training only managers to run quality circles, and not the staff in the retail outlets who were expected to participate in them;
- setting up circles where managers appointed themselves as leaders and made their secretaries keep the minutes. This maintained the existing hierarchy which quality circles are supposed to break out of;
- expecting staff to attend meetings outside working hours and without pay;
- ignoring real problems raised by the staff (about, for example, the outlets' opening hours) and focusing on trivia (were there enough ashtrays in the customer reception area).

Further reading

Beckford, J., *Quality: A Critical Introduction*, Routledge, London, 1998; 4th edn, 2002

Crosby, P., *Quality is Free: The Art of Making Quality Certain*, McGraw-Hill, 1979

Ishikawa, K., *What is Total Quality Control? The Japanese Way*, Prentice Hall, 1985

Juran, J., *Juran on Planning for Quality*, Free Press, New York, and Collier Macmillan, London, 1988

Scenario planning

Scenario planning (sometimes called "scenario and contingency planning") is a structured way for organisations to think about the future. A group of executives sets out to develop a small number of scenarios – stories about how the future might unfold and how this might affect an issue that confronts them.

The issue can be a narrow one: whether to make a particular investment, for example. Should a supermarket put millions into more out-of-town megastores and their attendant car parks, or should it invest in secure websites and a fleet of vans to make door-to-door deliveries? Or it can be much wider: an American education authority, for instance, contemplating the impact of demographic change on the need for new schools. Will the ageing of the existing population be counterbalanced by the rising level of immigration?

In Peter Schwartz's book *The Art of the Long View*, scenarios are described as:

> Stories that can help us recognise and adapt to changing aspects of our present environment. They form a method for articulating the different pathways that might exist for you tomorrow, and finding your appropriate movements down each of those possible paths.

Scenario planning has been used by some of the world's largest corporations, including Royal Dutch Shell, Motorola, Disney and Accenture. Two things lay behind its rapid growth in the 1970s:

- Widespread dissatisfaction with existing ways of planning. Many organisations realised how misleading were predictions based on straight-line extrapolations from the past. The oil price hikes of 1973 and 1978 dramatically and painfully brought home how vulnerable businesses were to sudden discontinuities. The unusually smooth path of economic progress since the second world war had lulled them into a false sense of continuity.
- Growing attachment to the idea that business can make better use of the non-rational side of human nature. At the head of Royal Dutch Shell's planning department at the time was Pierre Wack (see page

317), a Belgian who had been persuaded to give up the editorship of a Franco-German philosophy magazine to join the company.

The appeal of scenario planning increased further in the wake of the September 11th 2001 terrorist attacks in the United States and the greater perceived uncertainty of the 21st century. According to Bain & Company's annual survey of management tools, fewer than 40% of companies used scenario planning in 1999. But by 2006 its usage had risen to 70%. As a result of its scenario planning, the New York Board of Trade decided in the 1990s to build a second trading floor outside the World Trade Centre, a decision that kept it going after September 11th 2001.

In an article in *Harvard Business Review* in 1985, Wack wrote:

> *Scenarios deal with two worlds; the world of facts and the world of perceptions. They explore for facts but they aim at perceptions inside the heads of decision-makers. Their purpose is to gather and transform information of strategic significance into fresh perceptions.*

The process of scenario planning usually begins with a long discussion about how the participants think that big shifts in society, economics, politics and technology might affect a particular issue. From this the group aims to draw up a list of priorities, including things that will have the most impact on the issue under discussion and those whose outcome is the most uncertain. These priorities then form the basis for sketching out rough pictures of the future.

Scenario planning draws on a wide range of disciplines and interests, including economics, psychology, politics and demographics. The recommended reading list of Global Business Network, a leading adviser on scenario planning, includes Alexis de Tocqueville's *Democracy in America* as well as Peter Senge's *The Fifth Discipline* and *The Leopard*, Giuseppe Tomasi's sweeping tale of Sicilian family life.

Further reading

Lindgren, M. and Bandhold, H., *Scenario Planning: The Link Between Future and Strategy*, Palgrave Macmillan, 2009

Schwartz, P., *The Art of the Long View*, Doubleday/Currency, 1991; John Wiley & Sons, 1998

Wack, P., "The Gentle Art of Re-perceiving", *Harvard Business Review*, September–October 1985

Scientific management

Scientific management was the first big management idea to reach a mass audience. It swept through corporate America in the early years of the 20th century, and much management thinking since has been either a reaction to it or a development of it.

The idea was first propounded by Frederick Winslow Taylor (see page 309), partly in response to a motivational problem which at the time was called "soldiering" – the attempt among workers to do the least amount of work in the longest amount of time. To counter this, Taylor proposed that managers should scientifically measure productivity and set high targets for workers to achieve. This was in contrast to the alternative method, known as initiative and incentive, in which workers were rewarded with higher wages or promotion. Taylor described this method as "poisonous".

Scientific management required managers to walk around with stop watches and note pads carrying out time-and-motion studies on workers in different departments. It led to the piece-rate system in which workers were paid for their output, not for their time. Taylor's first publication, which came out in 1895, was called *A Piece-Rate System.*

He believed that "the principal object of management should be to secure the maximum prosperity for the employer, coupled with the maximum prosperity of each employee". The interests of management, workers and owners were, he maintained, intertwined. He wanted to remove "all possible brain work" from the shop floor, handing all action, as far as possible, over to machines. "In the past, the man has been first; in the future the machine must be first," he was fond of saying. He ignited a debate about man versus machine that continued far into the 20th century.

The famous book in which he enunciated his theories, *The Principles of Scientific Management,* had a strong impact on subsequent management thinking. It influenced people such as Frank and Lillian Gilbreth (see page 243), American time-and-motion experts; it influenced industrial psychologists, many of whom saw it as an insult to the human spirit and set out to show that allowing free rein to human initiative produced superior results; and it influenced industrialists like the Michelin brothers (of tyre fame).

At the core of scientific management lie four principles:

- Replace rule-of-thumb methods of doing work with ones based on scientific study of the tasks to be carried out.
- Select and train individuals for specific tasks.
- Give individuals clear instructions on what they have to do, then supervise them while they do it.
- Divide work between managers and workers, so that the managers plan "scientifically" what is to be done, and the workers then do it.

Peter Drucker (see page 235) once wrote that Taylor was "the first man in history who did not take work for granted, but looked at it and studied it. His approach to work is still the basic foundation". The trade union movement, however, always hated it. A union officer once said: "No tyrant or slave driver in the ecstasy of his most delirious dream ever sought to place upon abject slaves a condition more repugnant."

There is little space for Taylor's ideas in today's world of freewheeling teamwork. But the writings of people such as Michael Porter (see page 295) and Michael Hammer (see page 247), with their emphasis on breaking business down into measurable (and controllable) activities, hold more than a faint echo of Taylor's ideas.

Further reading

Gilbreth, F.B., *Primer of Scientific Management*, D. Van Nostrand, 1912

Taylor, F.W., *Two Papers on Scientific Management: A Piece-rate System and Notes on Belting*, George Routledge, 1919

Taylor, F.W., *The Principles of Scientific Management*, Harper and Brothers, 1911; reprint, Hive Publishing Company, 1986

Urwick, L. and Brech, E.F.L., *The Making of Scientific Management*, Management Publications Trust, 1945–6; reprint, 1965

Segmentation

Segmentation is the process of slicing the market for a particular product or service into a number of different segments. The segments are usually based on factors such as demographics, beliefs or the occasion of use of the product. One segment of the market for video cameras, for instance, might be the group of people who have new-born babies. Another could be the group of people visiting relatives who live abroad.

In their book *Breakthrough Imperatives*, Mark Gottfredson and Steven Schaubert say:

> *The goal of customer segmentation analysis is to identify the most attractive segments of a company's customer base (existing or potential) by comparing the segments' size, growth and profitability.*

The idea of segmentation has spread beyond its consumer origins. Human-resources departments now talk about segmenting their "customers" – that is, the different groups of employees within their own organisation. In a bank, for example, three such segments might be retail bank tellers, investment bank advisers and money-market traders.

Once different segments of a market have been identified, suppliers to that market can target their advertising and promotional efforts more accurately and more profitably. Different segments can be reached through the most appropriate channel: parents of new-borns through ante-natal clinics, for instance, and foreign travellers through airlines' websites.

Each market segment represents a group of potential customers with common characteristics. In consumer markets, segmentation is usually based on the following:

- **Demographic factors.** Gender, age, family size, and so on.
- **Geography.** In most countries there are marked differences in the consumer preferences of different regions. The consumption of wine in the north of England, for example, is very different from that in the south.
- **Social factors.** One classic segmentation is by income and occupation, but this is proving to be less and less useful. There

are a lot of extremely wealthy people who do not spend much, and vice versa. So the focus is shifting to lifestyle. In recent years, marketers have become more interested in categorising consumers as "generation xers" or "the millennial generation" rather than by the size of their bank accounts. Consumers are thought to have more in common with people from the same generation than with any other grouping.

Industrial markets have been notoriously more difficult to segment than consumer markets. Firms find it hard to decide which factors are most useful for categorising their corporate clients. Should it be size, industry sector, or geography? Computer-maker Hewlett-Packard segmented its big industrial customers into five categories based on the value of their purchases and the complexity of their IT systems.

Segmentation was in part a reaction against the mass-marketing tactics sparked off by Henry Ford when he said that customers could buy his Model T car "in any colour as long as it's black". Many of its classifications, however, have proved to be of little use. Baby boomers have been found to have little more in common than their defining characteristic: a birthdate in the years following the second world war. John Forsyth, a consultant, wrote in McKinsey Quarterly in 1999:

> Unfortunately, easy cases permitting marketers to establish meaningful differences among groups of customers and then to identify them – a phenomenon we call "actionable segmentation" – are rare.

The internet provides new opportunities for segmentation by offering continuous opportunities to capture information about customer behaviour. Consumers identify themselves and their characteristics by their electronic participation in particular interest groups, and by their general online behaviour.

Further reading

Coupland, Douglas, Generation X, St Martin's Press, 1991

Howe, N. and Strauss, W., Millennials Rising: The Next Great Generation, Vintage, 2000

Kotler, P. and Keller, K., Marketing Management, 14th edn, Prentice Hall, 2011

The Seven Ss

The Seven Ss is a framework developed in the late 1970s and early 1980s for analysing organisations and looking at the various elements that make them successful (or not). The framework has seven aspects, each of them beginning with the letter S, hence the mnemonic:

1 Strategy: the route that the organisation has chosen for its future growth.
2 Structure: the way in which the organisation is put together; how its different bits relate to each other.
3 Systems: the formal and informal procedures that govern everyday activity; today this inevitably involves the implementation of information technology.
4 Skills: the distinctive capabilities of the people who work for the organisation.
5 Shared values: originally called superordinate goals, the things that influence a group to work together for a common aim.
6 Staff: the organisation's human resources.
7 Style: the way in which the organisation's employees present themselves to the outside world, to suppliers and customers in particular.

The Seven Ss helped change managers' thinking about how companies could be improved. The theory told them that it was not just a matter of devising a new strategy and following it through (as they might have thought before). Nor was it a matter of setting up new systems and letting them generate improvements. To improve, companies had to pay attention to all seven Ss at the same time.

The seven were often subdivided into the first three (strategy, structure and systems), referred to as the hard Ss, and the last four, called the soft Ss. All seven are interrelated, so a change in one has a ripple effect on all the others. Hence it is impossible to make progress on one without making progress on all of them.

The theory was developed in the context of the astoundingly rapid progress of Japanese manufacturing companies in the 1960s and 1970s. Western companies, it was said, were better at the hard Ss. But it was because the Japanese combined both hard and soft that they were so much more successful.

Diagrammatically, the seven are usually represented in a circle to convey the idea that they are all of equal significance. No one of them is more important than any other, although Richard Pascale (see page 289), the theory's champion (see page 29), subsequently gave a special status to superordinate goals (also known as shared values). These, he said, "provide the glue that holds the other six together". This positioning of superordinate goals at the centre of the circle stimulated some of the subsequent work on corporate culture (see page 52), since culture is to some extent a combination of an organisation's superordinate goals and its style.

Just as the growth share matrix (see page 95) is powerfully associated with one of the leading strategy consultancies (the Boston Consulting Group), so the Seven Ss is linked with another (McKinsey & Company). It was the seedcorn from which grew the idea of excellence and one of the most popular business books ever written (*In Search of Excellence*). Excellent companies were those that excelled in all of the Seven Ss. Pascale subsequently expanded the idea in his book *The Art of Japanese Management*, in which he compared a Japanese company, Matsushita, with an American company, ITT, greatly to the credit of the former.

Further reading

Pascale, R., and Athos, A., *The Art of Japanese Management: Applications for American Executives*, Simon & Schuster, 1981

Six Sigma

This is an approach to quality improvement based on the statistical work of Joseph Juran (see page 255), one of two American pioneers of quality management in Japan (see Total quality management, page 191). Sigma is a Greek letter used in mathematics to denote standard deviation, a statistical measure of the extent to which a series of numbers or readings deviates from its mean. One Sigma indicates a wide scattering of the readings. If the mean is the required quality standard of a particular process or product, then One Sigma quality is not very good. The higher the number, the closer the readings come to total perfection. At the Six Sigma level, there are only 3.4 defects per million.

This may sound complicated, but in practice it has proved a popular way for managers to put quality management into effect. One of its great advantages is that it eschews the idea of aiming for "zero defects", or total perfection – a dauntingly inaccessible goal for most. It presents a system for improving quality gradually. Companies or operational groups move step-by-step up the Sigma ladder, the ultimate goal being to reach the Six Sigma state – still just short of perfection. Reasonably unsophisticated computer programs do the necessary calculations when fed with data on the goals (the specifications of the perfect product or process) and the organisation's actual achievements.

Six Sigma sounds like some sort of secret coven. Its advocates insist that it is no such thing. But it has certain attributes of the exclusive society. Anyone in an organisation who goes on a basic training course for a Six Sigma programme (and training is essential to an understanding of what it is about) is called a Green Belt. Anyone who is given the full-time job of leading a team that is embarking on a Six Sigma exercise is given further training and is called a Black Belt. Beyond this there are a special few who are trained even more, and they are called Master Black Belts. Their role is to champion the exercise throughout the organisation and to watch over the Black Belts and ensure that they are consistently improving the quality of their team's output.

In its annual report for the year 2000, chemicals giant DuPont reported:

Six Sigma implementation continues to gain momentum. At the *end of the year, there were about 1,100 trained Black Belts and over 3,400 active projects. The potential pre-tax benefit from active projects was $700m.*

Pioneered in the United States by Motorola in the 1980s (and registered by the company as its own trademark), Six Sigma became hugely popular in the 1990s after Jack Welch adopted it at General Electric. Mikel Harry and Richard Schroeder, the two men who introduced the method to Motorola, went on to set up the Six Sigma Academy, a consultancy which worked with companies such as Allied Signal, GE and ABB.

To achieve Six Sigma quality at GE, a process must produce no more than 3.4 defects per million "opportunities". An opportunity is defined as "a chance for non-conformance, or not meeting the required specifications". The company says: "Six Sigma has changed the DNA of GE. It is now the way we work – in everything we do and in every product we design".

However, Six Sigma has not been an unmitigated success for everybody. Robert Nardelli took it with him when he moved from GE to head up Home Depot. But in August 2007 the *Wall Street Journal* reported that he had angered the employees there greatly with his attempt to force it upon them.

Further reading

Pande, P.S., Neuman, R.P. and Cavanagh, R.R., *The Six Sigma Way*, McGraw-Hill, 2000

Pyzdek, T., *The Six Sigma Handbook: A Complete Guide for Greenbelts, Blackbelts, and Managers At All Levels*, McGraw-Hill, 3rd edn, 2009

Skunkworks

A skunkworks is a place (or sometimes the people who work in that place) designed to encourage the employees of large organisations to come up with original ideas. It usually consists of a small team taken out of their normal working environment and given exceptional freedom from their organisation's standard management constraints. The name is taken from the moonshine factory in a famous Al Capp cartoon series called "Li'l Abner".

All skunkworks are modelled on the Lockheed aircraft company's secret research-cum-production facility where, in the 1940s, staff were removed from the corporate bureaucracy and encouraged to ignore standard procedures in the hope that they would come up, in the first instance, with a high-speed fighter plane that could compete with those produced in Germany by Messerschmitt. So successful was the concept that the company continued with it, and its skunkworks came up with a number of other innovative products, including the notorious U2 spy plane.

The idea was soon copied by other large companies, including IBM, by then the largest of them all, although the name "Skunk Works" is a registered trademark of Lockheed Martin Corporation. In 1980 Big Blue used a skunkworks to break free from its suffocating mainframe mentality and to join the world of the PC, at a time when many of its rivals were unable to make the switch.

The skunkworks concept fell into disrepute when it began to be seen as just another cost centre – and one with attitude at that. But in the new workplace of the 21st century, where there is a heavy emphasis on teamwork and the right environment for teams to flourish, the skunkworks idea is being revived, but in slightly different guise. Much of Motorola's Razr mobile phone, for example, was developed in a new laboratory that the company set up in downtown Chicago, 50 miles from its main R&D facility in suburban Illinois. With lots of bright colours and no dividing walls, the building and design of the laboratory's workspace were very different from Motorola's main offices.

But the company's expectations of what the skunkworks should produce were also different. It was not left alone to think lofty scientific thoughts, but was regularly kept in touch with marketing, design and accounting folk to keep its feet firmly on commercial ground. The idea is not (as it used to be) that those in the skunkworks emerge at the end of the day with something that makes their competitors say "Wow". The idea is that they come out with something that makes their competitors' customers say "Wow".

Some companies adopted the skunkworks idea more widely. Malaysia Airlines set up what it called "laboratories", small groups of people brought together on an ad hoc basis to address specific issues – "raising revenues", for instance. The group stayed together for a month or so, until it fulfilled its agreed-upon "exit criteria". Working in a laboratory, said the airline's CEO, "is not a job; it's a calling".

Further reading

Bennis, W. and Biederman, P.W., *Organising Genius: The Secrets of Creative Collaboration*, Addison-Wesley, 1997; new edn, Nicholas Brealey, 1998

Rich, B.R., *Skunkworks: A Personal Memoir of my Years at Lockheed*, Back Bay Books, 1996

Span of control

A manager's span of control is the number of employees that he or she can effectively be in control of at any one time. It was once thought that there was a single ideal span of control based on some fundamental human capacity. Zealous hunters after this number were spurred on by the thought that once unearthed it would be the key to the perfect corporate structure. Organograms could then be built in a rigid and perfect manner for all time.

Over the years, however, there have been so many differing views about the optimum span of control that the unavoidable conclusion is that it is a matter of horses for courses. The ideal span is partly determined by the nature of the work involved. With craftsmen the number can be quite small because the level of supervision required is high. With mass production, however, the span of control can be many times higher because each worker has a clearly defined task to perform, requiring little regular oversight. The contemporary view is that spans depend on both the industry a firm is in and the firm itself.

Spans of control can be deliberately enlarged by making workers more autonomous and more capable of managing themselves. They can also be enlarged by increasing the number of rules and constraining the freedom of junior employees to make mistakes. As a span of control gets larger, it exponentially (and dramatically) increases the number of relationships among individuals within each management cell. One manager and six subordinates, for instance, create 222 relationships among the seven of them; one manager and 16 subordinates create over 500,000 relationships.

Managers were traditionally compensated in part according to the number of employees under their control. Those at the top are not only responsible directly for the employees who report to them, but also (indirectly) for the lower-level employees who report to their underlings. The route to higher rewards was to move up the pyramid by climbing the corporate ladder. In the delayered organisations of the 21st century this reward structure has had to be rethought.

As long ago as the early 1800s, Eli Whitney was experimenting by giving managers different spans of control at his gun factory in the United States. Almost 200 years later the experiments are still continuing.

Views on the ideal span of control have changed over time as thinking about corporate structure itself has changed. For the first 60 years of the 20th century, when managers favoured a structure based largely on military models, a consensus formed around the number six. After 1960, however, management styles began to change. Flatter, less hierarchical and more loosely structured organisations implied larger spans of control (see also Delayering, page 59). The consensus on the size of the ideal span rose to between 15 and 25. GE's guideline was that no managers should have more than 10–15 people reporting to them directly. There was also a widespread feeling that five layers was the maximum with which any large organisation could function effectively. Jack Welch, a former boss of GE, once wrote: "When there are a lot of layers, it usually means managers have too few people reporting to them."

The coming of the virtual organisation (see page 207) made managers take a new look at the concept. In a virtual organisation people work as independent self-contained units, either individually or in small teams. They have access to (electronic) information that lays down the boundaries within which they can be autonomous. But at the same time they are allowed to be completely free within those boundaries. In such an environment, the ideal span of control can be very large. Indeed, it can scarcely be called a span of control any longer; it is more a span of loose links and alliances.

Strategic alliance

A strategic alliance is a relationship between two or more organisations that falls somewhere between the extremes of an arm's-length sourcing arrangement on the one hand, and a full-blown acquisition on the other. It embraces things such as franchising, licensing and joint ventures.

Booz Allen & Hamilton, a firm of management consultants and an acknowledged expert in the field, defines a strategic alliance as:

> A co-operative arrangement between two or more companies in which:
> - a common strategy is developed in unison and a win-win attitude is adopted by all parties;
> - the relationship is reciprocal, with each partner prepared to share specific strengths with the other, thus lending power to the enterprise;
> - a pooling of resources, investment and risks occurs for mutual gain.

In general, there are two types of strategic alliance: a bilateral alliance (between two organisations) and a network alliance (between several organisations). The alliance between Royal Bank of Scotland (RBS) and Tesco, whereby the British supermarket chain provided the Scottish bank's services throughout its stores, was an example of the former; the Airbus consortium and the Visa card network were examples of the latter. In 2009, Tesco bought out RBS to give itself the potential to become a full bank in its own right.

Strategic alliances have many advantages: they require little immediate financial commitment; they allow companies to put their toes into new markets before they get soaked; and they offer a quiet retreat should a venture not work out as the partners had hoped. However, going into something knowing that it is (literally) not a big deal, and that there is a face-saving exit route, may not be the best way to make those charged with running it hungry for success.

The most popular use for alliances is as a means to try out a foreign market. Not surprisingly, therefore, there are more alliances in Europe and

Asia (where there are more foreign markets nearby) than in the United States. In some cases, alliances are used by companies because other means of entering a market are closed to them. Hence there have been many in the airline industry, where governments are sensitive about domestic carriers falling into foreign hands.

One thing crucial to a successful alliance is a degree of cultural compatibility. Companies are advised, for example, to pick on someone their own size. Alliances between the very big and the very small are hard to operate not least because of the different significance that the alliance assumes in each organisation's scale of things.

Alliances are often said to be like marriages. The partners have to understand each other's expectations, be sensitive to each other's changes of mood and not be too surprised if their partnership ends in divorce. Indeed, many companies build into their alliances a sort of pre-nuptial contract, an agreement as to what is to happen to their joint property in the event of a subsequent divorce.

Strategic alliances grew at a phenomenal rate in the 1990s. Some companies, such as General Electric and AT&T, set up several hundred. On one estimate, IBM cemented almost 1,000 strategic alliances during the decade. Booz Allen & Hamilton reckoned that more than 20,000 were formed worldwide in the period 1996–98.

Not all these alliances were successful. In 1998 BT and AT&T agreed to bundle their international assets into a single joint venture that started off with annual revenues of $11 billion, annual operating profits of $1 billion and some 5,000 employees. In 2001 the two companies agreed to unwind the alliance – at considerable cost.

Further reading

Bamford, J. and Ernst, D., "Managing an Alliance Portfolio", *McKinsey Quarterly*, No. 3, 2002

Doz, Y. and Hamel, G., *Alliance Advantage: The Art of Creating Value Through Partnering*, Harvard Business School Press, 1998

Steinhilber, S., *Strategic Alliances: Three Ways to Make Them Work*, Harvard Business School Press, 2008

Strategic planning

In ancient Greek, the word στρατηγια meant the art of generalship, of devising and carrying out a military campaign. The English word derived from it, strategy, was transferred from its military origins to the business world in the years before the ubiquitous MBA, at a time when a military career was considered a good qualification for a manager. As with the military, strategy was seen by businessmen as a high-level function fit only for the minds of leaders and a small cohort of the brightest and best. The planning of corporate strategy was usually a secretive operation that took place at irregular intervals.

The problems of strategic planning have attracted some of the best minds in both business and academia, but those minds have not agreed on a practice that works in all circumstances. Most can go along with the general guidelines laid down by Alfred Chandler (see page 225) – that strategic planning involves the articulation of long-term goals and the allocation of the resources necessary to achieve those goals. But beyond that there are few common themes.

Igor Ansoff (see page 215) pointed out a crucial distinction between strategic planning and what he called strategic management. Strategic management, he maintained, has three parts:

- strategic planning;
- the skill of a firm in converting its plans into reality; and
- the skill of a firm in managing its own internal resistance to change.

Ansoff's analysis was based on his observation that "as firms became increasingly skilful strategy formulators, the translation of strategy into results in the marketplace lagged behind. This created paralysis by analysis in strategic planning".

The popularity of strategic planning in the 1960s and thereafter gave a big boost to the fledgling business of management consulting. *Business Week* wrote that it "spawned a mini-industry of brainy consulting boutiques ... you could plot a strategy that would safely steer your company to uninterrupted triumph if only you thought hard enough".

By the late 1980s, however, strategic planning had gone out of fashion.

General Electric led the way when it axed its respected planning department in 1983. Its chief executive, Jack Welch, felt that the department's 200 or more senior executives were too involved with financial minutiae and not enough with new businesses and visionary markets. GE's strategic planning was passed to the bosses of its 12 main business units, who thereafter met every summer for full-day sessions on strategy.

It was not until the mid-1990s that strategic planning began to stage a revival. *Business Week* put the event on its cover in August 1996. "After a decade of gritty downsizing," it wrote, "Big Thinkers are back in corporate vogue." The arrival of the internet and the possibilities of e-commerce (see page 69) were compelling companies to think carefully about the new electronic business world. Disney, for instance, appointed senior executives specifically in charge of strategic planning for its online businesses.

On its reappearance, however, strategic planning took a different form. It evolved into a continuous process, not (as it had been) a discrete half-yearly or annual coven attended by a select few. Nokia, a mobile-phone company, said it was aiming to make strategy "a daily part of a manager's activity". EDS involved over 2,000 of its employees in a late 1990s strategic planning process. But Gary Hamel (see page 245) still found it "amazing that young people who live closest to the future are the most disenfranchised in strategy-creating exercises".

Further reading

Ansoff, H.I., *Corporate Strategy: An Analytic Approach to Business Policy for Growth and Expansion*, McGraw-Hill, 1965

Chandler, A., *Strategy and Structure: Chapters in the History of the American Industrial Enterprise*, MIT Press, 1969; reprint, 1990

Collis, D. and Rukstad, M., "Can You Say What Your Strategy Is?", *Harvard Business Review*, April 2008

Mintzberg, H., "Crafting Strategy", *Harvard Business Review*, July–August 1987

Porter, M., "What is Strategy?", *Harvard Business Review*, November–December 1996

Rumelt, R., Schendel, D. and Teece, D., *Fundamental Issues in Strategy, a Research Agenda*, Harvard Business School Press, 1995

Succession planning

The idea that finding a successor to the current chief executive of an organisation is a process that should be planned and executed methodically has gathered strength in recent years. It seems, however, to be one of those rare processes that get worse with practice. One survey of American quoted companies calculated that every day in 2006 six CEOs left their job – either because they were sacked or because they jumped just before being sacked.

There are two types of literature on succession planning:

- That which looks at ways of finding a successor to the family (or small private) business. The difficulties here are usually linked to the incumbent/founder's failure to take on board his own mortality, or his inability to tell his beloved second child that (after his death or retirement) there can be only one chief executive.
- That which looks at finding a successor to the chief executive of a large public corporation. The focus here has shifted in recent years to take in a wider constituency. Despite some writers' insistence that finding a successor is the biggest responsibility of any chief executive, no company now makes it a matter for the chief executive alone. If left to their own devices, chief executives, like the rest of us, are inclined to replace themselves with a clone (on the grounds that such a person is without doubt the best person for the job).

In both cases (in the family business and the public company), there is general agreement that it is not wise to leave the choice of a successor to the last minute. Any future chief executive needs to be groomed and to have a handover period when the baton of responsibility is passed from one to the other. "One of the biggest tasks I face as CEO", said Craigie Zildjian, CEO of the oldest family business in the United States, "is getting succession right."

Firms increasingly turn to outside headhunters or consultants to help them choose their next chief executive. These outsiders may suggest a suitable internal candidate or seek to entice an external candidate to the post. Until the last two decades of the 20th century, most chief executives of large companies were appointed from inside their organisations. Long experience of the company's business was considered an important qualification for the job. But by the end of the century many more high-flying managers were changing employer in mid-career. In 1988, on average, an executive worked for fewer than three employees in his lifetime; ten years later that average had risen to more than five. It has become increasingly common for new CEOs to be complete outsiders.

Several types of successor have been identified:

- **The inside outsider.** The employee whose leadership style is completely different from that of their predecessor. This sort of appointment is made by a company in need of a drastic change in strategic direction. A classic appointment of an inside outsider was that of Sir John Harvey-Jones as boss of ICI in 1982.
- **The outside insider.** The person who knows a lot about the company but does not actually work for it. Such a person has the objective view of the outsider without the complete ignorance that is the outsider's main drawback. Examples of outside insiders include the many management consultants who have gone on to head companies that they have advised.
- **The horse-race winner.** The internal candidate who is publicly set against other internal candidates and told to compete for the job. Classic examples of this are the three-horse race set up by Walter Wriston to decide on his successor at Citicorp in 1984 (the winner was the then youthful John Reed).
- **The boss's pet.** This is the candidate who is hand-picked and personally groomed by the existing chief executive over an extended period of time.

A growing number of former CEOs are being called back to run the companies that they have left (Michael Dell at Dell Computer, for instance, and Harry Stonecipher at Boeing). One returning CEO advised others that they should "think twice" before they do it. "It means not only that your successor failed, but that you did too – at succession planning."

Further reading

Lafley, A.G. and Tichy, N.M., "The Art and Science of Finding the Right CEO", *Harvard Business Review*, October 2011

Levinson, H., "Conflicts that Plague the Family Business", *Harvard Business Review*, March–April 1971

Zaleznik, A., "Managers and Leaders: Are they Different?", *Harvard Business Review*, May–June 1977

Supply-chain management

The fact that a number of companies (such as Wal-Mart, Zara, Dell and Toyota) have managed to record extraordinary success while doing quite ordinary things (such as running supermarkets, selling clothes or making computers or cars) has made managers more fully aware that what their organisations produce can matter a lot less than the way that they produce it. This holds true even in an age when the product life cycle (see page 153) is getting shorter and shorter, and more emphasis is being placed on technological product innovation as a means to add value.

Central to the way that companies produce things is the way that they manage their supply chains – the collection and distribution of all the inputs to the production process. Some companies take this to extremes. For example, Olam, a Singapore-based commodities trader, says that in practice it is "in the business of supply-chain management". It undertakes all the processes involved in getting soft commodities such as cocoa and coffee from the grower's farm to the factories of Olam customers such as Sara Lee. Its competitive advantage lies in the superiority of its processes, not its commodities.

Traditionally, the way companies ensured that the right components were ready at the right time was to hold huge stocks of them in warehouses which could be drawn down as and when required. When Toyota invented the just-in-time system (JIT – see page 107), all that changed. Companies became more aware of the cost of sitting on warehouses full of stock and tried to manage their supply chains so that inputs arrived only when they were needed. At the same time, as companies became more international, so the process crossed more borders and became more complex.

Of course technology helped. Much of the improvement in supply-chain management in recent years has come about because of improved information systems that enable managers to know more accurately (and more quickly) exactly what is where and when. Nevertheless, not all companies give supply-chain management a high priority. An article in *Harvard Business Review*, "Are You the Weakest Link in Your Company's Supply Chain", in September 2007 claimed that "the warehouses of many large companies still operate with 20-year-old technology, producing incomplete and unintegrated information flows". Some companies have been disappointed by the failure of business-to-business exchanges to develop on the internet and provide them with supplies more efficiently than via traditional routes.

The development of RFID (radio frequency identification) technology promises to enable firms to streamline the process even more. RFID involves implanting every package of goods with a small radio transmitter, enabling its owner to know exactly where it is every minute of the day. Following its movements could become a bit like being in an airplane watching a screen on which the progress of the plane is shown by an arrow moving across a map of the world.

In many cases improving the efficiency of supply chains also involves changing a company's relationships with its suppliers. Not all suppliers are prepared to bear the extra cost involved in (effectively) holding stock on their customers' behalf. Those that are want a greater commitment from those customers, which has led companies to become much closer to their suppliers, sometimes establishing a formal alliance with them and sometimes taking an equity stake in their business.

In East Asia in particular such links are common. Most of the suppliers to Toyota, for example, are based in or around Toyota City, the company's main manufacturing centre, a 45-minute drive from Nagoya in Japan. Toyota is, if not their only customer, certainly their most important one, and one they are prepared to go to considerable lengths to keep happy. When Toyota sets up a plant in another country, many of these suppliers follow and set up an operation of their own nearby.

Further reading

Boone T. and Ganeshan, R. (eds), *New Directions in Supply Chain Management: Technology Strategy and Implementation*, AMACOM (American Management Association), NY 2002

Hugos, M.H., *Essentials of Supply-Chain Management*, 3rd edn, Wiley 2011

Simchi-Levi, D., Kaminsky, P. and Simchi-Levi, E., *Managing the Supply Chain: The Definitive Guide for the Business Professional*, McGraw-Hill, 2004

Sustainability

The concept of sustainability came on to the corporate agenda via the UN World Commission on Environment and Development (more commonly known as the Brundtland Commission after the name of its chairman, Gro Harlem Brundtland, a former Norwegian prime minister). The commission, set up in 1983 to address growing concern about "the accelerating deterioration of the human environment and natural resources, and the consequences of that deterioration for economic and social development", introduced the idea of sustainable development, which it famously defined as development that "meets the needs of the present without compromising the ability of future generations to meet their own needs".

The commission recognised that this was a global issue which required global solutions. As the engines of much global economic growth, corporations were inevitably at the heart of any solution. They have a major impact on the human environment, not just through headline-grabbing accidents such as those at the Union Carbide factory in Bhopal, India, in 1984, which killed thousands, but also through the way they design their office buildings or run their fleets of vehicles. Moreover, corporations are, above all, consumers of natural resources, ever hungry for raw materials that can be manufactured into products and profits.

As consumers have become more aware of environmental issues they have begun to put pressure on companies to inject more sustainability into their strategic thinking. "Talent" too (see page 185) does not want to work for firms that destroy forests or fisheries, so it has also put pressure on firms to change. Between them, consumers and employees have made a strong business case for sustainability.

SustainAbility, a consulting firm, has identified six industrial sectors whose strategies, it believes, "will have profound impact upon the sustainability agenda". These are chemicals, energy, finance and capital markets, food and beverages, healthcare, and the knowledge economy. David Miliband, when Britain's environment minister, took it one step further. In November 2006 he said:

> Every industry needs to be an environmental industry in
> one sense or another. Every business needs to take resource
> productivity as seriously as it takes labour productivity.

Some firms began to do so. Hewlett-Packard went further than most in encouraging its suppliers to be socially and environmentally responsible while trying to attain high standards itself. It tried, for instance, to shift from air to sea transport wherever possible, to reduce carbon emissions.

Many companies, however, have not yet got the message. A report by the WWF says:

> Even the most visionary corporate leaders can be heard explaining that they are hitting a wall because: "our consumers won't buy our sustainable products; our investors demand next-quarter profits; the legislation is inconsistent and our global competitors can produce goods with little or no regard for the environment; or there is no business case for sustainability".

Further reading

Hawken, P , Lovins, A. and Lovins, L.H. , *Natural Capitalism: Creating the Next Industrial Revolution*, Little, Brown, 1999

Kiron, D. et al., "Sustainability Nears a Tipping Point", *Sloan Management Review*, Winter 2012

Porter, M. and Kramer, M., "Strategy and Society: The Link Between Competitive Advantage and Corporate Social Responsibility", *Harvard Business Review*, December 2006

Rainey, D., *Sustainable Business Development: Inventing the Future through Strategy, Innovation, and Leadership*, Cambridge University Press, 2006

SWOT analysis

SWOT is a handy mnemonic to help corporate planners think about strategy. It stands for Strengths, Weaknesses, Opportunities and Threats. What are an organisation's SWOTS? How can it manage them in a way that will optimise its performance? A second four-letter acronym is sometimes brought into play here: USED. How can the Strengths be Used; the Weaknesses be Stopped, the Opportunities be Exploited; and the Threats be Defended against?

Wikipedia credits the technique to Albert Humphrey, an academic at Stanford University, who based it on an analysis of *Fortune* 500 companies that he carried out in the 1960s and 1970s.

The process starts by listing a firm's attributes under the four headings; a particular strength, for example, might be a dedicated workforce or some currently valuable patent. These are then given scores according to what is seen as likely to be the company's business environment over the next few years. If a recession is beginning and employees have to be laid off, a dedicated workforce might be a weakness. If a boom is about to begin, however, it will be a strength.

The four features can be divided along two main dimensions:

- **Internal/external.** The internal features are the company's own strengths and weaknesses. Analysing them is a matter of analysing the state of the company. They are things that already exist. The external features are the organisation's opportunities and the threats to its future performance. These exist only on the horizon, and they are less easy to assess and measure. They arise from things like changes in technology, demography or government policy.
- **Positive/negative.** The positive things are the strengths and opportunities; the negative ones are the threats and weaknesses.

A SWOT analysis can be applied to different aspects of a company's business, such as its IT capability or its skills. The simplicity and intuitive wholeness of the framework have helped to make it extremely popular with both corporations and governments. An analysis of the competitive advantages and disadvantages of Germany in 1999 found that the country's strengths lay in its educated and skilled workforce. Among its weaknesses were its high labour and social costs.

Nevertheless, there has been no shortage of critics. One of the main criticisms is that, in the end, such an analysis invariably relies on subjective judgment. Objective measures of all the ingredients in the balance simply do not exist. Some say that this does not matter, because the process of doing the analysis is more important and revealing than the results of the analysis themselves. The journey is more important than the destination.

Further reading

Hill, T. and Westbrook, R., "SWOT analysis: it's time for a product recall", *Long Range Planning*, February 1997

Pickton, D.W. and Wright, S.W., "What's SWOT in strategic analysis?", *Strategic Change*, Vol. 7, No. 2, March–April 1998

Synergy

The word comes from ancient Greek: συνεργια means working together. Andrew Campbell and Michael Goold, two British academics, defined it as "links between business units that result in additional value creation". It is, they went on to say, "a Holy Grail for large multi-unit companies". It is something akin to the philosopher's stone: seeming to create extra value without consuming resources.

Synergy has been used as part of the justification for almost every takeover since Alexander moved into Egypt. In the 20th century the idea was refreshed by Ruth Benedict, an anthropologist. She used the word when writing during the second world war about communities where co-operation was rewarded and proved advantageous to all. The idea was picked up and transferred to the business world by Abraham Maslow (see page 267, and Hierarchy of needs, page 101). It fitted well with Maslow's non-authoritarian model of organisational structure.

The business gains from synergy are often not distinguished sufficiently well from those that come from combining two businesses in such a way as to create value. Synergy is passive; it happens when two things come together regardless of what else they do. If a company buys one of its major suppliers, the synergy comes from the fact that it is now a preferred customer, not from the subsequent reorganisation of the supplier's warehouses so that they are more conveniently located for their new owner.

Promises of synergy are rarely fulfilled. Campbell and Goold said: "Synergy initiatives often fall short of management's expectations." They quote the example of a firm of consultants where, to gain synergy, the IT specialists were merged with the strategy specialists, until the day when the IT people found that the strategy people were on a completely different scale of pay and perks. All the synergy gains were lost in an instant. The authors ended their article by quoting the physicians' creed: "First ensure you do no harm."

The synergy from mergers and acquisitions (M&A) is particularly elusive. Leon Cooperman, a senior executive at Goldman Sachs, when asked to name one big merger that had lived up to expectations, said: "I'm sure that there are success stories out there. But at this moment I draw a blank."

Michael Porter (see page 295), who looked closely at the activities of

33 large American companies between 1950 and 1986, found that 55% of their acquisitions were later divested. Of their forays into unrelated industries (the fashion at the time was for conglomerates), 74% were later divested.

Synergy fails to materialise in M&A for two main reasons:

- Managers give too much attention to financial and strategic aspects during the negotiation of the deal. All eyes are focused on striking the right price (whatever it is), not on extracting the full value.
- Managers underestimate the cultural differences between organisations. These can be particularly significant in deals that cross borders. An Anglo-French merger between packaging companies Metal Box and Carnaud, for instance, was notorious for the refusal of managers from different cultures to work with each other. It has been said that cross-border deals work well in the airline industry because people have gone into that particular business to meet and understand people from other cultures. The same cannot be said of people who go into packaging.

The unbundling of organisations, which often occurs after a prolonged period of mergers and acquisitions, involves a sort of reverse synergy. In this, three minus two equals more than one. This greater value is realised either through a capital gain from the sale of previously bundled assets (a process often referred to as asset stripping), or through an improvement in the margins on the unbundled businesses.

Further reading

Eisenhardt, K.M. and Galunic, D.C., "Co-Evolving: At Last a Way to Make Synergies Work", *Harvard Business Review*, January–February 2000

Goold, M. and Campbell, A., "Desperately Seeking Synergy", *Harvard Business Review*, September–October 1998

Hagel, J. III and Singer, M., "Unbundling the Corporation", *Harvard Business Review*, March–April 1999

Sirower, M.L., *The Synergy Trap*, Free Press, 2007

Talent

No one word demonstrated the shift in corporations' attention in the 1990s from processes to people more vividly than the single word "talent". Spurred on by a book called *The War for Talent*, written by three McKinsey consultants in the late 1990s, the word became common in management speak. "We need to cultivate the talent"; "Where are we going to find the talent essential to our future success?" Talent is a subset of what used to be called human resources, the people who work in organisations. It is, essentially, those individuals among that group who have the potential to add most value.

Behind the word lies the idea that more and more corporate value is going to be created by knowledge and by so-called "knowledge workers". Manual labour is worth less; knowledge (and the right use of it) is worth more. And people with such knowledge are (so the theory goes) in short supply. One CEO was reported as saying that not only did he not have enough talent to carry out the company's strategy, but he did not even have "the talent needed in HR to hire the missing managers". Moreover, the situation is likely to stay that way (and may even get worse) for some time to come.

This has significantly shifted the balance of power in the recruitment process. Companies used to be relaxed about finding enough qualified people to run their operations. What they could not find they would train, was the usual attitude. That might take some time, but in a world where people sought jobs for life (and the pensions that went with them) time was in the company's favour. But talent is not patient, and it is not faithful. Many companies have found themselves training employees only for them to go on and sell their acquired skills to their rivals. So now they look more for talent that is ready-made.

In their eagerness to please this talent, companies go to considerable lengths to appear especially attractive. They have, for instance, devoted a great deal of effort to the design of their websites, often the first port of call these days for bright young potential recruits. They have in many cases reconstructed their HR departments (see Human resources transformation, page 103), in part so that they can tailor their remuneration packages more finely for the individuals that they really require. And they have altered their approach to issues such as governance and environmental responsibility because they know that many of the talented people they are seeking want to work for ethical and responsible employers – almost more than they want the promise of a pension.

Talented people increasingly want to work in places where they can feel good about what they do for most of the day. What's more, in today's knowledge-based businesses, these young people are far more aware of their working environment, of "what's going on around here", than were their grandparents, who were often hired for their brawn rather than their brain. It is harder for today's businesses to disguise from their employees what they are up to – even when, as in cases such as Enron and WorldCom, they put a lot of effort into it.

Further reading

Bloom, B., *Developing Talent in Young People*, Ballantine Books, 1985

Martin, J. and Schmidt, C., "How to Keep Your Top Talent", *Harvard Business Review*, May 2010

Michaels, E., Handfield-Jones, H. and Axelrod, B., *The War for Talent*, Harvard Business School Press, 2001

Stahl, G. *et al.*, "Six Principles of Effective Global Talent Management", *Sloan Management Review*, Winter 2012

Theories X and Y

Theory X and Theory Y was an idea devised by Douglas McGregor (see page 273) in his 1960 book *The Human Side of Enterprise*. It encapsulated a fundamental distinction between management styles and has formed the basis for much subsequent writing on the subject.

Theory X is an authoritarian style where the emphasis is on "productivity, on the concept of a fair day's work, on the evils of feather-bedding and restriction of output, on rewards for performance ... [it] reflects an underlying belief that management must counteract an inherent human tendency to avoid work". Theory X is the style that predominated in business after the mechanistic system of scientific management (see page 159) had swept everything before it in the first few decades of the 20th century.

Theory Y is a participative style of management which "assumes that people will exercise self-direction and self-control in the achievement of organisational objectives to the degree that they are committed to those objectives". It is management's main task in such a system to maximise that commitment.

Theory X assumes that individuals are base, work-shy and constantly in need of a good prod. It always has a ready-made excuse for failure – the innate limitations of all human resources. Theory Y, however, assumes that individuals go to work of their own accord, because work is the only way in which they have a chance of satisfying their (high-level) need for achievement and self-respect. People will work without prodding; it has been their fate since Adam and Eve were banished from the Garden of Eden.

Theory Y gives management no easy excuses for failure. It challenges them "to innovate, to discover new ways of organising and directing human effort, even though we recognise that the perfect organisation, like the perfect vacuum, is practically out of reach". McGregor urged companies to adopt Theory Y. Only it, he believed, could motivate human beings to the highest levels of achievement. Theory X merely satisfied their lower-level physical needs and could not hope to be as productive. "Man is a wanting animal," wrote McGregor, "as soon as one of his needs is satisfied another appears in its place."

There are parallels with Abraham Maslow's hierarchy of needs (see page 101), and Maslow (see page 267) was indeed greatly influenced by McGregor. So much so that he tried to introduce Theory Y into a Californian electronics business, but found that the idea in its extreme form did not work well. All individuals, he concluded, however independent and mature, need some form of structure around them and some direction from others. Maslow also criticised Theory Y for its "inhumanity" to the weak, and to those not capable of a high level of self-motivation.

In his comic classic *Up the Organisation*, Robert Townsend (see page 313) wrote powerfully in support of Theory Y:

> People don't hate work. It's as natural as rest or play. They don't have to be forced or threatened. If they commit themselves to mutual objectives, they'll drive themselves more effectively than you can drive them. But they'll commit themselves only to the extent they can see ways of satisfying their ego and development needs.

Further reading

Lorsch, J. and Morse, J., "Beyond Theory Y", *Harvard Business Review*, May–June 1970

McGregor, D., *Leadership and motivation: essays*, MIT Press, 1966; 1969

McGregor, D., *The Human Side of Enterprise*, McGraw-Hill, 1960; annotated edn, McGraw-Hill, 2006

Townsend, R., *Up the Organisation*, Michael Joseph, 1970; reprinted as *Further Up the Organisation*, Coronet, 1985

Tipping point

The tipping point is an expression used in epidemiology that was taken by Malcolm Gladwell, a *New York Times* writer, and applied to other areas of life – including business – in his 2000 book *The Tipping Point*. The subtitle, *How Little Things Can Make a Big Difference*, explains more clearly what the whole thing is about.

In epidemiology the tipping point is that moment when a small change tips the balance of a system and brings about a large change; for example, when the normal spread of influenza throughout a population suddenly turns into an epidemic. In recent years the language of epidemiology has spread (like a virus?) within business. Managers talk about viral marketing (see page 205), the infectious enthusiasm of their teams, and "outbreaks" of corporate greed – and even, as was reported once about JetBlue, an American low-cost airline, an "outbreak of passenger abuse". A lot of this language owes its spread to the influence of the internet, where viruses are common and where dormant information can sometimes erupt suddenly and infect us all.

Gladwell says:

> *Ideas and behaviour and messages and products sometimes behave just like outbreaks of infectious disease. They are social epidemics. The Tipping Point is an examination of the social epidemics that surround us.*

He says he first came across the idea when, as a reporter on the *Washington Post*, he was covering the AIDS outbreak which, as he put it, "tipped in 1982, when it went from a rare disease affecting a few gay men to a worldwide epidemic".

A similar phenomenon occurs with films (*The Blair Witch Project* was a classic example, but it has worked also for both low- and big-budget movies) and books (think of *The Kite Runner* or *Eats, Shoots and Leaves*). And it happens with products and brands – the Hermes headscarf and the Prada handbag, for instance – but more particularly with techy ones such as the iPod or the BlackBerry.

Every marketing manager dreams that it will happen to his or her next product launch. Success in reaching a tipping point depends partly on the people who are spreading the epidemic (are they good spreaders? do they sneeze a lot when they have flu?); the nature of the epidemic itself (how easy is it to catch? can you breath it in, or is it only transmitted through unprotected sex?); and finally the context in which it is spread (among people who are in frequent close contact with others, or in the backwoods of Saskatchewan?)

Although a huge bestseller, Gladwell's book was described by *Publishers Weekly* as a "facile piece of pop sociology", and there is little in it of real value to managers, except perhaps for the message "don't be surprised". We always expect everyday change to happen slowly and steadily, says Gladwell. But, he adds:

> When crime drops dramatically in New York for no apparent reason, or when a movie made on a shoestring budget ends up making hundreds of millions of dollars, we're surprised. I'm saying, don't be surprised. This is the way social epidemics work.

Further reading

Gladwell, M., *The Tipping Point: How Little Things Can Make a Big Difference*, Little, Brown, 2000

Total quality management

Total quality management (TQM) is the idea that controlling quality is not something that is left exclusively to the "quality controller", a person who stands at the end of a production line checking final output. It is (or it should be) something that permeates an organisation from the moment its raw materials arrive to the moment its finished products leave.

TQM is a process-oriented system built on the belief that quality is a matter of conforming to a customer's requirements. Those requirements can be measured, and deviations from them can then be prevented by means of process improvements or redesigns.

The European Foundation for Quality Management (EFQM) said that TQM strategies are characterised by the following:

- The excellence of all managerial, operational and administrative processes.
- A culture of continuous improvement in all aspects of the business.
- An understanding that quality improvement results in cost advantages and better profit potential.
- The creation of more intensive relationships with customers and suppliers.
- The involvement of all personnel.
- Market-oriented organisational practices.

Total quality management was developed by a number of Japanese firms in the 1950s and 1960s. But it was built largely on the teachings of W. Edwards Deming (see page 233) and Joseph Juran (see page 255), two Americans who had quietly developed the principles in the aftermath of the second world war. With the help of books and articles such as David Garvin's 1983 description in *Harvard Business Review* of the way in which TQM and other techniques were putting Japanese companies streets ahead of their foreign competitors, the idea was later reclaimed by the United States and widely adopted by American business.

Europe, which has at times looked left out of this game of American-Japanese ping-pong, has also made occasional claims to be the fount of total quality. Raymond Levy, chairman of Renault, a French car company, said in the early 1990s:

> *Quality is representative of a culture which we Europeans have no reason to let others monopolise. The Europe of Descartes; the Europe of the Age of Reason and the Enlightenment; the Europe of the industrial and technological revolution of the last two centuries holds within itself all the elements of method and exactitude conveyed by the term "total quality".*

In the late 1990s there was something of a backlash against the implications of TQM, especially in the United States. Florida Power & Light, for example, the first American company to win the prestigious Deming Prize for quality management, cut its TQM programme because of its employees' complaints about the excessive amount of paperwork that it required. Douglas Aircraft, a subsidiary of McDonnell Douglas, cut its programme to next to nothing. *Newsweek* colourfully described the aircraft company's action: "At Douglas, TQM appeared to be just one more hothouse Japanese flower never meant to grow on rocky American ground."

Further reading

Crosby, P.B., *Quality is Free*, McGraw-Hill, 1979

Deming, W.E., *Out of the Crisis: Quality, Productivity and Competitive Position*, Cambridge University Press, 1986; 2nd edn, MIT Press, 2000

Garvin, D., "Quality on the Line", *Harvard Business Review*, September–October 1983

Juran. J.J. and Gryna, F.M., *Juran's Quality Control Handbook*, 4th edn, McGraw-Hill, 1988

Triple bottom line

The phrase "the triple bottom line" was first coined in 1994 by John Elkington, the founder of a British consultancy called SustainAbility. He argued that companies should be preparing three different (and quite separate) bottom lines. One is the traditional measure of corporate profit – the "bottom line" of the profit and loss account. The second is the bottom line of a company's "people account" – a measure in some shape or form of how socially responsible an organisation has been throughout its operations. The third is the bottom line of the company's "planet" account – a measure of how environmentally responsible it has been. The triple bottom line (TBL) thus consists of three Ps: profit, people and planet. It aims to measure the financial, social and environmental performance of the corporation over a period of time. Only a company that produces a TBL is taking account of the full cost involved in doing business.

In some senses the TBL is a particular manifestation of the balanced scorecard (see page 11). Behind it lies the same fundamental principle: what you measure is what you get, because what you measure is what you are likely to pay attention to. Only when companies measure their social and environmental impact will we have socially and environmentally responsible organisations.

The idea enjoyed some success in the turn-of-the-century *zeitgeist* of corporate social responsibility, climate change and fair trade. After more than a decade in which cost-cutting had been the number-one business priority, the hidden social and environmental costs of transferring production and services to low-cost countries such as China, India and Brazil became increasingly apparent to Western consumers. These included such things as the indiscriminate logging of the Amazon basin, the excessive use of hydrocarbons and the exploitation of cheap labour.

Growing awareness of corporate malpractice in these areas forced several companies, including Nike and Tesco, to re-examine their sourcing policies and to keep a closer eye on the ethical standards of their suppliers in places as far apart as Mexico and Bangladesh, where labour markets are unregulated and manufacturers are able to ride roughshod over social and environmental standards. It also encouraged the growth of the Fairtrade movement, which adds its brand to products that have been produced and traded in an environmentally and socially "fair" way (of course, that concept is itself open to interpretation). From small beginnings, the movement picked up steam. Nevertheless, the Fairtrade movement is still only small, focusing essentially on coffee, tea, bananas and cotton, and it accounted for little more than 0.5% of all UK grocery sales in 2009.

One problem with the triple bottom line is that the three separate accounts cannot easily be added up. It is difficult to measure the planet and people accounts in the same terms as profits – that is, in terms of cash. The full cost of an oil-tanker spillage, for example, is probably immeasurable in monetary terms, as is the cost of displacing whole communities to clear forests, or the cost of depriving children of their freedom to learn in order to make them work at a young age.

Further reading

Elkington, J., *Cannibals with Forks: the Triple Bottom Line of 21st Century Business*, Capstone, 1997

Savitz, A.W. and Weber, K., *The Triple Bottom Line: How Today's Best-Run Companies Are Achieving Economic, Social and Environmental Success – and How You Can Too*, Jossey-Bass, 2006

Willard, B., *The Sustainability Advantage: Seven Business Case Benefits of a Triple Bottom Line*, New Society Publishers, 2002

True and fair

The collapse of companies such as Enron and WorldCom in the aftermath of the internet bubble demonstrated the central role of accounting in good corporate governance (see page 43). Both companies manipulated their figures and then persuaded their auditors (Arthur Andersen in both cases) to sign off on accounts that were at best misleading, at worst downright criminal.

The cases highlighted a contrast between the modern American approach to accounting and the more old-fashioned British approach. America's accounting rules have developed in the context of the increasingly litigious nature of that country's corporate life. This has put pressure on American accountants to be very precise about what is and what is not permissible in company accounts.

In the UK, by contrast, accountants have tried to stick more closely to the old idea of "true and fair", of accepting that precision in accounting is a chimera, that the best you can hope for is that the figures appear (to an honest, independent expert of goodwill) to be as true and fair a reflection of the corporate reality as it is possible to achieve. In the UK, auditors are required to state whether the accounts they are signing show a "true and fair view" of the organisation's affairs.

Although this principle can overrule specific legal requirements, there is no precise legal definition of what true and fair means. Despite its vagueness, however, the Sarbanes-Oxley Act (American legislation passed in the wake of the Enron and WorldCom accounting scandals that is applicable to all companies quoted on an American stock exchange) reinstated the principle into American accounting.

For most of the 20th century, in the UK and the many countries that follow British accounting principles, the true and fair view held the upper hand over the strict rule-setters. It was the most inviolate of the four golden principles of accounting (and the only one not beginning with the letter C: the other three being continuity, consistency and conservatism).

Proponents of the case for "true and fair" were not helped by a general debasement of the accounting profession itself. In an era that declared itself to be all about change and innovation, it was common to denigrate "bean counters", people whose professional ethos was the antithesis of most of this. ("Creative" accountants, after all, are folk who fiddle the books.)

What's more, whereas a few decades ago an accountancy training was essential for a young manager aiming for the top, the MBA replaced it for aspiring young executives. They now want to go to top-ranking business schools where they do not, by and large, learn how to count beans.

Even chief financial officers have largely abandoned accountancy qualifications. In 2001, Spencer Stuart, an executive search firm, looked at the qualifications of the CFOs at *Fortune* 500 companies. Only one in five of them had a CPA (Certified Public Accountant) qualification; 35% of them had an MBA.

Two things in particular have compromised the accountants' vision of what is true and fair. One is their desire to do (more glamorous) things than accounting and auditing – in particular, consulting. Arthur Andersen, for example, earned $25m from its audit of Enron in 2000 and $27m in consulting fees from that company in the same year. The other distortion comes from the excessively familiar relationships that grow up in cases where an auditor remains with the same client for many years. At Enron, many of the employees in the company's accounts department had previously worked for Arthur Andersen, and vice versa.

Further reading

Flint, D., *A True and Fair View in Company Accounts*, Gee & Co, 1982

Parker, R.H. and Nobes, C.W., *An International View of True and Fair Accounting*, Routledge 1994

Rayman, A., *Accounting Standards: True or False?*, Routledge, 2006

Unique selling proposition

A unique selling proposition (USP) is a description of the qualities that are unique to a particular product or service and that differentiate it in a way which will make customers purchase it rather than its rivals.

Marketing experts used to insist that every product and service had to have a USP, at least one unique feature that could be distilled into a 60-second sales spiel, the equivalent of a single written paragraph. But this idea was usurped by the view that what really matters in marketing a product or service is its positioning, where it sits on the spectrum of customer needs. Shampoos, for instance, claim to meet all sorts of different customer needs and sit in all sorts of different positions – the need to wash dry hair or greasy hair, dark hair or blond hair, or the need to wash hair frequently or not so frequently. Few of them, however, can claim to have a unique selling proposition. All of them clean hair.

Uniqueness is rare, and coming up with a continuous stream of products with unique features is, in practice, extremely difficult. Philip Kotler (see page 261) said that the difficulty firms have in creating functional uniqueness has made them "focus on having a unique emotional selling proposition (an ESP) instead of a USP". He gives the example of the Ferrari car and the Rolex watch. Neither has a distinctive functional uniqueness, but each has a unique emotional association in the consumer's mind.

Uniqueness can be sought in a number of ways:

- By offering the lowest price. John Lewis, a British department store, used to claim that it was "never knowingly undersold". Its USP established it as the cheapest vendor (under certain prescribed conditions) of the items that it sold. But this is a rocky route to success, particularly at a time when there are firms prepared to sell (temporarily) at well below cost just to establish turnover. This was the case with many early internet retailing experiments. Moreover, buyers who base their purchasing decisions on price alone are often disloyal. Customers continue to go to John Lewis for many reasons other than its price promise.
- By offering the highest quality. This is the Rolls-Royce approach to selling.

- By being exclusive. In the information age, this is an increasingly common type of USP. More and more firms offer a unique packaging of information or knowledge.
- By offering the best customer service. Domino's Pizza became the bestselling brand in the United States on the basis of its USP: "Fresh, hot pizza delivered in 30 minutes or less, guaranteed." It did not promise high quality or low price, just fast delivery. A side benefit of a USP like this is that it compels the firm's employees to try that bit harder to achieve the promise. A firm that fails to fulfil the promise in its USP is condemned to a short future if it cannot quickly come up with a new one.
- By offering the widest choice. This is particularly appropriate to niche markets. A specialist cheese shop, say, can claim to offer a wider selection of cheeses than anyone else.
- By giving the best guarantee. This is particularly important in industries such as travel and catalogue selling, where customers pay for something upfront and then have to hope that what they think they have bought is eventually delivered.

Jay Abraham, a marketing consultant who once described himself as "the most expensive and successful marketing consultant on the planet", said that most businesses do not have a USP:

> [They have] only a "me too", rudderless, nondescript, unappealing business that feeds solely upon the sheer momentum of the marketplace. There's nothing unique; there's nothing distinct. They promise no great value, benefit, or service – just "buy from us" for no justifiable, rational reason.

Value chain

The value chain was first developed as a business idea in the second chapter of *Competitive Advantage: Creating and Sustaining Superior Performance* by Michael Porter (see page 295), first published in 1985. In it he wrote:

> A systematic way of examining all the activities a firm performs and how they interact is necessary for analysing the sources of competitive advantage. In this chapter, I introduce the value chain as the basic tool for doing so.

In the decade after the book was published, the idea became one of the most discussed and most misunderstood in the whole of the management arena. Each link in a value chain consists of a bundle of activities (value activities), and these bundles are performed by a firm to "design, produce, market, deliver and support its product". "Value activities are the discrete building blocks of competitive advantage," wrote Porter.

Rival firms may have similar chains, but they may also have very different ones. Porter quoted the example of People Express, one of the earliest of the low-cost airlines, and United Airlines, a more traditional firm. They were both in the same business, but there were significant differences in the way that, for example, they ran their boarding-gate operations, their aircraft operations and their crews. Differences such as these, claimed Porter, are a principal source of competitive advantage.

Critics of the idea focused on the difficulty in identifying the discrete building blocks. Without defining them carefully it is not possible to compare and contrast them with those of rivals and thereby to seek ways of gaining competitive advantage. Porter tried to help. He said:

> [Every value activity] employs purchased inputs, human resources (labour and management), and some form of technology to perform its function. Each value activity also uses and creates information ... the appropriate degree of disaggregation depends on the economics of the activities and the purposes for which the value chain is being analysed.

He also said a bit about what value chains were not. For instance: "Value activities and accounting classifications are rarely the same," he explained. But still, most firms found it hard to spot a value activity when it hit their factory floor. Non-manufacturing businesses found it even harder.

Since the idea of the value chain was first introduced, it has been taken in a number of different directions. One has attempted to extend it beyond the straightforward manufacturing processes for which it was, in its early form, most suited.

In 1993, Richard Norman and Rafael Ramirez argued that the value chain was outdated, suited to a slower changing world of comparatively fixed markets. Companies in the 1990s, they said, needed not just to add value but to "reinvent" it. This they could do by reconfiguring roles and relationships between "a constellation of actors" – suppliers, partners, customers, and so on. One company they pointed to as having done this particularly well was IKEA, a Swedish-based international retailer of home furniture.

Later, Jeffrey Rayport and John Sviokla applied the idea to the virtual world, the world of information, arguing that managers must pay attention to the way in which value chains work in both the tangible world of the market place and the virtual world of the market space. Just as companies take raw materials and refine them into products, so (increasingly) do they also take raw information and add value from a chain of five activities: information gathering, organising, selecting, synthesising and distributing.

Further reading

Baldwin, C., Clark, K., Magretta, J. and Dyer, J., *Harvard Business Review on Managing the Value Chain*, Harvard Business School Press, 2000

Krajewski, L., Ritzman, L. and Malhotra, M.K., *Operations Management: Processes and Value Chains*, 8th edn, Pearson Prentice Hall, 2007

Porter, M., *Competitive Advantage: Creating and Sustaining Superior Performance*, Free Press, New York, and Collier Macmillan, London, 1985; 2nd edn, Free Press, London and New York, 1988

Rayport, J.F. and Sviokla, J.J., "Exploiting the Virtual Value Chain", *Harvard Business Review*, January–February 1995

Value creation

Value creation is a corporation's *raison d'être*, the ultimate measure by which it is judged. Debate has focused on what is the most appropriate type of value for the corporation to create. Is it:

- the value that the stockmarket gives the company (its market value);
- the value shown in its balance sheet (the accounting or book value of its assets minus its liabilities);
- something based on its expected future performance – profits or cash; or
- none of these?

In the 1990s, the main emphasis of executives was on creating value for shareholders – a value that was reflected in movements of the company's stock price. But measures based on stockmarket values are subject to the same wild fluctuations as the market itself. In a rising tide, all boats get raised. But when macroeconomic changes force up markets generally, it does not mean that the value of each individual company in that market has changed similarly. Markets are often moved by sentiment that has little to do with the underlying value of individual corporations.

The dotcom frenzy at the end of the 1990s was proof of this. Small new internet firms were suddenly lifted into the stratosphere by investors' enthusiasm for their stocks. But their underlying value throughout the frenzy remained more or less unchanged – for many of them, that value was ultimately measured by a liquidator.

However, any measure based on book value has to get over the fact that accounting measures are not carved in stone. They can (and do) differ from country to country. It is also stymied by the fact that book values fail to take full account of intangible assets – things you cannot kick, like brands, patents or partnerships. These have come to assume a growing proportion of many companies' value, particularly in the high-tech sector where the most valuable assets walk in and out of the front door every day. At the start of this century, it was estimated that intangible assets could account for as much as half of the value of the entire American economy.

Measures that attempt to value a company based on its future prospects are no easy alternative. They soon run into the difficulty of quantifying what those prospects are. The popular idea that a company is no more than the net present value of its future cash flow depends on guessing first what that cash flow is going to be, and then what future interest rates are going to be. Interest rates are used to discount those cash flows and calculate their present value. These measures do, however, have the advantage of being independent of accounting rules, so they can be used to compare companies in different industries and countries.

A measure developed to overcome these problems is called EVA (economic value added). This is the measure of output (taken as operating profit after tax and some other adjustments) less input (taken as the annual rental charge on the total capital employed, both debt and equity). Managers have all the elements of this equation (costs, revenues, debt and capital expenditure) in their hands. So when it increases or decreases they have no one to praise or blame other than themselves. This makes it (in theory) a good benchmark against which to measure their bonuses and other perks.

Further reading

Bughin, J. and Copeland, T.E., "The Virtuous Cycle of Shareholder Value Creation", *McKinsey Quarterly*, No. 2, 1997

Grant, J., *Foundations of Economic Value Added*, Frank J. Fabozzi Associates, 1997; 2nd edn, John Wiley & Sons, 2002

Helfert, E., *Techniques of Financial Analysis: A Guide to Value Creation*, R.D. Irwin, 1963; 11th edn, McGraw-Hill, 2003

Morin, R.A. and Jarrell, S.L., *Driving Shareholder Value: Value-Building Techniques for Creating Shareholder Wealth*, McGraw-Hill, 2000

Stern, J. and Shiely, J.S., *The EVA Challenge: Implementing Value-added Change in an Organization*, John Wiley & Sons, 2001

Vertical integration

Vertical integration is the merging together of two businesses that are at different stages of production – for example, a food manufacturer and a chain of supermarkets. Merging in this way with something further on in the production process (and thus closer to the final consumer) is known as forward integration.

Vertical integration can be contrasted to horizontal integration, the merging together of businesses that are at the same stage of production, such as two supermarkets, or two food manufacturers. Merging with something further back in the process (if a food manufacturer were to merge with a farm, say) is known as backward integration. The integration of two organisations that are in completely different lines of business is sometimes referred to as conglomerate integration.

Businesses are downstream or upstream of each other depending on whether they are nearer to or further away from the final consumer (the "sea", as it were, to which the river of production flows).

The benefits of vertical integration come from the greater capacity it gives organisations to control access to inputs (and to control the cost, quality and delivery times of those inputs). In line with the changing organisational structure of the late 20th century, however, this logic became less compelling. In the late 1990s, consultants McKinsey & Company wrote:

> Whereas historically firms have vertically integrated in order
> to control access to scarce physical resources, modern firms
> are internally and externally disaggregated, participating in a
> variety of alliances and joint ventures and outsourcing even
> those activities normally regarded as core.

Some of the best known examples of vertical integration have been in the oil industry. In the 1970s and 1980s, many companies that were engaged primarily in exploration and the extraction of crude petroleum decided to acquire downstream refineries and distribution networks. Companies such as Shell and BP came to control every step involved in bringing a drop of oil from its North Sea or Alaskan origins to a vehicle's fuel tank.

The idea of vertical integration was taken a step further by Dell Computer, one of the most successful companies of the 1990s. Michael Dell, its founder, said that he combined the traditional vertical integration of the supply chain with the special characteristics of the virtual organisation (see page 207) to create something that he called "virtual integration". Dell assembles computers from other firms' parts, but it has relationships with those firms that are more binding than the traditional links between buyer and supplier. It does not own them in the way of the vertically integrated firm but through exchanges of information and a variety of loose associations it achieves much the same aim – what Michael Dell calls "a tightly co-ordinated supply chain".

Vertical integration is a difficult strategy for companies to implement successfully. It is often expensive and hard to reverse. Upstream producers frequently integrate with downstream distributors to secure a market for their output. This is fine when times are good. But many firms have found themselves cutting prices sharply to their downstream distributors when demand has fallen just so they can maintain targeted levels of plant utilisation.

The vertically integrated giants of the computer industry, firms such as IBM, Digital and Burroughs, were felled like young saplings when at the end of the 1970s Apple formed a network of independent specialists that produced machines far more efficiently than the do-it-all giants.

Further reading

Dell, M., Magretta, J. and Rollins, K., "The power of virtual integration: an interview with Dell Computer's Michael Dell", *Harvard Business Review*, March–April 1998

Harrigan, K.R., *Vertical Integration, Outsourcing and Corporate Strategy*, Beard Books, 2003

Stuckey, J. and White, D., "When and When Not to Vertically Integrate", *McKinsey Quarterly*, No. 3, 1993

Viral marketing

Viral marketing involves choosing a small group of well-connected individuals to launch a product or service via the internet or their mobile phones. The idea is that their approval will spread rapidly via their online network of connections, create a buzz around the product being marketed and result in millions of sales. The most desirable individuals for viral marketing are those with what is known as high social networking potential (SNP). A person's SNP is a combination of the size of their online social network and their power to influence that network.

Viral marketing is meant to work like the spread of an epidemic. If every infected person infects, in turn, more than one other, the epidemic spreads rapidly. If every prospect reaches more than one other, sales rise rapidly. At the height of the dotcom boom there were few business plans that did not include viral marketing as a central part of their strategy.

Viral marketing moved into a new phase with the growth of online social networks such as YouTube and Facebook. On such networks information gets pulled out by the participants instead of being pushed out via e-mail. It gives the virus greater potential to multiply. But as the internet grows more diffuse and more commonplace, most people's SNP seems bound to decline.

Few marketing viruses are known to have succeeded on anything like the scale of Hotmail, commonly considered to be the father of viral marketing. Hotmail's success was based partly on the fact that it was free – viral marketing seems to work well when there is a free element to what is being marketed (as there often is with online services). Whenever someone sent a Hotmail e-mail message, for example, there was a note at the bottom saying, "Get your private, free e-mail at www.hotmail.com".

Viral marketing also works well with products and services that peer groups want to be associated with. That was the case, for example, with *The Blair Witch Project*, a film that became a box-office success in America largely through viral marketing among university students. And it worked well for the launch of a British pop group called the Arctic Monkeys, whose first record went to the top of the British charts in 2005 thanks largely to being marketed by fans on the internet.

The term viral marketing is said to have been first coined by Jeffrey Rayport, a Harvard Business School academic, in a 1996 article for the magazine *Fast Company*. The idea really took off with the growth of the internet and e-commerce. Word-of-mouth has long been recognised as a powerful marketing tool; e-word of mouth seemed to have the potential to be so much more so.

But word-of-mouth marketing works a lot better among young chatter-boxes than it does among middle-aged recluses. Likewise, if web surfers don't pass on information, weary perhaps from too many messages that threaten all sorts of awfulness if they are not passed to at least ten people in less than ten minutes, or just web-weary in general, then the effect of viral marketing soon fizzles out. The virus can quickly lose its power to infect.

Further reading

Aral, S. and Walker, D., "Forget Viral Marketing – Make the Product Itself Viral", *Harvard Business Review*, June 2011

Sernovitz, A., *Word of Mouth Marketing*, Kaplan Press, 2009

The virtual organisation

It is widely alleged that the business organisation of the future will be virtual. But precise definitions of what it means to be a virtual organisation are hard to find. The origin of the phrase, though, is clear. It comes from the expression "virtual reality", an experience in which electronically created sounds and images are made to resemble reality. A virtual company resembles a normal traditional company in its inputs and its outputs. It differs in the way in which it adds value during the journey in between.

The virtual organisation has an almost infinite variety of structures, all of them fluid and changing. Most of them need virtually no employees. A New York insurance company was once started from scratch by someone whose overriding aim was to employ nobody but himself. The UK's Virgin Group briefly held 5% of the British cola market with just five employees. This was achieved by tightly focusing on the company's core competence: its marketing. Everything else, from the production of the drink to the distribution of it, was done by someone else. A virtual organisation relies for the most part on a network of part-time electronically connected freelances, sometimes referred to as e-lances.

The virtual organisation has few physical assets, reflecting the fact that adding value is becoming more dependent on (mobile) knowledge and less dependent on (immobile) plant and machinery. Hollywood is often cited as a template for the virtual organisation. The way that movies have been made since the industry freed itself from the studio system (where everyone from Bette Davis down to the doorman was a full-time employee) has been virtual. A number of freelances, from actors to directors via set builders and publicity agents, come together with a common purpose: to make a movie, to tell a story on celluloid. They then go their separate ways and another (unrelated) bunch of people (with a similar set of skills) comes together to make another movie. And so it goes on, very productively.

Linked to the idea of the virtual organisation is the idea of the virtual office, a place where space is not allocated uniquely to individual employees. People work as and when they need to, wherever space is available. This practice is commonly referred to as hot-desking. The virtual office has the advantage of providing a different vista every day. But it makes it difficult to form close relationships with colleagues.

In *Rethinking the Future*, Lester Thurow, once the dean of Sloan School of Management, gave a vivid portrayal of the virtual office:

> You walk in and there's an electronic board that says room 1021 is empty. You go to 1021. You have your personal telephone number. You call up your computer code. You press a button and your family picture is up on the flat-screen TV set on the wall. And that's your office for as long as you're there. The minute you leave, it ceases to be your office.
>
> We know why you don't do that at the moment; human beings like to have a cave. But the first company that figures out how to make this work will save 25% on office space, 25% on telephones, 25% on computers. These will be the low-cost producers, and low-cost producers will inherit the earth.

AT&T, an American telecoms company, reckons that it saved over $500m between 1991 and 1998 by reorganising its office space along virtual lines.

The process of defining the virtual organisation is a gradual one. As companies withdraw more and more into their core competencies, so they become more virtual. The virtual organisation is able to leverage this core into almost any industrial sector. Thus it can be in the pensions business and the railway business at the same time (as was the Virgin organisation in the UK). It can then rapidly desert any one of those businesses, and equally rapidly move into something completely different by establishing strategic alliances with organisations that have the essential skills that it lacks. And it can do this anywhere in the world.

The virtual organisation is inevitably ephemeral because it has no repository of long-term memory, no individuals who have worked for the same organisation for years and years. Nor has it any long-term geographical presence or a local community that remembers "Old Mr Chambers from way back".

Further reading

Davidow, W.H. and Malone, M.S., *The Virtual Corporation: Structuring and Revitalizing the Corporation for the 21st Century*, HarperBusiness, 1992

Handy, C., "Trust and the Virtual Organisation", *Harvard Business Review*, May–June 1995

Vision

A vision is the image that a business must have of its aims and goals before it sets out to reach them. It is a bit like the old saying: "If you don't know where you're going, then for sure you won't get there." Warren Bennis (see page 217) said of vision:

> To choose a direction, an executive must first have developed a mental image of the possible and desirable future state of the organisation. This image, which we call a vision, may be as vague as a dream or as precise as a goal or a mission statement.

In the early 1960s, John Kennedy had a vision of putting a man on the moon by 1970, and in 1969 Neil Armstrong and Buzz Aldrin landed there. In the 1980s, Sanford Weill had a vision of making American Express the leading investment bank within five years. IBM's vision at the time was still vaguer: to provide the best service of any firm in the world.

Great leaders create visions. In *Dynamic Administration*, Mary Parker Follett, an American political scientist, wrote:

> The most successful leader of all is the one who sees another picture not yet actualised. He sees the things which belong in his present picture but which are not yet there.

This description of Napoleon is by Louis Madelin, his contemporary and biographer:

> He would deal with three or four alternatives at the same time and endeavour to conjure up every possible eventuality – preferably the worst. This foresight, the fruit of meditation, generally enabled him to be ready for any setback, nothing ever took him by surprise … perhaps the most astonishing characteristic of his intellect was the combination of idealism and realism which enabled him to face the most exalted visions at the same time as the most insignificant realities. And, indeed, he was in a sense a visionary, a dreamer of dreams.

For a vision to have any impact on the employees of an organisation it has to be conveyed in a dramatic and enduring way. Metaphor is often useful: "a chicken in every pot" is a standard off-the-shelf vision for a politician promising a programme of rapid economic improvement.

Jan Carlzon, the leader of Scandinavian Airline Systems (SAS) in the 1980s, once outlined his vision for the "Passenger Pleasing Plane". With seating never more than two abreast and higher roofs, Carlzon said that his starting point was: "An aircraft which the passenger wants. Then we can add on engines and the cockpit, not the other way around." Unfortunately Carlzon did not survive in the industry long enough to turn this particular vision into reality.

Jim Collins (see page 229) and Jerry Porras were largely responsible for a revival of interest in the "visioning thing" in the mid-1990s with their bestselling book *Built to Last*. It related corporate longevity to a company's vision and to its goals. The average age of the authors' sample of enduringly successful companies was 97. They claimed that:

> *The lessons of these companies can be learned and applied by the vast majority of managers at all levels. Gone forever – at least in our eyes – is the debilitating perspective that the trajectory of a company depends on whether it is led by people ordained with rare and mysterious qualities that cannot be learned by others.*

The authors have been criticised for the fact that 17 out of the 18 companies they examined were American. (The one outsider was Sony.) Experience of corporate longevity is undoubtedly greater in Europe and Japan than it is in the United States. It would have been interesting if Collins and Porras had looked closely at corporate experience of the visioning thing in these places.

Further reading

Collins, J.C. and Porras, J.I., "Building Your Company's Vision", *Harvard Business Review*, September–October 1996

Collins, J.C. and Porras, J.I., *Built to Last: Successful Habits of Visionary Companies*, HarperBusiness, New York, 1994; 10th edn, Random House Business Books, 2005

Ibarra, H., "Women and the Vision Thing", *Harvard Business Review*, January 2009

Zero-base budgeting

O nce upon a time a business's annual budget was drawn up on the basis of the previous year's budget. To each item that appeared last year, managers would add a certain percentage. The percentage would be determined more or less arbitrarily, although it would probably be related in some indeterminate way to the rate of inflation, the company's overall strategy and the manager's frame of mind on that day.

For many years it was acknowledged that this was not an ideal way to allocate a company's scarce financial resources. It encouraged managers to focus on the cost increases from year to year rather than on the under-lying costs themselves. It also took account inadequately of the changing environment in which a company operated. For example, increasing last year's expenditure by the rate of inflation "plus some" was, at some stage, sure to have left a business way behind its rivals.

Nobody came up with anything better until Peter Pyhrr, a manager at Texas Instruments (TI) in Dallas, developed the idea of zero-base budgeting. Each year he prepared his budgets as if last year's figures had not existed. Every assumption had to be rethought from scratch and then justified. It was not acceptable to use last year's expenditure as a benchmark for this year's budgeted costs, and then only to have to justify the increase in that expenditure. In effect, zero-base budgeting treats all claims on financial resources as if they were entirely new claims for entirely new projects.

A basic requirement of zero-base budgeting is that managers prepare their budgets for their operations at the lowest possible level. They are then required to calculate the costs and benefits of making a particular business decision that would lead to an incremental increase from that level. Breaking the budget down into different decision packages in this way makes it easier for senior managers to make choices among competing claims on scarce resources.

Other companies rapidly adopted the idea. It has also been used exten-sively by local and national governments and by health and education authorities, areas where the budgeting process has traditionally rolled over from one year to the next with its underlying assumptions rarely questioned.

Criticism of zero-base budgeting focuses on the practical difficulties of implementation, and on the fact that it is very time-consuming. Traditional incremental budgeting retains the great advantage of simplicity. One author has claimed that "recent history has indicated that zero-base budgeting is very susceptible to political influence and pressures". In recent years it has largely fallen into disuse, at least outside the public sector.

Further reading

Pyhrr, P., *Zero-base Budgeting: A Practical Management Tool for Evaluating Expenses*, John Wiley & Sons, 1973; reprint, 1977

PART TWO
MANAGEMENT GURUS

Igor Ansoff

BORN: 1918
DIED: 2002
NATIONALITY: American

Notable publications
Corporate Strategy: An Analytic Approach to Business Policy for Growth and Expansion, McGraw-Hill, 1965
Strategic Management, Wiley, 1979; republished 2007

Notable quotations
Paralysis by analysis.

I begged, borrowed and stole concepts and theoretical insights from psychology, sociology and political science. And I attempted to integrate them into a holistic explanation of strategic behaviour.
(About his book, *Strategic Management*)

Background

Igor Ansoff was the father of modern strategic thinking. When Gary Hamel (see page 245) referred to the origins of corporate strategy he paid Ansoff an indirect compliment: "Strategy didn't start with Igor Ansoff, neither did it start with Machiavelli," he wrote. "It probably did not even start with Sun Tzu. Strategy is as old as human conflict." In other words, Ansoff came of a great line passing through Machiavelli and Sun Tzu.

Born in Vladivostok of a Russian mother and an American diplomat father, Ansoff spent the first 18 years of his life in Russia before moving to New York, where he studied mechanical engineering and physics. In 1950 he joined the Rand Corporation, an influential think-tank of the time, where he worked on strategic problem-solving for NATO, developing theories that he subsequently came to apply to business.

He then worked for Lockheed, an aerospace company, and became a vice-president before moving on in 1963 to become an academic, first at the Carnegie Institute of Technology in Pittsburgh, then as founding dean of the Graduate School of Management at Vanderbilt University in Nashville, Tennessee.

Ansoff's 1965 book on corporate strategy, the first to concentrate solely on the subject, was described by Henry Mintzberg (see page 275), a consistent critic of Ansoff, as "the most elaborate model of strategic planning [see page 173] in the literature". Although it started with a simple aim, "to produce a resource-allocation pattern that will offer the best potential for meeting the firm's objectives", it soon got too bogged down in detail for many readers. It contained a series of rigorous processes and checklists designed to help managers reach strategic decisions.

Ansoff himself came to recognise that too often it resulted in "paralysis by analysis", and in his later work he moved away from this rigid approach, seeking to find ways of introducing flexibility into the planning process. At the same time he abandoned his search for big universal management prescriptions, believing that each organisation has to make strategic decisions on its own, dependent on its own unique environment.

Ansoff divided management decision-making into three: strategic; administrative; and operating, a classification that has been adopted by many subsequent writers. Several of his other ideas were picked up by other gurus and made more famous – competitive advantage (by Michael Porter, see pages 37 and 295), core competence (by Gary Hamel and C.K. Prahalad, see pages 41, 245 and 297) and "sticking to your knitting" (by Tom Peters, see page 293), for example.

In 1974 he moved to Brussels and worked at the European Institute of Advanced Studies in Management, a time that he described as "the most important phase of my intellectual development". Out of this experience he wrote *Strategic Management* (1979). In 1983 he returned to the United States to become professor of strategic management at the United States International University. He also set up his own consulting business in San Diego, southern California.

Warren Bennis

BORN: 1925
NATIONALITY: American

Notable publications
With Nanus, B., *Leaders: The Strategies for Taking Charge*, Harper & Row,
    1985; 2nd edn, HarperBusiness, 1997
Why Leaders Can't Lead, Jossey-Bass, 1989
With Thomas, R., *Geeks and Geezers*, Harvard Business School Press,
    2002
With Biederman, P.W., *Still Surprised: A Memoir of a Life in Leadership*,
    Jossey-Bass, 2010

Notable quotations
Managers do things right. Leaders do the right thing.

*I think a lot of the leaders I've spoken to give expression to their feminine
side. Many male leaders are almost bisexual in their ability to be open and
reflective ... Gender is not the determining factor.*

*Leadership is an endless subject and endlessly interesting because you can
never get your conceptual arms fully around it. I always feel rather like a
lepidopterist chasing a butterfly.*

Background
Warren Bennis is a laid-back silver-haired professor at the University of
Southern California who has been an influential authority on leadership
for decades. He has been consulted on the subject by at least four American
presidents and by some of the best-known occupants of corporate boardrooms around the world.

His fundamental tenet is that leaders are made, not born. The worst
problem they can face, says Bennis, is "early success. There's no opportunity to learn from adversity and problems". Other myths about leadership that he dismisses are that it is a rare skill; that leaders are charismatic
(most of them are quite ordinary people); and that leaders control and
manipulate (they do not; they align the energies of others behind an
attractive goal).

Being a leader is very different from being a manager, says Bennis. So being a manager in an organisation is not necessarily the best training for being the leader of that organisation. But it is the only training that most CEOs get for the job. Managers, however, can learn to be leaders. "I believe in 'possible selves'," Bennis has written, "the capacity to adapt and change."

In *Leaders: The Strategies for Taking Charge*, Bennis lists four competencies that leaders need to develop:

- forming a vision which provides people with a bridge to the future;
- giving meaning to that vision through communication;
- building trust, "the lubrication that makes it possible for organisations to work";
- searching for self-knowledge and self-regard.

Bennis argues that to become a good leader, a person first has to develop as an individual. In particular that means learning not to be afraid of being seen as vulnerable. Leadership qualities, he maintains, can only emerge from an "integrated self". Howard Schultz, the founder and chairman of the Starbucks chain of coffee shops, says that Bennis once told him that to become a great leader you have to develop "your ability to leave your own ego at the door, and to recognise the skills and traits that you need in order to build a world-class organisation".

Bennis has also argued that leaders take a different attitude to failure from run-of-the-mill managers, thinking of it not so much as the end of a phase, but rather the beginning of one imbued with knowledge gained from the failure.

Bennis was greatly influenced by Douglas McGregor (see page 273). In the late 1960s he tried to run the college where he was provost along the lines of McGregor's Theory Y. But he found that, in practice, it was not possible to leave all staff to their own self-motivating devices. Many people seemed to need more structure and direction than McGregor's scheme would allow.

Marvin Bower

BORN: 1903
DIED: 2003
NATIONALITY: American

Notable publication
The Will to Manage: Corporate Success through Programmed Management,
McGraw-Hill, 1966

Notable quotation
If you looked after the client, the profits would look after themselves.

Background
For many years the management consulting business was dominated by
one firm. It advised the world's biggest corporations and some of its biggest
countries about high-level strategy. So outstanding was it that it became
known simply as "The Firm". That firm, McKinsey, was the creation of one
man. Not James O. McKinsey, the man whose name hangs over its front
door (and who died young of pneumonia in 1937), but Marvin Bower, the
most powerful influence on the firm in the 65 years from James McKinsey's death to his own, at the age of 99, in 2003.

Bower modelled the consultancy on the lines of a professional law firm,
establishing a set of values by which it was to be guided. For example,
clients' interests were supposed to have precedence over growth in the
firms' revenues. His approach to consulting was heavily influenced by the
legal profession, which had been his first choice of career. After studying
at Harvard Law School he applied to work for a firm in Cleveland, where
he had been raised. But his grades were not good enough, so he went back
to the then young Harvard Business School, gained an MBA and returned
to a job with the law firm as a corporate lawyer.

In 1933 he joined McKinsey's fledgling firm when its only office was
in Chicago. He then set up a branch in New York and, after McKinsey's
death, helped rebuild the company around its New York operation. He
was managing director from 1950 to 1967. *BusinessWeek* said of Bower
that he was "the very image of America's 'Organisation Man' [see William
Whyte, page 321] in the 1950s ... immaculately dressed in a Brooks Brothers

dark suit, a starched white shirt, and a hat". For years he insisted that McKinsey consultants wear hats. He was also famously outspoken and not afraid to confront clients. A colleague once recalled an occasion when he bellowed out, "The problem with this company, Mr Little, is you." "It happened to be totally accurate," added the colleague. "That was the end of our work with that client. But it didn't bother Marvin."

Bower often turned down clients when he did not believe that they were prepared for change. He declined to work for Howard Hughes, for example, and refused to help the American government devise a scheme to bail out American Motors, a car company.

McKinsey's approach to its work – offering high-level strategic advice – has left it vulnerable to the criticism that it does not stick around to follow through the consequences of that advice. It has a reputation for arrogance, sometimes explained away as a manifestation of total concentration on its clients. The Economist once wrote of an ex-member of the firm: "He suffers the lack of self-doubt common in former McKinsey consultants."

Several of Bower's alumni became famous in their own right – Tom Peters (see page 293), Kenichi Ohmae (see page 281) and Richard Pascale (see page 289), for instance, are all included separately in this compendium of gurus. Even the next generation of management gurus seems to have benefited from a spell at the Firm. Both Donald Sull (see Active inertia, page 7) and Pankaj Ghemawat (see page 239) worked for McKinsey before moving on to academic careers.

Warren Buffett

BORN: 1930
NATIONALITY: American

Notable quotations

As a group lemmings have a rotten image. But no individual lemming has ever received a bad press.

I want to give my kids just enough so that they would feel that they could do anything, but not so much that they would feel like doing nothing.

Background

Although more of an investment guru than a management guru, Warren Buffett made his billions (and became the richest man in the world) from the success of the companies owned by his investment vehicle, Berkshire Hathaway, a publicly quoted company. He has described the extent of his involvement in these companies as being limited to the allocation of capital and people. "Charles T. Munger, Berkshire Hathaway's vice-chairman, and I really have only two jobs," he once said (Charles T. Munger being his long-time closest associate). "One is to attract and keep outstanding managers to run our various operations. The other is capital allocation." That includes setting the compensation of the chief executive.

Buffett is known as "the Sage of Omaha", after the town where he was born and where he spent most of his life, and much is made of his small-town homespun values. He likes to play the ukulele and he played and sang for Chinese TV in early 2012. He also plays bridge (with Bill Gates, among others) in his modest home in Omaha. His one conceit is a corporate jet, but that is second-hand and named "The Indefensible".

Buffett, however, is not really a small-town boy made good. His father, Howard Buffett, was a stockbroker who won a seat in Congress when Warren was a boy, and the family moved to Washington, DC, for a while. Then Buffett went to the Wharton School in Philadelphia, the top business school in the United States for finance and for those heading for the higher reaches of Wall Street. He left before he completed his course, but finished his studies at New York's almost equally prestigious Columbia Business School. From there, in 1951, he started to make his living by investing on the stockmarket. He was greatly influenced by Ben Graham, who wrote a classic book on investment, *Security Analysis* (1934), and had been his tutor at Columbia.

Buffett famously avoided the high-tech sector during the turn-of-the-century dotcom boom and bust, but in recent years he has suffered from a high involvement with the less-than-stellar insurance industry. Berkshire Hathaway's annual report contains a closely observed "letter to shareholders", written by Buffett, which is a mixture of homespun wisdom and market savvy. The company's annual meeting is held in the Q-West centre in downtown Omaha and is attended by as many as 20,000 investors from all over the world. "We have embraced the 21st century," wrote Buffett in one of his letters, "by entering such cutting-edge industries as bricks, carpets, insulation and paint – try to control your excitement."

In June 2006 he gave Berkshire Hathaway shares worth over $30 billion to the Bill and Melinda Gates Foundation, the biggest single charitable donation in history.

Dale Carnegie

BORN: 1888
DIED: 1955
NATIONALITY: American

Notable publications
Public Speaking: A Practical Course for Businessmen, Association Press, 1926
How to Win Friends and Influence People, The World's Work, Kingswood,
Surrey, 1913; new edited edn, Vermilion, 2007

Notable quotations
*Don't criticise, condemn or complain; give honest and sincere appreciation;
and arouse in the other person an eager want.*

*A person's name is, to that person, the sweetest and most important sound
in any language.*

Background
Unlike many of the gurus in this book, Dale Carnegie did not emerge
from an urban immigrant background and/or a brilliant academic career.
He was born Dale Breckenridge Carnagey into a poor farming family, and
he struggled through college in Warrensburg, Missouri. But he had one
exceptional skill – he was an extraordinary public speaker and he first
established a reputation as a teacher of public speaking at night school in
New York's YMCAs. So successful were his courses that he turned them
into a popular textbook and went on to found the Dale Carnegie Institute
of Effective Speaking and Human Relations.

Carnegie's first lesson was "Don't Criticise", and he quoted examples
of famous folk, such as Abraham Lincoln, Clark Gable and Marconi,
who he claimed took care not to criticise others. His second lesson was,
always try to see the issue from the other person's point of view. Why,
for example, would that particular person want to do a particular task for
you? He recognised that a key motivator for many people is the desire to
feel important, the nourishment of their self-esteem. He nourished his
own self-esteem in 1916 by hiring the Carnegie Hall, named after Andrew
Carnegie, where he gave a lecture to a packed house.

Carnegie was one of the first to provide what he called "in a nutshell" summaries of the different chapters of his books, a practice that is now almost universal in management writing.

Although the first edition of *How to Win Friends* ran to only 5,000 copies, since then more than 15m copies have been sold. Carnegie's books have been reprinted many times over the years. In 1997, over 40 years after his death, *How to Win Friends and Influence People* was still on the bestseller lists in Germany.

Alfred Chandler

BORN: 1918
DIED: 2007
NATIONALITY: American
ACHIEVEMENT: Pulitzer Prize for *The Visible Hand*

Notable publications
Strategy and Structure: Chapters in the History of the American Industrial Enterprise, MIT Press, 1969, reprint, 1990
The Visible Hand: The Managerial Revolution in American Business, Belknap Press and Harvard University Press, 1977
With Deams, H. (eds), *Managerial Hierarchies: Comparative Perspectives on the Rise of Modern Industrial Enterprises*, Harvard University Press, 1980

Notable quotations
The visible hand.

Unless structure follows strategy, inefficiency results.

You can't do today's job with yesterday's methods and still be in business tomorrow

Background

Almost single-handedly, Alfred Chandler invented the study of business history. He was first and foremost a historian, and completed his PhD at Harvard University in 1952. Ten years later he published his classic business book, *Strategy and Structure*, in which he argued that all successful companies must have a structure that matches their strategy (and not, as many had assumed until then, the other way round).

He based his theory on an extensive study of large American corporations between the years 1850 and 1920 – corporations such as Du Pont, General Motors and Sears, Roebuck. It was a time when businesses were developing from single-unit, centrally managed operations into umbrella-type structures where a number of comparatively autonomous units shared certain overheads, in particular the strategic planning (see page 173) function.

Chandler was an early advocate of the centralise/decentralise dichotomy, encouraging companies to co-ordinate strategic planning from the centre while leaving individual business units free to get on with the day-to-day running of their operations. The visible hand of management, he maintained, had replaced Adam Smith's invisible hand of market forces because it co-ordinated the flow of goods and services from producers to consumers more efficiently than did purely market mechanisms.

He found the origins of modern management hierarchies in the rapid growth of the American railroads. Local decision-making there was required on and near the track, but at the same time there was a need for a headquarters to co-ordinate the different local operations. The structure was forced on the organisation by outside events.

During the second world war Chandler served in the US navy, where he saw at first hand the operation of a large organisation. He then taught at MIT and Johns Hopkins University before going on to Harvard Business School in 1971, where he became the first holder of an endowed chair in business history.

His academic work covered a wide range of subjects. He was one of a group of editors of the authorised editions of the letters and papers of two American presidents: Theodore Roosevelt and Dwight D. Eisenhower. He also wrote biographies of Henry Varnum Poor, his great-grandfather and one of the founders of the Standard & Poor's information business, and of Pierre du Pont, founder of the chemicals company that still bears his family's name.

Clayton Christensen

BORN: 1952
NATIONALITY: American

Notable publications
With Bower, J., "Disruptive Technologies, Catching the Wave", *Harvard Business Review*, January–February 1995
The Innovator's Dilemma, Harvard Business School Press, 1997; HarperBusiness 2000
With Raynor, M., *The Innovator's Solution*, Harvard Business School Press, 2003
"How Will You Measure Your Life?", *Harvard Business Review*, July/August 2010

Notable quotations
There is something about the way that decisions get made in successful organisations that sows the seeds of eventual failure ... Many large companies adopt a strategy of waiting until new markets are "large enough to be interesting". But this is not often a successful strategy.

There are times at which it is right not to listen to customers.

Background
A tall, soft-spoken Mormon academic at Harvard Business School, "Clay" Christensen sprang to prominence on the strength of one book, *The Innovator's Dilemma*. Its subtitle contains the essence of what the book is about: *When New Technologies Cause Great Firms to Fail.* The favourable reaction to the book showed that Christensen had put his finger on a problem that many managers at the time (1997 – early in the cycle of the dotcom boom) were able to recognise, the problem of how to identify breakthrough technologies when your customers will not.

Managers are trained to invest in products and services that are most in demand, yet some of the most dramatic technological innovations come from products where initial demand may be poor. Christensen cited the examples of the mobile phone, digital photography and internet shopping.

Central to the book is his distinction between two types of innovative technology. There are what he calls sustaining technologies, which merely improve existing products or services, and disruptive technologies (see page 63), which completely change the nature of a market or business. Sustaining technologies improve the quality of CDs; disruptive technologies come up with the iPod and the digital downloading of sound.

The term "disruptive technology", which Christensen had first used in a 1995 article in *Harvard Business Review*, quickly became part of every ambitious manager's vocabulary. Alerted to the fact that something like digital photography could arrive in a sort of flanking movement and almost bring down a company of the size and vintage of Kodak (because it was so committed to sustaining an old technology), managers went on the look-out for disruptive technologies and the small start-ups that might first harbour them. Bankers, for instance, feared that any upstart with an ATM and an advertising budget might be able to provide all the services that they had assumed could only be distributed through thousands of acres of prime real estate.

In his second book, *The Innovator's Solution*, Christensen replaced the term disruptive technology with the phrase "disruptive innovation", since it was not the technology *per se* that was disruptive in such cases but the way in which it was used in a business context – that is, the innovation itself.

Christensen has won the McKinsey award for the best article published in *Harvard Business Review* in a year four times. Born in Salt Lake City, Utah, he was a missionary in Korea from 1971 to 1973 on behalf of the Mormon church. He speaks Korean and has published an essay about his beliefs called "Why I Believe". He is also a keen scoutmaster and the father of five children.

Jim Collins

BORN: 1958
NATIONALITY: American

Notable publications
With Porras, J.I., *Built to Last: Successful Habits of Visionary Companies*,
   HarperBusiness, 1994; 10th edn, Random House Business Books, 2005
Good to Great, Random House Business Books, 2001
With Hansen, M.T., *Great by Choice*, HarperBusiness, 2011

Notable quotations
The purpose of bureaucracy is to compensate for incompetence and lack of discipline – a problem that largely goes away if you have the right people in the first place.

A great company will have many once-in-a-lifetime opportunities.

Background
Jim Collins is a former Stanford Business School professor who found himself with a publishing sensation when he expanded his Stanford research – about what it takes to make companies endure – into a book. *Built to Last*, published in 1994, enabled Collins to retire from teaching. This and his other book, *Good to Great*, published in 2001, have become the Harry Potters of management literature, hugely popular and holding the promise of magic. *Good to Great* became the bestselling business book of all time, overtaking the long-standing holder of the title, *In Search of Excellence*, by Tom Peters (see page 293).

Collins excels at the American method of empirical business research. He gathers masses of data about a group that he wishes to study (in the case of his first book, enduringly excellent companies), compares it with a "carefully selected" control group that is not enduringly excellent and then sets out to find statistically significant differences. It is a painstaking method that takes time.

He says that *Built to Last* took six years to research, and *Good to Great* took five years of work by a team of 21 assistants in Collins's own "management laboratory" in Boulder, Colorado, near the mountains that he loves to climb. Although Collins can command enormous fees on the business lecture circuit, he moves only rarely away from Boulder.

The subtitle of *Built to Last* is *Successful Habits of Visionary Companies*, and Collins is very into the vision/mission thing. Enduringly successful companies, he says, have a clear mission. Setting that mission can be done in four different ways:

- By targeting. This can be precise, as was that of the Wal-Mart supermarket chain, which in 1976 set itself the target of being a $1 billion company within four years – a goal that it achieved. Or a target can be less precise; for example, Merck's 1979 target of becoming "the pre-eminent drug-maker worldwide in the 1980s".
- By identifying a common enemy. This is perhaps most famously embodied in Honda's three-word mission statement – "Yamaha wo tsubusu" ("We will crush Yamaha") – proving that Japanese firms are as fiercely competitive among themselves as they are abroad. Nike, a sports-shoe manufacturer, also thrived on a mission to defeat its enemy, first adidas, then Reebok.
- By setting up a role model. This is less common than the first two and crops up in the form of "To be the IBM of the real-estate business" or "To be the Rolls-Royce of the shoe industry".
- By an internal transformation. This is often used by old organisations in need of a shake-up. Procter & Gamble, for instance, determined at one time to provide its workers with steady employment following a period when it had become known for its rapid hire-and-fire policies.

Stephen Covey

BORN: 1932
NATIONALITY: American

Notable publications
The Seven Habits of Highly Effective People, Simon & Schuster, 1989
The Eighth Habit: From Effectiveness to Greatness, Free Press, 2005

Notable quotation
Human beings are not things needing to be motivated and controlled; they are four dimensional – body, mind, heart, and spirit.

Background

Like Clayton Christensen (see page 227) Stephen Covey is a Mormon, born in Utah and educated at Harvard Business School. While Christensen was a missionary for the church in Korea, Covey served his time in the UK.

He then became a professor of organisational behaviour at Brigham Young University before setting up the Covey Leadership Center (following the phenomenal success of his best-known book). *The Seven Habits of Highly Effective People* carried the spirit of the self-help movement into management. It packaged it into a formula that managers are familiar with, distilling it into seven simple compartments that anyone can get their head around in less time than it takes to travel from one airport lounge to the next.

Covey studied a number of books about personal success before writing his own. These included Dale Carnegie's *How to Win Friends and Influence People* (see page 223) and *Self-Help*, the 1859 quintessentially Victorian classic by Samuel Smiles, a no-nonsense Yorkshireman (new edition, Oxford Paperbacks, 2002).

The Wikipedia entry for Covey once alleged that he had "recast" much of the seven habits from a 1966 Peter Drucker article called "The Effective Executive", in which Drucker wrote "effectiveness, in other words, is a habit" and in which there is a chapter called "First Things First" – itself one of Covey's seven habits.

Covey designed a two-by-two matrix for deciding which things to put first, dividing activities into the important and the urgent. So activities can be urgent and important, not urgent but important, urgent but not important and neither urgent nor important. Effective people, said Covey, concentrate on the second of these – the non-urgent important activities. By so doing, they minimise the chances of there being activities of the first kind – urgent and important.

His full set of seven consists of:

- Be proactive.
- Begin with the end in mind.
- Put first things first.
- Think win/win.
- Seek first to understand, then to be understood.
- Synergise – learn to work with others to the benefit of all parties.
- Sharpen the saw – taken from the metaphor of the woodcutter who doesn't stop to sharpen his saw because he's too busy chopping down a tree.

His later work has moved into a more spiritual field and has aimed to broaden the applicability of the seven habits outside the corporate arena – for stay-at-home mums, for example, and for troubled teenagers. He has expanded his seven habits to eight, the eighth being: Find your voice and inspire others to find theirs. In his book *The Eighth Habit*, Covey says it is not enough to be effective in what he calls "the knowledge-worker age". "The challenges and complexity we face today", he says, "are of a different order of magnitude."

Covey is the father of nine children and the grandfather of about 50. In 2003 he received the National Fatherhood Award, which he says is "the most meaningful award" he has ever received.

W. Edwards Deming

BORN: 1900
DIED: 1993
NATIONALITY: American
ACHIEVEMENT: The Order of the Sacred Treasure, second class, the highest Japanese award ever given to foreigners

Notable publication
Out of the Crisis: Quality, Productivity and Competitive Position,
    Cambridge University Press, 1986; 2nd edn, MIT Press, 2000

Notable quotations
If I had to reduce my message for management to a few words, I'd say it all had to do with reducing variation.

I think I was the only man in Japan in 1950 who believed my prediction – that within five years manufacturers the world over would be screaming for protection [from Japanese imports]. It took four years.

Background
W. Edwards Deming was a physicist/statistician with a PhD from Yale who applied the ideas of a little-known American mathematician, Walter Shewhart, to business processes. Deming later said that Shewhart had an "uncanny ability to make things difficult". There was always a need for an interpreter of his findings. The most surprising thing is that Deming did not do this first in his native America, but in Japan.

Born in Iowa and raised on his grandfather's chicken farm, Deming joined the US Census Bureau in 1939 and, after the second world war, was sent to Japan to advise on a census that was taking place there. He stayed on to advise Japanese businessmen how to inject quality into their manufacturing industry. At the time Japan was notorious in the Western world for the shabby goods that it produced. By the late 1970s the roles had been reversed: Japan was producing the quality stuff while America's car industry was in crisis and its standard-bearers of quality were Coca-Cola and McDonald's.

It gave Americans some solace at the time to discover that behind the

Japanese quality miracle had been two Americans that few of them had heard of: Joseph Moses Juran (see page 255) and W. Edwards Deming. Juran, an electrical engineer, had also gone to Japan after the second world war and begun to teach middle managers about quality. Juran focused more on the human-relations aspects of quality, while Deming's approach involved demonstrating that all business processes are vulnerable to a loss of quality through statistical variation. Management, he argued, was responsible for 85% of that variation. Reduce the variation, increase the quality, was the foundation of his advice.

Deming's method for bringing this about was built on what became known outside Japan as the "quality circle" (see page 155) and inside Japan as the "Deming circle". These circles consisted of groups of workers who sought to improve the processes that they were responsible for in four stages. First came the planning of how to do it followed by the implementation of that plan. Then workers would check the variance from anticipated outcomes and take any corrective action that was necessary.

To this day, Japanese industry awards a prestigious annual prize to companies that have demonstrated exceptional improvements in quality. It is called the Deming Prize.

Deming was lauded on his return to the United States and conducted seminars around the country until he was in his 90s. Several big American firms, including Ford Motor Company, came to credit him with transforming their product quality and their profits. Over a number of years he came to distil his advice for managers into "14 points", which ranged from quality-related items such as "Cease dependence on mass inspection. Build quality into the product from the start", to more human issues such as "Remove barriers to pride in workmanship".

Deming was a modest man who loved music and sang in a choir.

Peter Drucker

BORN: 1909
DIED: 2005
NATIONALITY: Austrian-American
ACHIEVEMENT: The American Presidential Medal of Freedom, 2002

Notable publications
The End of Economic Man, Heinemann, 1939
The Concept of the Corporation, John Day & Co, 1946
The Practice of Management, Harper, New York, 1954; Heinemann,
    London, 1955; revised edn, Butterworth-Heinemann, 2007
The Age of Discontinuity, Heinemann, 1967
The Effective Executive, HarperBusiness, (paperback) 1993

Notable quotations
There are many books I could have written that are better than the ones I actually wrote. My best book would have been Managing Ignorance, and I'm very sorry I didn't write it.

There is only one definition of business purpose: to create a customer.

The real discipline comes in saying "no" to the wrong opportunities.

In the next economic downturn there will be an outbreak of bitterness and contempt for the super-corporate chieftains who pay themselves millions.
(Written in 1997)

Background
The most enduring guru of them all, Peter Drucker was the author of more than three dozen books, translated into almost as many languages. In 1997 *McKinsey Quarterly* said: "In the world of management gurus, there is no debate. Peter Drucker is the one guru to whom other gurus kowtow." But unlike some of those that might have kowtowed to him, Drucker was a guru with charm who never set out to diminish others. Some commentators have remarked that although he was firmly embedded in the human-relations school of management – along with Douglas McGregor (see page 273) and Warren Bennis (see page 217), for example – the guru he himself most admired was Frederick Winslow Taylor (see page 309), the

father of "scientific" management (see page 159).

Though born in Vienna, Drucker started his professional life in Frankfurt as a financial reporter, and he never lost his journalistic eye for a witty aphorism or a memorable metaphor. His writing is never dull, but nor is it superficial, in a field where both dullness and superficiality are common. He brought to it a Renaissance breadth of knowledge, and was as likely to refer to his beloved Jane Austen as to Taylor. Rosabeth Moss Kanter (see page 257) once wrote: "In the Drucker perspective ... quality of life, technological progress and world peace are all the products of good management ... at root, Drucker is a management Utopian, descended as much from Robert Owen [see page 285] as Max Weber [see page 319]."

Drucker moved to England in the early 1930s and thence to America in 1937, where he stayed until his death 68 years later. He started in the United States as a correspondent for a number of British newspapers. From 1950 to 1972 he was professor of business at New York University Graduate School of Business. In 1971 he moved to California to help develop one of the country's first executive MBAs at Claremont Graduate University, and its business school is now named after him.

From his first management book, *The Concept of the Corporation*, published in 1946, to his last article, "What Makes an Effective Executive" (which won the prestigious McKinsey award for the best article to appear in *Harvard Business Review* in 2004), Drucker never failed to sympathise with the difficulties of managers and the demands of their task. In his 1954 book *The Practice of Management*, he argued that management was one of the major social innovations of the 20th century, primarily a human activity, not a mechanical or an economic one. He pioneered the idea of the corporation as a social institution.

In *The Concept of the Corporation*, Drucker argued strongly in favour of decentralised decision-making at a time when corporate role models such as General Motors were concentrating more and more power in their headquarters. He argued that the assembly line, so embedded at the heart of industrial efficiency, was in fact very inefficient because it only allowed things to be done in sequence. He also introduced the idea of management by objectives (see page 121), aiming for long-term goals by setting a series of short-term ones. In 1969 he coined the phrase "knowledge worker".

Drucker thought of himself as a loner, as someone well outside the mainstream of management education. "I have always been a loner," he said once. "I work best outside. That's where I'm most effective. I would be a very poor manager. Hopeless. And a company job would bore me to death. I enjoy being an outsider."

Henri Fayol

BORN: 1841
DIED: 1925
NATIONALITY: French

Notable publication
General and Industrial Management, 1916 (in French); Sir Isaac Pitman,
London, 1949 (in English)

Background

While American manufacturing processes were being revolutionised by
Frederick Winslow Taylor (see page 309), France's were being overturned
by Fayolism, a system devised by an engineer, Henri Fayol, who became
something of a hero for rescuing a troubled mining company and turning
it into one of France's most successful businesses.

Though born in Istanbul, Fayol spent all his working life as a manager
at Compagnie de Commentry-Fourchambeau-Decazeville, a big French
mining conglomerate. For the last 30 years of his working life (1888–1918)
he was managing director of the company. He is the founding father of
what has become known as the administration school of management.
At its heart is Fayol's five-point breakdown of managerial responsibility
into planning, organising, co-ordinating, commanding and controlling, a
division which has pervaded much management thinking since.

"Command and control" became the slogan for the authoritative style
of management fashionable through the 1950s and 1960s, though Fayol's
method was more nuanced than this. His "commanding", for instance,
included energising employees, while controlling included adapting the
overall plan to changing circumstances.

Fayol's theory stood in stark contrast to that of Taylor, his contemporary.
Fayol himself said: "Taylor's approach differs from the one we have
outlined in that he examines the firm from the bottom up. He starts with
the most elemental units of activity – the workers' actions – then studies
the effects of their actions on productivity, devises new methods for
making them more efficient, and applies what he learns at lower levels
to the hierarchy." Fayol's approach was top-down, he looked at the organisation from the point of view of senior managers.

He also looked for general management principles that could be applied to a wide range of organisations – business, financial or government. He was a great believer in the value of specialisation and the unity of command, that each employee should be answerable to only one other person. Like W. Edwards Deming (see page 233) after him he distilled his thinking about management into 14 principles, ranging from specialisation to unity of command (one worker, one boss).

Fayol was scarcely known outside his native France until a quarter of a century after his death when his most important work, *General and Industrial Management*, was finally translated into English. His influence then spread rapidly, and persisted. As late as 1993, he was being listed in one poll as the most popular management writer of all time.

Pankaj Ghemawat

BORN: 1960
NATIONALITY: Indian

Notable publications
Games Businesses Play, MIT Press, 1997
Strategy and the Business Landscape, Addison Wesley Longman, 1999; 2nd edn, Pearson Prentice Hall, 2006
Redefining Global Strategy, Harvard Business School Press, 2007
"The Risk of Not Investing in a Recession", *Sloan Management Review*, Spring 2009
"The Cosmopolitan Corporation", *Harvard Business Review*, May 2011

Notable quotations
Globalony.

Managers who believe the hype of a flat world do so at their own risk. National borders still matter a lot for business strategists.

Globalisation's future is more fragile than you know.

Background

Pankaj Ghemawat is one of the younger representatives of the Indian gurus of management – men who straddle cultures, American, European and Asian, and throw new light on corporate behaviour, and particularly its global aspect.

Ghemawat follows in the steps of Sumantra Ghoshal (see page 241), whose early work was on managing across borders, and C.K. Prahalad (see page 297), whose later field of interest was "the base of the pyramid" – helping businesses to work with poorer customers. In 1991 Ghemawat became the youngest-ever full professor at Harvard Business School, no mean achievement. He gained a PhD in business economics from Harvard University and then went to work for consulting firm McKinsey & Company in London for a couple of years before returning to Harvard to teach.

His main area of interest is globalisation (see page 93), and his main thesis is that the world is not flat – in direct contradiction to a hugely bestselling book by Thomas Friedman, a *New York Times* columnist, called *The World is Flat*. The subtitle of Ghemawat's latest book, *Redefining Global Strategy*, is *Crossing Borders in a World Where Differences Still Matter*.

Friedman went on a whistle-stop tour of manufacturing and service industries around the world and concluded that everywhere is becoming the same mix of 24/7 sameness and that everyone is competing in the same single global economy. Ghemawat calls this "globalony" and argues that companies with a global reach need to pay careful attention to regional differences and modify their strategy accordingly. If the world were truly flat, foreign direct investment, which passes across borders, would account for a far greater percentage of global investment than the mere 10% which it currently represents. What works well in San José still does not necessarily go down so well in Bangalore or Shanghai.

Ghemawat goes on to argue that these differences need not necessarily be seen as a stumbling block, to be evened out at the earliest opportunity. They are the source of commercial opportunities which firms can take advantage of. The provision of health-care services, for example, is as uneven around the world as it ever was. It is just differently uneven.

In 2006, as befits a professor of global strategy, Ghemawat moved across the Atlantic, from Harvard to IESE, a Barcelona-based school that persistently ranks high among European business schools.

Sumantra Ghoshal

BORN: 1948
DIED: 2004
NATIONALITY: Indian
ACHIEVEMENT: Founding dean of the Indian School of Management, Hyderabad

Notable publications

With Bartlett, C., *Managing Across Borders*, Harvard Business School Press, 1989

With Bartlett, C., "Matrix Management: Not a Structure, a Frame of Mind", *Harvard Business Review*, July–August 1990

Birkinshaw, J. and Piramal, G. (eds), *Sumantra Ghoshal on Management: A Force for Good*, Pearson Education, 2005

Notable quotations

The most important source of a nation's progress is the quality of its management.

You cannot have faith in people unless you take action to improve and develop them.

Businesses are spinning tops. Let the momentum slacken and the top will fall.

Background

A soft-spoken physicist from Calcutta, Sumantra Ghoshal began his career with Indian Oil Corporation. By the time he moved on to management academia he had had a solid grounding in corporate life. After gaining doctorates at Harvard and MIT, he worked at INSEAD, a leading European business school in Fontainebleau, France, and London Business School before dying at the age of 55.

Ghoshal's influence far exceeded his written output. He was an inspiring lecturer, a popular colleague and a gentle man. He first made his mark in a seminal critique of the widely used matrix form of organisational structure in which managers report in two directions – along both functional and geographic lines. Written with his close collaborator,

Christopher Bartlett, the article argued that this dual reporting leads to "conflict and confusion". In large multinationals, "separated by barriers of distance, language, time and culture, managers found it virtually impossible to clarify the confusion and resolve the conflicts".

Bartlett and Ghoshal argued that companies need to alter their organisational psychology (their shared norms and beliefs) and their physiology (the systems that allow information to flow around the organisation) before they start to redesign their anatomy (the reporting lines). Their work set off a search for new metaphors for organisational structures, borrowing in particular from psychology and biology – for example, the corporate DNA and the left brain of the organisation.

Typical of Ghoshal's colourful communication was what he called his "springtime theory". He would tell his audiences about his annual visit to Calcutta to see his parents in July. "Imagine the heat," he would say, "the humidity, the noise, the dirt. It sucks up all your energy, drains your brain, and exhausts your imagination." And then he would take them to the forest of Fontainebleau, near INSEAD, where he was a professor at the time, and point to "the smell of the trees, the crispness in the air, the flowers, the grass underfoot. How one's heart lifts up, how the energy and creativity bubble away." Go through the door of any business, he would say, and you can tell whether it is Calcutta or Fontainebleau. A manager's task is to create a working environment that is like Fontainebleau, not Calcutta.

Shortly before he died, Ghoshal wrote one of his most contentious papers, in which he suggested that much of the blame for corporate corruption in the early 2000s could be laid at the feet of business schools and the way they try to teach management as a science. Such a method has no room for morality. Thus, argued Ghoshal, "business schools have actively freed their students from any sense of moral responsibility". Ghoshal's criticism of business education mirrors that of Henry Mintzberg (see page 275) and Warren Bennis (see page 217).

Despite the enormously high regard in which managers held Ghoshal's seminal work, *Managing Across Borders*, Bartlett (his co-author) said after his death: "Borders never meant much to Sumantra." He was more inspired (and inspiring) as a teacher and conversationalist than as a writer.

Frank and Lillian Gilbreth

BORN: Frank 1868; Lillian 1878
DIED: Frank 1924; Lillian 1972
NATIONALITY: American
ACHIEVEMENT: Lillian Gilbreth was included in the US National
Women's Hall of Fame in 1995

Notable publication
Psychology in the Workplace, 1912–13

Notable quotations
Therbligs.

Because they come cheaper by the dozen.

Background

Frank and Lillian Gilbreth brought together two of the main streams of
management thinking over the past 100 years. On the one hand, they
followed the pioneering work in time and motion studies begun by
Frederick Winslow Taylor (see page 309), and on the other they developed
the study of workplace psychology. Frank, who began his working life as
a bricklayer, closely observed the ways in which different men performed
the task and came to conclusions about the most efficient way. In one
case he increased the rate of laying bricks from 1,000 a day to 2,700 a
day. Lillian wrote a thesis on the psychology of management and her
first notable publication, *Psychology in the Workplace*, was serialised in a
journal of the Society of Industrial Engineers.

The two subdivided workers' hand movements into 17 different units,
which they called "therbligs" (Gilbreth backwards, except for the t and
the h). Doctors to this day owe a debt to them, since it was Frank who
first came up with the idea that surgeons should use a nurse as "a caddy"
to hand them their instruments as and when they were needed. Previously surgeons had searched for and fetched their own instruments while
operating.

The Gilbreths are generally considered as one unit. But Frank married
Lillian when he was 36, after he had done much of his time-and-motion

work and years after he had set up his own engineering consulting business. He died only 20 years later, after the couple had produced 12 children, who limited the amount of time they had to work together.

Lillian lived on for another 48 years after Frank's death, continuing to work and give seminars for much of that time. Famously, she travelled to Europe a few days after her husband's death in 1924 to fulfil a speaking engagement in Prague that he had undertaken. She was a redoubtable woman, forging a career in a discipline – management in the engineering industry – where women were not at the time taken seriously. Often called "the first lady of management", she was also the first female member of the American Society of Mechanical Engineers.

In recent years the Gilbreths' work has largely disappeared from the management canon, with time-and-motion studies mostly associated with Taylor. The couple are best remembered for a book written by two of their 12 children (Ernestine and Frank junior). Called *Cheaper by the Dozen* (first published in 1946), it has been turned into films and TV series that have little to do with the real lives of the Gilbreths, apart from the fact that they had 12 children. And even that was not quite the truth, since one of their children (the second) died of diphtheria when she was only six years old. They never actually had 12 offspring alive at the same time.

The title of the book was taken from the answer Frank is alleged to have given when people asked him how he came to have so many children: "Because they come cheaper by the dozen."

Gary Hamel

BORN: 1954
NATIONALITY: American

Notable publications
With Prahalad, C.K., *Competing for the Future*, Harvard Business School
 Press, 1994
"Strategy as Revolution", *Harvard Business Review*, July–August 1996
With Breen, B., *The Future of Management*, Harvard Business School
 Press, 2007
"First, Let's Fire All the Managers", *Harvard Business Review*, December 2011

Notable quotations
Core competencies are the collective learning in the organisation ... core competence does not diminish with use. Unlike physical assets, which do deteriorate over time, competencies are enhanced as they are applied and shared.

Strategy didn't start with Igor Ansoff, neither did it start with Machiavelli. It probably did not even start with Sun Tzu. Strategy is as old as human conflict.

Management was designed to solve a very specific problem – how to do things with perfect replicability, at ever-increasing scale and steadily increasing efficiency. Now there's a new set of challenges on the horizon. How do you build organisations that are as nimble as change itself?

Background
Gary Hamel started his working life as a hospital administrator before taking a PhD and becoming an academic, sharing his time between London and Chicago. He brought a new focus to the subject of corporate strategy, building his reputation with the idea of core competencies (see page 41), a theory that he first propounded in 1990 in a paper written with C.K. Prahalad (see page 297), an Indian academic. "Core competencies," they wrote, "are the collective learning in the organisation, especially how to co-ordinate diverse production skills and integrate multiple streams of technologies" – in short, they are the things that an organisation does exceptionally well.

This idea dovetailed with the phenomenon of outsourcing (see page 143), which allowed companies to hand over to others the processes and operations (such as IT or book-keeping) which were not "core" to their business. They were thus freed to concentrate on the things that they did best.

Hamel took corporate strategy away from the precision of traditional planning. He saw it in terms of dramatic change, of revolution. Strategic innovation, he said, will be the main source of competitive advantage (see page 37) in the future. Traditional strategic planning, he argued, is not strategic; rather it is a calendar-driven ritual about plans and planning. Great strategies come from challenging the status quo. He quoted Anita Roddick, the founder of Body Shop, who is said to have said: "I watch where the cosmetics industry is going and then walk in the opposite direction."

The brightness of Hamel's star was dimmed somewhat at the end of 2001 by the collapse of Enron, a once high-flying energy company that imploded into bankruptcy, leading to long terms of imprisonment for its leading executives. In his book *Leading the Revolution*, Hamel (along with others) had held Enron up as an exemplar of his style of revolutionary strategic innovation – just before the company disintegrated. He had also lauded a number of large Japanese companies whose business models stalled badly in the last years of the 20th century.

In his most recent book, *The Future of Management*, the feisty Hamel stuck his neck out again. "Management is out of date," he says. "Like the combustion engine, it's a technology that has largely stopped evolving, and that's not good." What then does the future of management hold? Hamel timidly won't say. "My goal in writing this book was not to predict the future of management, but to help you invent it," he wrote. Useful things to bear in mind, he suggested, are the need for companies to have purpose, to seek out ideas from the fringes, and to embrace the democratising power of the internet. *The Economist* commented that none of this "will be news to anyone who has been in business for more than a few minutes".

Michael Hammer

BORN: 1948
DIED: 2008
NATIONALITY: American

Notable publications
"Re-engineering Work: Don't Automate, Obliterate", *Harvard Business Review*, July–August 1990
With Champy, J., *Reengineering the Corporation: A Manifesto for Business Revolution*, HarperBusiness, New York, 1993; revised updated edn, HarperCollins, 2004
"Deep Change: How Operational Innovation Can Transform Your Company", *Harvard Business Review*, April 2004

Notable quotation
When accessible data is combined with easy-to-use analysis and modelling tools, frontline workers – when properly trained – suddenly have sophisticated decision-making capabilities. Decisions can be made more quickly and problems resolved as soon as they crop up.

Background
Michael Hammer was a professor of computer science at MIT in Boston when he came up with the biggest business idea of the 1990s – re-engineering (see Business process re-engineering, page 25) – which he defined as "the fundamental rethinking and radical redesign of business processes to achieve dramatic improvements in critical measures of performance". The terms process improvement, process excellence and process innovation all came from him.

The idea, first propounded in an article in *Harvard Business Review*, was later expanded into a book that Hammer wrote with James Champy, the founder of CSC Index, a consulting firm. The book sold several million copies.

So popular was re-engineering that one survey in the 1990s showed it to have been adopted by almost 80% of *Fortune* 500 companies. It was often blamed for the widespread lay-offs that became part of almost every company's radical redesign at that time.

Hammer, whose writing could be surprisingly vivid, once wrote: "A company that does not focus resolutely on its customers and the processes that produce value for its customers is not long for this world." Process improvements come from "walking in the customer's shoes", finding out what it is that customers really want, and then designing processes to meet that demand.

By 1997 Hammer had taken the view that: "Processes are the key organisational theme for companies in the 21st century. Excellence in processes is what is going to distinguish successful organisations from the also-rans." He added, mindful of the main beneficiaries of most novel business ideas: "Capability at helping companies to achieve process excellence is what's going to distinguish leading consulting companies from those sweeping up after the elephants."

Hammer never managed to repeat his success. He opened his own management-education firm, Hammer and Company, and worked on the idea of "the process enterprise". If you really want to make re-engineering successful, he argued, you need a whole new type of organisation.

In 2004 he published a paper, "The invention and deployment of new ways of doing work", on operational innovation. In this he pointed out that many companies – from Dell to Toyota to Southwest Airlines – have flourished not because of what they do but because of how they do it. They simply "out-operate" their rivals. Hammer went on to say that operational innovation, which "may appear unglamorous or unfamiliar to many executives ... is the only lasting basis for superior performance". A bold claim, indeed, since phenomena such as Apple and Google continue to thrive because of their innovative products and services.

Charles Handy

BORN: 1932
NATIONALITY: Irish

Notable publications
The Empty Raincoat, Hutchinson, 1994
The Gods of Management, Pan, 1985; new edn, Arrow, 1995
The Age of Unreason, Hutchinson Business, 1989; 2nd edn, Arrow, 1995
Myself and Other More Important Matters, Heinemann, 2006

Notable quotation
I told my children when they were leaving education that they would be well advised to look for customers not bosses.

Background
Charles Handy is the son of an Irish Protestant vicar whose broad interests spread from religion and philosophy to the organisation of the workplace. In *The Gods of Management* he identified four different management cultures which he likened to four Greek gods: Apollo, Athena, Dionysus and Zeus. His vivid use of metaphor and his accessible writing style have made his books extremely popular. It was once said of Peter Drucker (see page 235) that he was a man "practising the scholarship of common sense". Charles Handy added "I would like that to be said of me."

Handy began his career as an employee of Royal Dutch Shell, an Anglo-Dutch oil company, and was sent to work on a drilling operation in the jungles of Borneo, where he made mistakes and was given (as he put it) a chance to redeem himself. He later vividly described how little relation his life on the job had to the goal he had been given by corporate headquarters – namely, to maximise the company's return on equity. Handy's subsequent written work has almost always been a search for ways in which companies can go beyond the pure pursuit of profit. How can they be transformed into communities and soar above being mere properties to be bought and sold?

Based for most of his working life in Britain, Handy became the country's leading management spokesperson. He came up with catchy concepts such as "the shamrock organisation" (which, like the eponymous plant, has three leaves: management; specialists; and an increasingly flexible labour force) and "portfolio working", a lifestyle in which the individual holds a number of "jobs, clients and types of work" all at the same time.

Handy's main interest was organisations, and his message was that they are "not machines that can be neatly designed, mapped, measured and controlled". He once used his experience of moving his kitchen seven times within the same house as a lesson to managers who try to fit "a modern organisation into old-fashioned spaces".

He had a key role in shaping British management education in the 1960s and 1970s. After a year in Boston observing MIT's way of teaching business, he returned to the UK, a country that had no management education other than the ersatz activities that then passed for it – an accountancy training or a spell in the British army. On his return he helped set up London Business School, drawing heavily on educational programmes (the MBA in particular) that he had much admired in America.

Later on he seemed to have some regrets about this. While accountants were not trained to be managers, he wrote in *Myself and Other More Important Matters*, "the way they and their kindred professions of law, medicine and architecture had been educating their future professionals did seem to have stood the test of time. They all consistently mixed formal learning with some form of apprenticeship." As *The Economist* once said of Handy, "More common sense is what he stands for, and fewer common rooms."

Geert Hofstede

BORN: 1928
NATIONALITY: Dutch

Notable publications
Culture's Consequences: International Differences in Work-Related Values,
Sage, 1980
Cultures and Organisations: Software of the Mind, Profile Books, London,
1994; 2nd edn, McGraw-Hill, New York, 2005

Notable quotation
*Culture is more often a source of conflict than of synergy. Cultural
differences are a nuisance at best and often a disaster.*

Background
The man who put corporate culture on the map – almost literally – Geert
Hofstede defined culture along five different dimensions. Each of these
he measured for a large number of countries, and then made cross-
country comparisons. In the age of globalisation (see page 93), these have
been used extensively by managers trying to understand the differences
between workforces in different environments.

A Dutch academic who has (unusually) never worked or studied in
America, Hofstede taught at INSEAD, near Paris, in the 1970s and spent
much of the 1990s in Hong Kong. He also taught for long spells at Maas-
tricht University and the University of Tilburg. Early in his career he
worked for IBM, where he carried out the research on which his career
and reputation subsequently rested. What has become known as the
Hofstede Cultural Orientation Model is based on his study between 1967
and 1973 of IBM employees in 40 different countries.

Initially, the model classified culture along four different dimensions:

- Individual versus collective (IDV). This refers to the extent to
  which individuals expect only to look after themselves and their
  immediate families, compared with the extent to which there is a
  tight social framework in which people expect the groups to which
  they belong to look after them. This is sometimes reflected in the

use of words such as "I" and "we", "my" and "our".

- ◪ Power distance index (PDI). This refers to the extent to which a society accepts that power in institutions and organisations is distributed unequally. Countries where PDI is low generally favour decentralised organisations, whereas those with a high level of PDI are more accepting of centralised authority.
- ◪ Uncertainty avoidance index (UAI). This is the extent to which employees feel threatened by ambiguity, and the relative importance that they attach to rules, long-term employment and steady progression up a well-defined career ladder.
- ◪ Masculinity (MAS). This refers to the nature of the dominant values in the organisation. For example, is it predominantly influenced by masculine values such as assertiveness and monetary focus, rather than feminine values such as concern for others and the quality of relationships?

Hofstede subsequently added a fifth dimension after carrying out a study of Chinese managers and workers during his time in Hong Kong. This he called long-term orientation (LTO), which refers to the different time frames used by different people and organisations. Those with a short-term view are more inclined towards consumption and to maintaining face by keeping up with the neighbours. With a long-term attitude, the focus is on preserving status-based relationships and thrift.

Hofstede has subsequently developed his work into a system for scoring individual countries according to their culture. The differences can be dramatic and surprising. Greece, for instance, scores 112 on the UAI dimension while Denmark, a fellow member of the European Union, scores only 23. Less surprisingly perhaps, Sweden scores only five on the MAS of its organisations, while persistently chauvinistic Japan scores 95. On LTO, China excels with a score of 118, while the not-so-far-away Philippines scores a mere 19.

Elliott Jaques

BORN: 1917
DIED: 2003
NATIONALITY: Canadian

Notable publications
The Changing Culture of a Factory, Tavistock Publishing, 1951
Measurement of Responsibility: A Study of Work, Payment and Individual Capacity, Tavistock Publishing, 1956; reprint, Heinemann Educational, 1972
A General Theory of Bureaucracy, Heinemann, 1976; reprint, Gower, 1986
"In Praise of Hierarchy", *Harvard Business Review*, 1990

Notable quotations
Any experienced manager, whatever his or her job, takes the great importance of time for granted. Things have to be done on time, planning is done about time, and organising is done to achieve things in time.

It is never possible to tell from an organisation chart just who is manager of whom; in effect, it is a wise manager (or subordinate) who knows his own subordinate (or manager).

Background
In *The Strategy Paradox*, a book published in 2007 and written by Michael Raynor, a consultant and co-author with Clayton Christensen (see page 227) of *The Innovator's Solution*, the author says: "For my money, the most undeservedly ignored management researcher of the modern era is Elliott Jaques (pronounced 'Jacks'). The Canadian-born psychologist's work on the nature of hierarchy spans half a century and is based on extensive field data on how people behave at work and how they feel about their roles."

Jaques decided that jobs could be defined in terms of their time horizon. For example, a director of marketing might be worried about marketing campaigns for next year, while a salesman on the road is worried about reaching his targets for the week. Jaques also believed that people had a "boss" and a "real boss". The boss was the person to whom they were nominally responsible, while the real boss was the person to whom they turned to get decisions crucial to the continuation of their work.

The sales manager in charge of a salesforce would not have a longer time horizon than the people in his salesforce. So when a salesman wanted a decision on something affecting his ability to deliver to his clients, he would go over the head of the sales manager for that decision. Jaques called this "level skipping", and identified it as a dangerous pathology in any hierarchy.

He then looked at the time horizons of people, their bosses and their real bosses, and he found that people with a time horizon of less than three months treated those with a horizon of 3-12 months as their real bosses, and so on up the scale. He identified seven different time horizons, from three months to 20 years, and argued that organisations, no matter how complex, should have seven levels of hierarchy, each corresponding to a different managerial time horizon. Jaques's theory has come to be known as RO (requisite organisation).

Much of Jaques's work was carried out in the UK. Although a graduate of the University of Toronto and the Johns Hopkins Medical School in Baltimore, he was a founding member of the Tavistock Institute of Human Relations in London, and much of the research on which his theories were based was carried out at Glacier Metal between 1948 and 1965. His first important book, *The Changing Culture of a Factory*, was about his research at Glacier, and he subsequently wrote *The Glacier Project Papers* (1965) with the company's managing director, Wilfred Brown.

Raynor and others have speculated as to why Jaques has not been more widely recognised for his achievement. One suggestion is that neither he nor Brown felt the work of management academics had scientific validity. So they never quoted them, and the management academics returned the compliment. "The net impact has been the isolation of this theory from the main dialogue on management and organisations," speculates one commentator.

Joseph Juran

BORN: 1904
DIED: 2008
NATIONALITY: American

Notable publications
Quality Control Handbook, McGraw-Hill, 1951; *Juran's Quality Handbook*, 5th edn, McGraw-Hill, 1999
Managerial Breakthrough: A New Concept of the Manager's Job, McGraw-Hill, 1964

Notable quotation
My belief is that historians in later decades will look back on the 21st century as the century of quality, much as the 20th century has been the century of productivity, largely following Frederick Taylor's model.

Background

An American who emigrated from Romania when he was eight, three years after his father had first gone to the United States to seek work, Joseph Juran led a remarkable life – not the least of it being that he lived to the age of 103.

As a young man he studied electrical engineering and was a keen chess player. He then went to work for Western Electric in the inspection department at its famous Hawthorne factory, just outside Chicago. It was here, while Juran was on the payroll, that Elton Mayo (see page 271) carried out what has become one of the most famous experiments in industrial psychology.

During the second world war Juran was seconded to work for the government in Washington, streamlining shipment processes for the Lend-Lease Administration. While there he came across the work of Vilfredo Pareto and was the first to name the 19th century Italian professor of political economy's "80/20 rule" – the rule that the top 20% of any country's population accounts for (more or less) 80% of its total income – "Pareto's Principle of Unequal Distribution". Juran extended the principle to quality control, stating, for instance, that most defects in production are the result of a small percentage of the causes of all defects – what he described as "the vital few and the trivial many".

His influences were eclectic. He once said that anthropologist Margaret Mead's book *Cultural Patterns and Technical Change* was highly influential in his ideas on how to "re-engineer" business quality. He recognised that cultural resistance to change was one of the biggest problems in reforming quality.

It was only after the war, however, that Juran moved into the arena for which he is most famous. He left Western Electric to become a freelance consultant on quality control. In 1954 he was invited to Japan to give a series of lectures which were subsequently credited by the Japanese with having been the basis of their quality-focused post-war industrial economy. He thus joined W. Edwards Deming (see page 233) in management mythology as one of the two Americans who, unappreciated in their own fast-food country for their ideas about quality, had gone abroad to find recognition.

Juran always emphasised the difference in approach between himself and Deming. He said that Deming was more focused on the statistical analysis of quality whereas he, Juran, was more concerned about the human input, teaching people how to introduce what he called CWQM (company-wide quality management).

CWQM was divided into three, into what has become known as the Juran Trilogy: quality planning, quality control and quality improvement. The first involves identifying customers and their needs so that these can be satisfied; the second is about developing processes to produce goods that can meet those needs; and the third is about constantly trying to improve those processes.

Rosabeth Moss Kanter

BORN: 1943
NATIONALITY: American

Notable publications
Men and Women of the Corporation, Basic Books, 1977; 1993
The Change Masters, Simon & Schuster, 1983
When Giants Learn to Dance: Mastering the Challenge of Strategy,
    Management, and Careers in the 1990s, Simon & Schuster, 1989;
    Unwin, 1990
"How Great Companies Think Differently", Harvard Business Review,
    November 2011
"Courage in the C-Suite", Harvard Business Review, December 2011

Notable quotations
The powerless live in a different world ... they may turn instead to the ultimate weapon of those who lack productive power, oppressive power.

Confidence isn't optimism or pessimism, and it's not a character attribute. It's the expectation of a positive outcome.

Background
One of the few women in recent years to have achieved genuine guru status, Rosabeth Moss Kanter hit the management headlines in 1977 with her first book, *Men and Women of the Corporation*, which won an award as the best book of the year on social issues. In it she introduced the concept for which she has ever since been best known: empowerment (see page 73).

Kanter carries the name of her first husband, Stuart Kanter, who died in 1969. In 1977 she set up a consultancy, called Goodmeasure, with her second husband, Barry A. Stein.

She is a sociologist by training. Her doctoral thesis was on communes and she was an associate professor of sociology at Brandeis University between 1966 and 1977. She moved to Harvard Business School in 1986 and for many years held the post of professor of business administration. She was the last academic to be editor, from 1989 to 1992, of *Harvard*

Business Review. Since her tenure the post has been in the hands of professional editors and journalists.

Her interests are broad. In 2007, a year before the first American presidential election in which a woman stood a real chance of winning, she wrote *America the Principled: Six Opportunities for Becoming a Can-Do Nation Again*. In it, among other things, she talked about education, a workplace social contract and international relations. (In 1988 she had been an adviser to the Democrat George Dukakis in his unsuccessful presidential campaign.)

Her first big management book, *Men and Women of the Corporation*, was an examination of one particular large corporation (which she calls Indsco) and the effect of power and powerlessness on behaviour and relationships within it. Kanter argued that structural issues – the structure of opportunities, the structure of power and the proportions of people from different groups – explained the behaviour of these groups within Indsco. It was not the behaviour of women, for example, that determined their relative lack of success within corporate life, but the structure of the organisations for which they were working. If there was to be any progress on issues such as the glass ceiling (see page 91), it would come about because organisations changed, not people. Kanter did not reserve her arguments for women alone – they applied equally to other powerless minorities within corporate life.

In *The Change Masters* (1983), she looked at ways in which this change might be brought about by examining six companies that were successful at it (her so-called change masters). Such companies have open communications systems and decentralisation of resources. In *When Giants Learn to Dance* (1989), the last of what is in effect a trilogy, Kanter likened the world of global competition to a "corporate Olympics". The winners in these "games" would be non-hierarchical, co-operative and focused on processes – the way things are done. They would also, she said, have a dose of humility.

Kanter's books embrace some complex ideas and are supported by a wealth of research, all of which has led to her being branded as "the thinking woman's Tom Peters" (see page 293). A large selection of her writing was gathered together in *Rosabeth Moss Kanter on The Frontiers of Change* (Harvard Business School Press, 1997).

Robert Kaplan and David Norton

BORN: 1940 (Kaplan)
NATIONALITY: American

Notable publications
"The Balanced Scorecard: Measures that Drive Performance", *Harvard Business Review*, January–February 1992
The Balanced Scorecard: Translating Strategy into Action, Harvard Business Press, 1996
Kaplan with Cooper, R., "Make Cost Right: Make the Right Decisions", *Harvard Business Review*, September–October 1988

Notable quotation
What you measure is what you get.

Background

Robert Kaplan and David Norton are the two halves of the most inseparable double-act in management. Whereas Tom Peters (see page 293) and Robert Waterman's book *In Search of Excellence* is more famous than anything Kaplan and Norton have written, the two McKinsey consultants split up early in their careers. Frank and Lillian Gilbreth (see page 243), though married for 20 years, did a lot of their most admired work separately. Kaplan and Norton have published very little individually.

Kaplan graduated in electrical engineering from MIT and followed that with a PhD in operations research from Cornell. He taught at Carnegie Mellon University in Pittsburgh before becoming a professor at Harvard Business School. Norton is a consultant, the founder of a firm called Renaissance Solutions. Their central area of interest is measurement, improving the ways we measure corporate performance, and over the past 20 years they have been the main promoters of two big new ideas in the area: activity-based costing (see page 9) and the balanced scorecard (see page 11).

The two have been highly successful at spotting shortcomings in traditional accounting procedures and suggesting improvements. Norton is alleged to have been responsible for the expression "the balanced scorecard", which he came up with after playing a game of golf with a senior IBM executive. The executive said that what he needed to measure the performance of his company was a scorecard like the one he used for a round of golf.

The idea was based on a variation of an old adage: "What gets measured gets done." The two men started with the premise that what you measure is what you get. Measure financial results and you get financial results. Measure things like innovation and customer satisfaction and you will get those too.

The first line of their 1996 book on the balanced scorecard reads: "Imagine entering the cockpit of a modern jet airplane and seeing only a single instrument there." They used the analogy to suggest that it should be equally uncomfortable to go into a corporation and find only a single instrument for guiding it along its future strategic direction – that is, the traditional financial balance sheet.

Business: The Ultimate Resource (A & C Black, 2006) comments that "elaborating, explaining and applying the basic concept [of the balanced scorecard] seems to have become a small industry". Norton has said that 60% of large American companies use some sort of scorecard combining financial and non-financial measures.

The idea that a firm's performance should be measured by both financial and non-financial yardsticks struck a chord with those keen to further the idea of corporate responsibility, both social and environmental. The "triple bottom line" (see page 193) – of people, planet and profit – was built on Kaplan's ideas. In 2007 he wrote a Harvard Business School case study on a South American company (called Amanco). It had innovatively embraced both social and environmental measures within its balanced scorecard, which it called a "sustainability scorecard".

Philip Kotler

BORN: 1931
NATIONALITY: American

Notable publications
Marketing Management: Analysis, Planning, Implementation and Control, Prentice Hall, 1967; 14th edn, 2011
With Lee, N., *Social Marketing: Influencing Behaviour for Good*, 4th edn, Sage Publications, 2011

Notable quotations
Marketing is not the art of finding clever ways to dispose of what you make. Marketing is the art of creating genuine customer value. It is the art of helping your customers become better off.

I operate on the assumption that "progress" is possible, even in the face of much contradictory evidence. I prefer to believe that human beings can improve their condition by applying collective intelligence to solving shared problems.

Good companies will meet needs. Great companies will create markets.

Background
Kellogg School of Management, Northwestern University's business school, located a few miles north of Chicago on the shores of Lake Michigan, frequently ranks among America's top ten business schools. But in one discipline it stands head and shoulders above the rest. Its marketing department is regarded by industry as second to none. Philip Kotler, who has been a professor of marketing at the school for over 40 years, is largely responsible for that.

His book *Marketing Management*, first published in 1967, is a classic textbook which has already run to more than a dozen editions. It applied rigorous analysis and mathematical methodology to the practice of marketing, something that had never been done before. Its influence over the past four decades has been monumental – even as the book itself has become ever more monumental (the 12th edition has over 800 pages). Gary Hamel (see page 245) said of it: "There are few MBA graduates alive who have not ploughed through Kotler's encyclopaedic textbook and have not benefited enormously from doing so ... I can think of few other books ... whose insights would be of more practical benefit to the average company."

Together with Theodore (Ted) Levitt (see opposite), Kotler was responsible for lifting marketing out of the disrepute in which it had once been held, changing it from being the slicker part of sales to being a recognised strategic function in its own right. Eventually Kotler came to see marketing as being about the exchange of values between two parties and, as such, a social activity, not just a business one. He coined the term "social marketing", defined by Wikipedia as "the systematic application of marketing (along with other concepts and techniques) to achieve specific behavioural goals for a social good".

Kotler has always seen marketing as something that evolves over time, and his book has also moved with the times. It was at first focused on transactional marketing, but it now pays much more attention to relationship marketing, the idea of customer loyalty as the means to build a whole series of sales out of a single transaction.

Kotler has also stretched marketing outside the business arena, writing articles, for instance, about how to apply marketing to health-care organisations, to individuals (celebrities) and even to countries.

By training, Kotler was an economist, studying first at the University of Chicago under Milton Friedman, a free-market evangelist, before moving on to do a PhD at MIT under Paul Samuelson, a Nobel Prize-winning Keynesian economist. The two economists' opposing philosophies so frustrated him that he switched for a while to mathematics, and at that time had his first introduction to people who were teaching marketing.

Theodore Levitt

BORN: 1925
DIED: 2006
NATIONALITY: American

Notable publications
"Marketing Myopia", *Harvard Business Review*, July–August 1960
The Marketing Imagination, Free Press, 1983
"The Globalisation of Markets", *Harvard Business Review*, May–June 1983

Notable quotations
Creativity is thinking up new things. Innovation is doing new things.

What I've achieved, I think, is to make myself effective in some way, kept myself intellectually curious, alive and productive, and made myself interesting to myself.

Background

Born in Germany where his father was a cobbler, Theodore (usually known as Ted) Levitt emigrated to the United States with his parents at the age of ten. Despite his origins, he was drafted into the US army and served in Europe in the second world war. After the war he gained a PhD in economics from Ohio State University. He was then an academic at Harvard Business School for some 30 years and started teaching marketing there at a time when, legend has it, he had never previously read a book on the subject.

Levitt is famous for two things in particular: an article published in 1960 ("Marketing Myopia"); and his resignation almost 30 years later from the editorship of the publication in which that article first appeared – *Harvard Business Review*.

The article, written only a year after he had joined the Harvard Business School faculty, can be seen as a turning point in the acceptance and respectability of marketing. It argued that companies had paid too much attention to producing products and too little to satisfying customers. He pointed out, for instance, that the train had lost out to the airplane and the motor car because it thought it was in the business of running trains rather than that of providing customers with transport.

The message may sound old hat now, but it was revolutionary at the time and almost 1m copies of the article have been sold in the years since it first appeared. After it, Philip Kotler (see page 261) could follow with his more intellectually rigorous analysis of marketing and his framework for taking it further. Before it, marketing was about little more than the four Ps: product, price, place and promotion.

Levitt's resignation from *Harvard Business Review*, which he once described as "a magazine written by people who can't write for people who won't read", was over an article about women in management. In his four years in the job he had controversially transformed the publication from a dry academic journal to a readable management magazine that featured cartoons. "If people don't read what you write," he once said, "then what you write is a museum piece." Some argued that if you raised the price of the magazine in the way that he had done during his editorship then you also risked becoming a museum piece. He was succeeded in the post by the almost equally controversial Rosabeth Moss Kanter (see page 257).

Levitt is sometimes credited with coining the term "globalisation" (see page 93) in a 1983 article, "The Globalisation of Markets". Although the term had undoubtedly been in use before – the *New York Times* said it was used in other senses "at least as early as 1944" – it was Levitt who first popularised (marketed?) it as referring to the spread of corporations around the globe.

"Gone are accustomed differences in national or regional preferences," he said at the time (a view echoed by Thomas Friedman in *The World is Flat* a quarter of a century later), allowing companies like Coca-Cola and McDonald's to sell identical products around the world. It was never a view that received universal acceptance, however. Kotler disagreed with it, as have gurus from a later generation, arguing that regional and national differences remain as crucial as ever, and that companies ignore them at their peril.

James March

BORN: 1928
NATIONALITY: American

Notable publications
With Simon, H., *Organizations*, John Wiley & Sons, 1958; 2nd edn,
  Blackwell, 1993
With Cyert, R., *A Behavioral Theory of the Firm*, Prentice Hall 1963; 2nd
  edn, Blackwell Business, 1992
The Pursuit of Organizational Intelligence, Blackwell, 1999
Explorations in Organizations, Stanford University Press, 2008

Notable quotation
*The protections for the imagination are indiscriminate. They shield bad
ideas as well as good ones – and there are many more of the former than
the latter. Most fantasies lead us astray, and most of the consequences of
imagination for individuals and individual organisations are disastrous.*

Background
James March is the gurus' guru, a man who once came second in just
such a poll to the incomparable Peter Drucker (*Harvard Business Review*,
December 2003; see page 235). An unostentatious academic who spent
most of his life on the faculty of Stanford University, described by *Harvard
Business Review* as "a polymath whose career has encompassed numerous
disciplines ... he has taught courses on subjects as diverse as organisational psychology, behavioural economics, leadership, rules for killing
people, friendship, decision-making, models in social science, revolutions,
computer simulation and statistics". A polymath indeed.

He is best known for his work on the behavioural theory of organisations, working at one time with Herbert Simon (see page 305), the definer of
the idea of satisficing, with whom he wrote a classic book, *Organizations*.
In this, and in the book he wrote with Richard Cyert, he developed a theory
about the "boundedness" of managers' behaviour. Just as consumers go
for the satisfactory rather than the "best" decision when purchasing, so
managers go for the less-than-rational decision when on the job, because
they are necessarily restricted by human and organisational limitations.

In a more recent paper, which he entitled "The Hot Stove Effect", after Mark Twain's point that cats who learn to avoid hot stoves learn to avoid cold ones too, March warned that the way in which we learn to reproduce success results, inevitably, in a bias against both risky and novel alternatives.

John Padgett, a professor at the University of Chicago, wrote in the journal *Contemporary Sociology* that "Jim March is to organisation theory what Miles Davis is to jazz ... March's influence, unlike that of any of his peers, is not limited to any possible subset of the social science disciplines; it is pervasive".

March has also written seven books of poetry and made a film (called *Don Quixote's Lessons for Leadership*). His background notes to the film include a short prose poem:

> *Quixote reminds us*
> *That if we trust only when*
> *Trust is warranted, love only*
> *When love is returned, learn*
> *Only when learning is valuable,*
> *We abandon an essential feature of our humanness.*

His love of language has led him to create some colourful metaphors – the garbage-can theory of organisational choice, for instance, which defines an organisation as "a collection of choices looking for problems; issues and feelings looking for decision situations in which they might be aired; solutions looking for issues to which they might be the answer; and decision-makers looking for work". Problems and solutions flow in and out of the garbage can. Which problems get attached to which solutions is largely a matter of chance.

Abraham Maslow

BORN: 1908
DIED: 1970
NATIONALITY: American

Notable publications
"A Theory of Human Motivation", *Psychological Review*, Vol. 50, 1943
Motivation and Personality, Harper New York 1954; 3rd edn revised
    Frager, R. *et al.*, Harper & Row, 1987
Hoffman, E., *The Right to be Human: a Biography of Abraham Maslow*,
    McGraw-Hill, 1999
Kaplan, A. (ed.), *Maslow on Management*, John Wiley & Sons, 1998

Notable quotations
What conditions of work, what kinds of work, what kinds of management, and what kinds of reward or pay will help human stature to grow healthy, to its fuller and fullest stature? Classic economic theory, based as it is on an inadequate theory of human motivation, could be revolutionised by accepting the results of higher human needs, including the impulse to self-actualisation and the love for the highest values.

One's only rival is one's own potentialities. One's only failure is failing to live up to one's own possibilities. In this sense every man can be a king and must therefore be treated like a king.

A musician must make music, an artist must paint, a poet must write, if he is to be ultimately happy. What a man can be, he must be. This need we may call self-actualisation.

        [Self-actualisation stood at the pinnacle of Maslow's "hierarchy of needs".]

Background
Abraham Maslow was born in New York, the eldest of seven children of Russian immigrant parents. As a young man, he displeased them greatly by choosing to study psychology (at the University of Wisconsin) rather than law in New York, and by choosing to marry his cousin Bertha Goodman.

    Maslow is undoubtedly the most influential anthropologist ever to have worked in industry. From his anthropological research among the Blackfoot Indians of Alberta, Canada, he claimed to have found "almost the same range of personalities as I find in our society". He then worked in industry before becoming a professor of psychology at Brandeis University in Massachusetts. In the 1950s he became a leader of the humanistic school of psychology, a "third force" that he hoped would break through the divide between Freudian psychology and behaviourism. His thinking was original in that it was based on observations of normal behaviour, rather than on aberrations and mental sickness.

He is best known as the creator of the hierarchy of needs (see page 101), a framework for thinking about human motivation. His intention was not that this should be applied particularly to the workplace, but managers soon saw the relevance of Maslow's framework to compensation packages.

Maslow was described by Peter Drucker (see page 235) as "the father of humanist psychology". But Drucker took issue with Maslow's hierarchy, complaining that he had not seen that "a want changes in the act of being satisfied". Hence "as a want approaches satiety its capacity to reward, and with it its power as an incentive, diminishes fast". And so (as we now know well) top executives can never be paid enough for them to be satisfied.

Maslow considered authoritarianism to be an aberration. The authoritarian characteristic, he said, "is the most important single disease afflicting man today – far more important than medical illnesses ... the most widespread of all diseases ... pandemic ... even in the United States, even in this classroom". People who achieve self-actualisation, he maintained, are democratic in outlook, not authoritarian.

Self-actualisation, at the top of his pyramid of needs, is the state that has most fascinated followers of Maslow. What is it? Who has achieved it? Maslow helped a bit by giving a list of people he felt had reached self-actualisation: Abraham Lincoln, Thomas Jefferson, Albert Einstein, Eleanor Roosevelt, William James, Albert Schweitzer, Benedict Spinoza and Aldous Huxley, as well as 12 unnamed people alive at the time Maslow did his research.

He then helped further by describing what it was that motivated people at this level. These people, he claimed, sought after truth, rather than dishonesty; uniqueness, not bland uniformity; completion, rather than incompleteness; simplicity, not unnecessary complexity; playfulness, not grim, humourless, drudgery; and self-sufficiency, not dependency.

Maslow died in semi-retirement in California where he had moved because of ill-health.

Konosuke Matsushita

BORN: 1894
DIED: 1989
NATIONALITY: Japanese

Notable quotations

No matter how deep a study you make, what you really have to rely on is your own intuition and, when it comes down to it, you really don't know what's going to happen until you do it.

Every person has a path to follow. It widens, narrows, climbs and descends. There are times of desperate wanderings. But with courageous perseverance and personal conviction, the right road will be found. This is what brings real joy.

Background

In the West, Matsushita was little more than a well-known Japanese conglomerate until John Kotter, a management academic and recognised authority on leadership, wrote a book called *Matsushita Leadership* (Simon & Schuster, 1997), which won the *Financial Times* global business book of the year award and handed the little-known (and by then dead) founder of the eponymous company, Konosuke Matsushita, the mantle of global leadership greatness.

The opening paragraph of Kotter's book sets the scene for what Matsushita has come to represent – the corporate leader as anti-hero:

> *By many standards, he didn't look like a great leader. Early pictures of Konosuke Matsushita show an unsmiling young man whose ears stick out like airplane wings. He never grew taller than five feet five inches nor weighed more than 135 pounds. Unlike his rival Akio Morita at Sony, he was neither charismatically handsome nor internationally recognised. Unlike most well-known western politicians, he didn't excel at public speaking, and in later years his voice grew increasingly frail. He rarely displayed speed-of-light intellectual skills or warmed an audience with hilarious anecdotes. Nevertheless, he did what*

all great leaders do – motivate large groups of individuals to improve the human condition.

He had none of the attributes of contemporaneous leaders in the West – of macho chauvinists like Jack Welch at General Electric, or of colourful characters like Sir John Harvey-Jones of Britain's ICI. But still he could inspire large groups of individuals and he was known in Japan as the "god of management". Kotter's book set out to explore how he did it, through early hardship and a never-ending thirst for learning.

Matsushita was the son of a landowner who lost all his money, forcing Konosuke to go out to work in Osaka well before he was 16. He started as an electrician at Osaka Electrical Light Company, but then he invented a new sort of light socket and, at the age of 23, set up a company with his brother-in-law, Toshio Iue, to manufacture it. At first he produced his electrical goods under the brand name National, but later he introduced the name Panasonic, for which the company is best-known today. He ruled his companies with a considerable degree of paternalism and offered his workers employment for life.

In his later years he took to explaining his social philosophy and wrote a number of books. One of them, *Developing a Road to Peace and Happiness through Prosperity*, sold several million copies. Matsushita died at the age of 94, recognised before his death as one of the richest men in the world.

Elton Mayo

BORN: 1880
DIED: 1949
NATIONALITY: Australian

Notable publications

The Human Problems of an Industrial Civilization, Macmillan, London, 1933; 2nd edn, Harvard University Press, 1946

The Social Problems of an Industrial Civilization, Routledge and Kegan Paul, 1949; later edn with appendix, 1975

Notable quotation

Human collaboration in work ... has always depended for its perpetuation upon the evolution of a non-logical social code which regulates the relations between persons and their attitudes to one another. Insistence upon a merely economic logic of production interferes with the development of such a code, and consequently gives rise in the group to a sense of human defeat.

Background

One of the few Australians to have appeared on anybody's list of famous management gurus, Elton Mayo was born in Adelaide on Boxing Day 1880 and studied psychology at the city's university. He followed an academic career and became professor of philosophy at the then new University of Queensland. After the first world war he was involved in research into shell shock, which he later likened to the condition of certain industrial workers.

At the age of 43 he won a scholarship to do research at the University of Pennsylvania's Wharton School. Three years later, in 1926, he moved to Harvard Business School to become a professor of industrial research. Between 1929 and 1937 Mayo's wife lived in the UK, where their two daughters were at school, while Mayo himself stayed at Harvard. The family got together almost only during the summer holidays. For the rest of the year Mayo corresponded with his wife almost daily, creating a remarkable series of letters that exists to this day.

While at Pennsylvania he became involved in the research for which he subsequently became world famous. One department of a spinning mill in Philadelphia had a labour turnover rate of 250% – that is, nobody stayed in a job for more than five months – while the average for other parts of the company was 6%. After introducing rest breaks and other improvements in working conditions, Mayo and his colleagues found that within a year the labour turnover rate fell to the average elsewhere in the company. Mayo concluded that social factors were a more powerful motivator in the workplace than financial rewards.

After this he was invited to take part in a series of experiments being carried out at Western Electric's Hawthorne factory outside Chicago which produced telephone equipment. Here the working conditions had been altered, as at the spinning mill in Philadelphia. But there was one important difference. When, for instance, the level of lighting in the workplace was increased, productivity rose, as was expected. But then when the lighting was dimmed, productivity again increased. And that had not been expected.

Mayo concluded that the key factor was the workers' feeling that they were being involved in the changes to their working conditions. They were being asked what they thought about them, both before and after they happened. Mayo believed that conflict between managers and workers was inevitable as long as workers were ruled by "the logic of sentiment" and managers by the "logic of cost and efficiency". Only when each party appreciated the position of the other (through discussion and compromise) could conflict be avoided.

This sounds much like common sense today, but following Frederick Winslow Taylor (see page 309) and his time-and-motion studies, it was almost revolutionary. Indeed, it has defined the major schism in management thinking ever since – between the humanistic school (represented by such people as Mayo and Douglas McGregor – see opposite) and the more "scientific" school (of people such as Taylor and Michael Hammer – see page 247).

Despite his close association with the Hawthorne experiments, it was not Mayo himself who conducted them but two of his assistants, Fritz Roethlisberger and William Dickson. Roethlisberger went on to say that although neither the data nor the results were Mayo's, the interpretations and conclusions were. Without those interpretations, the data could still be gathering dust in some archive to this day.

Mayo spent the last two years of his life working in the UK, which he had visited as a student. He died in Guildford, Surrey. A brother, Sir Herbert Mayo, became president of the Law Council of Australia.

Douglas McGregor

BORN: 1906
DIED: 1964
NATIONALITY: American

Notable publication
The Human Side of Enterprise, McGraw-Hill, 1960; annotated edn,
    McGraw-Hill, 2006

Notable quotations
*Behind every managerial decision or action are assumptions about human
nature and human behaviour.*

*Man is a wanting animal. As soon as one of his needs is satisfied another
appears in its place.*

Background

Douglas McGregor died at the comparatively young age of 58 in 1964. He
had a fairly straightforward academic career, lecturing at Harvard University and at MIT, where he set up the industrial-relations department and
became one of the first Sloan professors. He became president of Antioch
College in 1948 but returned to MIT after six years and remained there
until his death.

He had an informal teaching style, which many of his students
remembered with affection, often sitting with his feet up on the lecture
desk. When not sitting, he was invariably jangling keys and coins in his
pockets.

McGregor did not publish much; but what he did publish had a great
impact. In 1993 he was listed as the most popular management writer of
all time, alongside Henri Fayol (see page 237). Like many of the gurus who
appear in these pages, he was not necessarily the first to come across the
idea associated with him. But he was the first to "name" it. Because of his
facility with metaphor and his easy writing style, the idea subsequently
became his.

A social psychologist by training, McGregor was strongly affected by
work he did as a young man at his grandfather's institute for transient

labourers in Detroit. Close to Abraham Maslow (see page 267), and greatly influenced by him, McGregor became a significant counter to the thinking and influence of scientific management (see page 159). His central idea is that there are two fundamentally different styles of management. One of them he called Theory X and the other Theory Y (see page 187). Theory X is authoritarian, assuming that individuals only ever work reluctantly. Theory Y is liberating and assumes that people will do almost anything if they are committed to the overall goals of their organisation.

Although McGregor's book on the theory was not published until 1960, he first outlined it in a speech at MIT's Sloan School of Management in April 1957. In *Frontiers of Excellence* (Nicholas Brealey, 1994) Robert Waterman revealed that Theory Y had been a secret weapon in Procter & Gamble's competitive armoury for many years. A senior P&G executive had invited McGregor in the mid-1950s to set up a detergent plant in Augusta, Georgia, along the lines of Theory Y. The executive, back from the Korean war, was convinced that military-style command-and-control management did not work in corporate life.

The Augusta plant was run in a non-hierarchical way with self-motivating teams along the lines of Theory Y, and by the mid-1960s it was 30% more productive than any other P&G plant. The principle was subsequently applied to other P&G plants, but the company kept the story secret for almost 40 years, regarding it as a competitive advantage.

Many leading management figures of recent years, including Rosabeth Moss Kanter (see page 257), Warren Bennis (see page 217 – who was a student of McGregor's at MIT) and Tom Peters (see page 293), have acknowledged that much of modern management thinking goes back to McGregor. Bennis says, "Just as every economist, knowingly or not, pays his dues to Keynes, we are all, one way or another, disciples of McGregor."

Some, however, have criticised his ideas as being tough on the weaker members of society, those who need guidance and who are not necessarily self-starters. There are, moreover, conspicuous examples of companies that have followed Theory Y precepts and yet foundered: DEC (Digital Equipment Corporation), steered by its charismatic founder, Ken Olsen, for one.

Shortly before he died, McGregor was developing an outline for something he called Theory Z, an answer to many of the criticisms of Theories X and Y. But his thoughts were never widely published.

Henry Mintzberg

BORN: 1939
NATIONALITY: Canadian

Notable publications
"The Manager's Job: Folklore and Fact", *Harvard Business Review*, 1975
The Structuring of Organisations: A Synthesis of the Research, Prentice
    Hall, 1979
Mintzberg on Management, Free Press, 1989
Managers not MBAs, Berrett-Koehler, 2004
Strategy Safari, Financial Times/Prentice Hall, 2008
Managing, Berrett-Koehler, 2009

Notable quotations
*The pressures of his job drive the manager to be superficial in his actions –
to overload himself with work, encourage interruption, respond quickly to
every stimulus, seek the tangible and avoid the abstract, make decisions in
small increments, and do everything abruptly.*

*Cognitive learning no more makes a manager than it does a swimmer. The
latter will drown the first time he jumps into the water if his coach never
takes him out of the lecture hall, gets him wet and gives him feedback on his
performance.*

Background
Henry Mintzberg is a consistently contrary Canadian academic who
sometimes seems to be undermining the very industry that he works in.
A professor at McGill University in Montreal for 40 years, he has been
controversial at least since a 1975 *Harvard Business Review* article in which
he examined what a number of managers in different industries actually
did, day in, day out, and found that they were not the robotic paragons of
efficiency that they were usually made out to be.

On the contrary, he found the average manager "jumping from topic
to topic". "He thrives on interruptions and more often than not disposes
of items in ten minutes or less. Though he may have 50 projects going,
all are delegated." In a study of British managers at the time, he found

that they worked without interruption for more than half an hour "about once every two days". He also found that senior managers spent more than three-quarters of their time in oral communication. "In other words," he concluded, "the job of managing is fundamentally one of processing information, notably by talking and especially by listening." To be a good manager you have to be a good listener.

After studying individual managers, Mintzberg demonstrated the breadth of his interest by turning his attention to individual organisations, and came up with what was subsequently an influential division of organisational structures into five:

- **The simple structure.** A young company before its entrepreneurial founder has had to let go of some of the strings. Such organisations are often autocratic and, as Mintzberg put it, vulnerable to a single heart attack.
- **The machine bureaucracy.** A company with many layers of management and a mass of formal procedures.
- **The professional bureaucracy.** An organisation that is cemented together by some sort of professional expertise, such as a hospital or a consultancy. This is usually the most democratic type of organisation, partly because it is often set up as a partnership.
- **The divisionalised form.** A structure where there is little central authority, but whatever there is is clearly defined. It is the form most frequently found among modern multinationals.
- **The adhocracy.** The type of organisation frequently found in the computer world, full of flexible teams working on specific projects. It is also the structure found in Hollywood and, said Mintzberg, it is the structure of the future.

In *Managers not MBAs*, Mintzberg moved on to another recurring theme of his – that the MBA, the bread-and-butter course of many business schools and the *sine qua non* of fast-track management careers, "prepares people to manage nothing". Synthesis, not analysis, he said, "is the very essence of management", and the MBA course teaches only analysis.

He pointed out that Ford's Robert McNamara and Enron's Jeffrey Skilling were both near the top of their class at Harvard Business School. But though they were brilliant analysts and star MBA students, they made lousy leaders. MBA graduates, says Mintzberg, are "glib and quick-witted ... not committed to particular industries but to management as a means of personal advancement". They are definitely not good listeners.

Akio Morita

BORN: 1921
DIED: 1999
NATIONALITY: Japanese

Notable publication
Made in Japan, Collins, 1987

Notable quotations
Think globally, act locally.

The public does not know what is possible. We do.

Background

More than any other individual, Akio Morita personified the integration of Japanese industry into the global community from the 1960s to the end of the century. Founder and creator of Sony, he moved his family to the United States in 1963 in order to better understand the American consumer and make Sony a truly global brand – a brave move for a man from a then still insular society. He, more than anyone, put Japanese industry on the map.

As a young man Morita had been expected to go into the family's 300-year-old *sake* business. But after service in the Japanese navy in the second world war he set up a small electronics company, Tokyo Telecommunications Engineering, along with a friend from the navy, Masaru Ibuka. Ibuka was to be the engineering genius behind the brand which Morita created.

In the 1950s the company produced a small transistor radio, which was its breakthrough product. The transistor had been invented in America, but Morita had bought a licence from Bell Laboratories to produce it in Japan. By the end of the decade the company was exporting its production to America and Europe.

In 1958 the company changed its name. Morita and Ibuka are said to have trawled dictionaries for weeks before coming up with the word Sonus, the Latin for sound, which they modified to Sony because, it is said, "sony boys" is Japanese for whizz kids. Three years later it became the first Japanese company to be listed on the New York Stock Exchange.

The transistor radio was followed by transistor televisions and videotape recorders. But music was the company's first focus, and Morita, taken by the fact that young people liked listening to music wherever they went, persuaded Sony (with virtually no supporting market research and against the wishes of many colleagues) to come out in 1980 with what became known as the Sony Walkman.

It was a phenomenal worldwide success and turned Sony into a truly household name everywhere. In 1998 it was declared the number one consumer brand in America, ahead of Coca-Cola and Marlboro cigarettes, the more usual chart toppers. Morita would have seen that as the natural outcome of his famous view of globalisation (see page 93) – "think globally, act locally". In America Sony was American. Only in Japan was it Japanese.

Morita continued to work and play ferociously (he loved water-skiing, tennis and scuba diving), and was due to become chairman of the *keidanran*, Japan's powerful but deeply conservative association of big industrialists. It would have been a remarkable appointment for a man who had dragged himself and his corporation into the rapidly globalising world, but on the day his appointment was due to be announced he had a stroke (at the age of 72, in the early morning, while on the tennis court). From then until his death he remained in a wheelchair.

Ikujiro Nonaka

BORN: 1935
NATIONALITY: Japanese

Notable publications

"The Knowledge-Creating Company", *Harvard Business Review*,
  November–December 1991
With Takeuchi, H., *The Knowledge-Creating Company: How Japanese
  Companies Create the Dynamics of Innovation*, Oxford University
  Press, 1995

Notable quotations

*Knowledge is active, based upon your own subjective beliefs. Information
is transient; but knowledge is eternal. Knowledge is about aspiring to truth,
goodness and beauty.*

*In the US, middle managers are denigrated as cancer. We see middle
managers playing a key role in facilitating the process of organisational
knowledge creation. They serve as the strategic "knot" that binds top
management with front-line managers.*

Background

Akio Morita (see page 277), Kenichi Ohmae (see page 281) and Ikujiro
Nonaka constituted a bridge that connected Japanese industry and
management with that of the rest of the world. Morita was the busi-
nessman, the founder and creator of Sony; Ohmae was the consultant,
an ex-McKinsey man who wrote books that explained Japanese business
practices to the rest of the world; and Nonaka was the behind-the-scenes
professor, cross-fertilising ideas from one culture to another.

  Nonaka's education and his teaching straddled the Pacific. He spent
five and a half years gaining a PhD and an MBA from the University
of California at Berkeley. Then in 1997 he was appointed Xerox distinguished professor of knowledge at Haas School of Business at Berkeley,
before returning across the Pacific in 2000 when he was appointed
a professor at the graduate school of international strategy at Japan's
Hitotsubashi University. There he was one of the main drivers behind

the development of business studies on the campus.

His particular field of interest was the process of knowledge creation within corporations – not a typical field of management study for Japan, which has been more innovative in areas such as operations and strategy. With Hirotaka Takeuchi, a colleague at Hitotsubashi University, whom he first met when they were both students at Berkeley, he developed during the 1990s the idea that one of the main ways in which companies create wealth is by creating knowledge, and that this is (and will continue to be for some time) a main source of competitive advantage (see page 37).

Much of their work is built on an examination of the different concepts of knowledge in the East and the West. In their book *The Knowledge-Creating Company*, the two academics differentiated between what they called implicit and explicit knowledge: the former is the Eastern type; the latter is familiar to the West. Implicit knowledge is intuitive, ambiguous and non-linear; explicit knowledge is the exact opposite, laid down in manuals, analysed and stored in databases.

They outlined a four-stage process by which an organisation develops knowledge. They gave it an acronym, SECI, which stands for socialisation, externalisation, combination/creation and internalisation. These are the means by which knowledge is "amplified throughout the organisation, creating a spiral model of knowledge creation".

Nonaka also coined the term "Ba" to describe a meeting place of minds in an organisation. Ba can be physical – an office or a coffee shop – or it can be mental – shared experiences or the organisational culture. The word has come to be used quite widely. In his book *The Wealth of Knowledge*, Thomas Stewart, the then editor of *Harvard Business Review*, described Ba as "a mental space rather than a physical one; it is shared context, which allows people to work together knowing that they are ... singing from the same song sheet".

Kenichi Ohmae

BORN: 1943
NATIONALITY: Japanese

Notable publications
The Mind of the Strategist, McGraw-Hill, 1982
Triad Power: The Coming Shape of Global Competition, Free Press, 1985
The Borderless World: Power and Strategy in the Interlinked Economy,
    Collins, 1990; Fontana, 1992

Notable quotations
The word "overseas" has no place in Honda's vocabulary, because it sees itself as equidistant from all its key customers.

In the long run, the corporation that is genuinely interested in its customers is the one that will be interesting to investors.

Background

Kenichi Ohmae is the only internationally renowned Japanese guru known for his thinking about strategy rather than about operations. Indeed, he is often referred to as "Mr Strategy". Like Akio Morita (see page 277) and Ikujiro Nonaka (see page 279), Ohmae translated Japanese business culture and strategy into English. His books are full of Japanese examples, and they helped familiarise Western audiences with Japan's management breakthroughs – for instance, the introduction of the just-in-time (JIT – see page 107) system at Toyota. At the same time, Ohmae took American and European ideas and interpreted them for a Japanese audience.

First trained as a nuclear scientist at the Tokyo Institute of Technology and at MIT in Boston, Ohmae became head of McKinsey & Company's Tokyo office in the early 1970s. From there he was an early observer and commentator on the phenomenon of globalisation (see page 93).

In his later books, *Triad Power* and *The Borderless World*, he expounded the view that companies which did not have a full presence in the world's three main trading blocs (Europe, North America and the Pacific Rim) were dangerously vulnerable to competition from those that did. In *The*

Mind of the Strategist, he set out to show how exceptional Japanese strategists (such as Konosuke Matsushita – see page 269 – and Soichiro Honda, often men who had had no formal business education) used vision and intuition to turn their ideas into action. For many in the West, who believed Japanese industry was built on rational analysis and the subjugation of individual creativity, it was an eye-opener.

Ohmae was also influential in spreading the idea that a major difference between Japanese corporations and their Western counterparts was the time frame within which they worked. Japanese firms look to the longer term, whereas Western firms, driven by the demands of their stockmarkets, are more focused on short-term profits. He argued that this difference led Western companies to pay too little attention to their customers.

Ohmae was a man of many parts in a country whose people are known for specialisms rather than broad interests. An accomplished clarinettist and a motor-cycle enthusiast, he said that he was more interested in "society, social systems and large corporate activities on a global scale" than in the strategic plans of companies that think global but act local. In 1995, at the same time as he left McKinsey after more than 20 years, he wrote a book called *The End of the Nation State*. That same year he stood for election as governor of Tokyo, equivalent to being mayor of London or New York. He failed to win the election, however, and in 1997 he joined the school of public and social research at UCLA in California.

Taiichi Ohno

BORN: 1912
DIED: 1990
NATIONALITY: Japanese

Notable publications

Workplace Management, Productivity Press, 1982

With Mito, S., *Just in Time for Today and Tomorrow*, Productivity Press,
1988

Background

Taiichi Ohno is not so much a guru, more a symbol of Japan's manufacturing resurgence after the second world war. Born in Dalian, in eastern
China, he joined Toyota Automatic Loom Works between the wars. This
was the first business of the Toyoda family until it was sold to a British
company, Platt Brothers, and the family decided to invest the money that
it gained from the sale in manufacturing motor cars.

Ohno switched to work as a production engineer for Toyota, a carmaker,
towards the end of the second world war, at a time when its productivity
was way below that of America's mighty Detroit-based industry. Toyota's
boss decreed that it "must catch up with America within three years".
Or else.

Ohno decided there was no reason other than inefficiency and waste-
fulness why Toyota's productivity should be any lower than that of
Detroit. Hence he set out to eradicate inefficiency and eliminate waste
in the part of the production process that he was responsible for. This
became the core of the so-called Toyota Production System (TPS) that
he and others subsequently developed between the mid-1940s and the
mid-1970s. Several elements of this system have become familiar in the
West: for example, *muda* (the elimination of waste), *jidoka* (the injection
of quality) and *kanban* (the tags used as part of a system of just-in-time
stock control).

But it was not a smooth path. Ohno met regular resistance when he
first set out to persuade the company to radically change its manufacturing processes. A big part of his story is about the power of Japanese
persistence, of how he kept asking repeatedly why the company needed

to (expensively) stockpile vast quantities of components for its production line – until eventually was born the just-in-time (JIT) method of stock control (see page 107).

Ohno often described the TPS as being rather like a supermarket, which he had first seen (and been impressed by) on his trips to America to look at car-production systems. In the TPS, each production process sets out its wares for the next process to choose from, just as a supermarket does. Thus production is "pulled" by the demand down the line rather than, as in previous assembly-line systems, being "pushed" by the production rate higher up the line.

The success of the TPS was helped to some extent by the fact that Toyota's main factory in Japan is situated in Toyoda City, near Nagoya, where there is a classic "cluster" of car-industry suppliers and manufacturers. With its main suppliers never more than a few miles away, it was easy for Toyota to choose parts on demand and ensure that they arrived at its doors precisely as and when it needed them. With more far-flung manufacturing networks, it is obviously harder to apply JIT.

Ohno's fame was spread to some extent by the telling of his story in books and articles translated into English. For example, in *The Mind of the Strategist*, an influential and early insight into Japanese strategic thinking written by Kenichi Ohmae (see page 281), Ohno is cited as a great example of his country's perseverance. "If instead of accepting the first answer, one ... persists [like Ohno] in asking 'Why?' four or five times in succession," wrote Ohmae, "one will certainly get to the guts of the issue, where fundamental bottlenecks and problems lie."

Robert Owen

BORN: 1771
DIED: 1858
NATIONALITY: British

Notable publication
A New View of Society, R. Watts, 1817; Kessinger Publishing, 2004

Notable quotation
Train any population rationally, and they will be rational. Furnish honest and useful employments to those so trained, and such employments they will greatly prefer to dishonest or injurious occupations. It is beyond all calculation the interest of every government to provide that training and that employment, and to provide both is easily practicable.

Background

Robert Owen lived in an age before management gurus existed, and by the end of his life he had moved far from his early years in management. He became a renowned social reformer, partly responsible for the co-operative movement in Britain, and the founder of a utopian community in New Harmony, Indiana. Although Owen himself died in Britain, all his seven children settled in the United States.

In the late 18th century, at the dawn of the Industrial Revolution, Owen found himself, aged 19, the owner of a textile factory in the then booming city of Manchester, soon to be known as "Cotton Capital". Working conditions in factories at the time were appalling – children aged five or six would work up to 15 hours a day. Owen set out to change that. But he did not take his eye off the purpose of the factories: to make a profit. He was one of the first to appreciate that workers can be more productive if they are managed rather than governed; if they are left to their own devices rather than being continually given orders.

In an era when machinery was the driver of industrial success, Owen switched the spotlight on to the human machines behind the machines. "If due care as to the state of your inanimate machines can produce such beneficial results," he wrote, "what may not be expected if you devote equal attention to your vital machines, which are far more wonderfully constructed."

On a visit to Scotland, Owen – a Welshman then working in England – met his future wife, Caroline Dale, and subsequently bought a mill that his father-in-law owned in New Lanark, outside Glasgow. It was here that his most advanced management experiments took place. But all of them were funded through the profits of the business, although at one stage he did buy out his partners so that the company's investment returns could be allowed to be less than the other investors might have been expecting.

Owen's most famous experiment was the so-called silent monitor system. Above each machinist's workstation there was a wooden cube with a different colour painted on each face. The factory superintendents rated the quality of each worker's output each day and turned the cube so that the colour responding to their work was showing for all to see.

Owen provided his workers with housing and schools for their children, none of whom were allowed to work in his factory. His experiments soon became world famous because not only were they humane, but they were also for a time exceedingly successful. At one stage New Lanark was producing annual returns of over 50%. Visitors came from far and wide, and included a future tsar of Russia. Almost a century after his death, one well-known management consultant, Lyndall Urwick, wrote of Owen that "generations ahead of his time, he preached and practised a conception of industrial relations which is, even now, accepted in only a few of the most progressive undertakings".

C. Northcote Parkinson

BORN: 1909
DIED: 1993
NATIONALITY: British

Notable publications
Parkinson's Law: The Pursuit of Progress, Penguin Classics, 1957
The Law and The Profits, John Murray, 1960

Notable quotations
Work expands to fill the time available for its completion.

The chief product of an automated society is a widespread and deepening sense of boredom.

The man who is denied the opportunity of taking decisions of importance begins to regard as important the decisions he is allowed to take.

Background

C. (for Cyril) Northcote Parkinson was not a guru in the traditional sense. Rather, he stands in the line of Laurence Peter (see page 291) and Scott Adams (of "Dilbert" fame) as the author of a humorous glance at management life which rang true in all four corners of the earth. Parkinson's first calling was as a naval historian, and his PhD thesis at London University was entitled "War in the Eastern Seas, 1793–1815". For the rest of his life he continued to write naval history and a number of fictional stories set at sea, in much the same genre as C.S. Forester and Patrick O'Brian.

But it is for his non-naval book, *Parkinson's Law*, that he is best known. The book expanded on an article by him first published in *The Economist* in November 1955. Illustrated by Britain's then leading cartoonist, Osbert Lancaster, the book was an instant hit. It was wrapped around the author's "law" that "work expands to fill the time available for its completion". Thus, Parkinson wrote, "an elderly lady of leisure can spend the entire day in writing and dispatching a postcard to her niece at Bognor Regis ... the total effort that would occupy a busy man for three minutes all told may in this fashion leave another person prostrate after a day of doubt, anxiety and toil."

Parkinson's barbs were directed first and foremost at government institutions – he cited the example of the British navy where the number of admiralty officials increased by 78% between 1914 and 1928, a time when the number of ships fell by 67% and the number of officers and men by 31%. But they applied almost equally well to private industry, which was at the time bloated after decades spent adding layers and layers of managerial bureaucracy.

Gary Hamel (see page 245) commented more than 40 years after Parkinson's book was written: "Yes, I know that bureaucracy is dead ... we're not slaves to our work, we've been liberated ... right? Well then, why does a re-reading of *Parkinson's Law*, written in 1958 at the apex of corporate bureaucracy, still ring true?"

Parkinson's Law has been applied in many different contexts. There is the IT version, for instance: "Data expands to fill the space available for storage." Or the road transport version: "Traffic expands to fill the roads available for it."

Married three times, Parkinson travelled widely. He lived and worked in Malaysia in the 1950s before spending time as a visiting professor at Harvard and at the universities of Illinois and California at Berkeley. He never ceased to be amused by the celebrity status that the book subsequently gave him. For instance, Ronald Reagan, when governor of California, asked him to explain why the number of painters on San Francisco's Oakland bridge had increased from 14 to 72 once a labour-saving paint sprayer had been introduced.

Richard Pascale

BORN: 1938
NATIONALITY: American

Notable publications
With Athos, A., *The Art of Japanese Management: Applications for American Executives*, Simon & Schuster, 1981
Managing on the Edge, Simon & Schuster, 1990
"Surfing the Edge of Chaos", *Sloan Management Review*, Spring 1999
With Parsons, G., "The Summit Syndrome", *Harvard Business Review*, May 2007

Notable quotations
If there is one prescription, it is that there is no prescription.

Nothing fails like success.

If it ain't broke, break it.

Background

Richard Pascale worked as a consultant at McKinsey & Company in the late 1970s alongside Tom Peters (see page 293) at a time when Americans thought they were being overwhelmed by Japan's industrial superiority. Peters and Pascale looked at the issue from different sides of the same coin and each wrote a huge bestseller which became the basis for their subsequent careers – in Pascale's case as an academic and consultant (to companies such as BP, Intel and GE).

Peters exhorted Americans not to despair because they still had some excellent companies. Pascale exhorted them to look at what it was that Japanese companies were doing better than them, and to learn their lessons. In his 1981 book, *The Art of Japanese Management*, he compared the Japanese company Matsushita with the American company ITT, greatly to the credit of the former. But it was in the softer sides of management rather than in such things as strategy and structure that Pascale concluded that the Japanese excelled.

Pascale became even better known for another Japanese company that he looked at closely, where he uncovered what is now known as the "Honda Effect". Disputing the Boston Consulting Group's view that the Japanese car company's success in North America was due to its long-term focus and planning, Pascale went and talked to a number of Honda executives about the company's entry into the United States. And he found that it had been the result more of a series of miscalculations, rapid readjustments and chance than of any clear rational progression along a planned strategy.

"Organisational agility", he decided, was the key to Honda's success, and much of his writing thereafter addressed this idea of agility. Honda, he said, exists "in a sort of restless, uneasy state, which enables it to get a great deal out of its people and itself as an entity". Henry Mintzberg (see page 275) followed up the debate with an article in the *California Management Review* (in summer 1996) entitled "The Honda Effect Revisited".

After spending 20 years on the faculty of Stanford's graduate school of business, Pascale moved to Oxford University's Saïd Business School as an associate fellow. His later work focused on the idea of complexity, drawing parallels between large organisations and complex scientific systems.

He focused on four commonalities in particular:

- that prolonged equilibrium in either type of system is a precursor to death;
- that innovation occurs close to the edge of chaos;
- that all living things demonstrate a capacity for self-organisation; and
- that when you tamper with living things, you face the law of unintended consequences.

It is perhaps the first – that to do nothing is not a viable option – that has attracted most attention at a time when the rate of corporate change has been accelerating sharply.

Laurence Peter

BORN: 1919
DIED: 1990
NATIONALITY: Canadian

Notable publication
With Hull, R., *The Peter Principle*, William Morrow, New York, 1969

Notable quotations
In a hierarchy, every employee tends to rise to his level of incompetence.

The man who is willing to meet you halfway is usually a poor judge of distance.

Bureaucracy defends the status quo long past the time when the quo has lost its status.

An intelligence test sometimes shows a man how smart he would have been not to have taken it.

Background

Not many management gurus have their name adopted for a principle, especially when they are not really a guru at all. The Peter Principle is encapsulated in the phrase: "In a hierarchy, every employee tends to rise to his level of incompetence." It first appeared on the cover of a book of the same name, written by Laurence J. Peter, a teacher and professor of education, and Raymond Hull, and it has since become part of the English language.

Written in a mock 19th-century style and illustrated with 19th-century engravings from *Punch*, a British humorous magazine, the book was an instant hit. Peter's Corollary stated: "In time, every post tends to be occupied by an employee who is incompetent to carry out its duties" or "The cream rises until it sours." As one reviewer wrote at the time: "There is a chilling touch of truth behind the whole thing."

Although Peter applied the principle first to the educational world with which he was familiar, it was not long before industrial organisations realised that it applied just as well to many of them. Most hierarchies are familiar with the outstanding finance director who is promoted to be an outstandingly disastrous CEO. Taken to extremes, the Peter Principle is a deeply depressing idea. It means that all employees who are not already hopeless at their job are merely in transit to a desk where they will be.

Peter's (tongue-in-cheek) solution to this "philosophy of despair" was to recommend "creative incompetence". Anyone can avoid disastrous promotion by creating "the impression that you have already reached your level of incompetence. Creative incompetence will achieve the best results if you choose an area of incompetence which does not directly hinder you in carrying out the main duties of your present position."

Peter and Hull suggested tactics such as:

- occasionally parking your car in the space reserved for the company president;
- arranging to receive a fake threatening phone call in the office and then pleading, within earshot of as many people as possible, "Don't tell my wife. If she finds out, this will kill her."

The success of Peter's book came out of the blue. *The Peter Principle* sold over 1m copies, a remarkable feat for a book of its type at the time, and it spent no less than 33 weeks on the American bestsellers' list. Hull was an unknown Canadian journalist and Peter was a Canadian teacher who had also been a counsellor, school psychologist, prison instructor and consultant. Above all, though, Peter had an extraordinarily well-tuned ear for the quotable quote, and in all walks of life – for example, he once wrote: "Television has changed the American child from an irresistible force to an immovable object."

Tom Peters

BORN: 1942
NATIONALITY: American

Notable publications
With Waterman, R.H., *In Search of Excellence: Lessons from America's Best-run Companies*, Harper & Row, New York, 1982; Profile Books, London, 2004
Thriving on Chaos: Handbook for a Management Revolution, Alfred A. Knopf, 1987
The Little Big Things: 163 Ways to Pursue Excellence at Work, HarperBusiness, 2010

Notable quotations
Excellent companies are both centralised and decentralised.

After 50 (combined) years of watching organisations thrive and shrivel, we held to one, and only one, basic belief: to loosen the reins, to allow a thousand flowers to bloom and a hundred schools to contend, is the best way to sustain vigour in perilous gyrating times. [with Robert Waterman]

Background

Tom Peters was the co-author of what was for over 20 years the best-selling business book of all time. *In Search of Excellence*, written with his fellow McKinsey consultant Robert Waterman, was first published in the United States in 1982 and subsequently sold millions of copies. It came out at a time when corporate America was feeling overwhelmed by Japan's evident superiority in manufacturing and needed reminding that there was still excellence to be found back home.

It is not, however, as a writer that Peters was best known in his later years. He became the first (and most outstanding) exponent of the late 20th-century phenomenon of the management lecture. He stood at the forefront of a new generation of management experts who took their wisdom off the bookshelf and into the classroom. Energetic, lively and entertaining, he wowed crowds of executives in conference halls from Hamburg to Hong Kong, the leader of a regular (and highly influential) migration of American gurus spreading the gospel of American management excellence to all corners of the earth. He peddled his theories of excellence with the exuberance and evangelistic zeal of a 19th-century cough-syrup salesman.

Peters served in the US navy in the late 1960s and then worked in the White House as an adviser on drug abuse. But he based the ideas in "Excellence" (as the book has become known) on experience that he and Waterman gained when working with American companies as management consultants for McKinsey & Company in the late 1970s and early 1980s. There they had been in contact with a fellow consultant, Richard Pascale (see page 289), who had used McKinsey's framework of the Seven Ss (see page 163) to explain the growing superiority at that time of Japanese industry and management methods.

Kathryn Harrigan, professor of business leadership at Columbia Business School, attributed some of the book's success to the fact that: "Americans are into cults, particularly the cult of the personality. They are all looking for the recipe of success, and Tom Peters made the best job of that. People knew exactly where to place him."

Robert Waterman was the opposite of Peters. Shy and introspective, he stayed on at McKinsey long after Peters had left. He eventually set up his own consultancy in San Francisco. The two authors never wrote another book together, although each separately wrote several. Peters started *Thriving on Chaos*, his second book, with the memorable line: "There are no excellent companies." This was after several of the so-called excellent companies in the first book had chalked up some far-from-excellent performances.

The focus of Peters's later work was the management of continuous change in a chaotic world. His books became ever more populist. *Re-imagine*, published in 2003 by Dorling Kindersley, a publisher famous for its artwork, contained lots of short sidebars, exclamation marks and pictures of things such as frogs leaping.

Michael Porter

BORN: 1947
NATIONALITY: American
ACHIEVEMENT: Member of Presidential Commission on Industrial Competitiveness, 1983

Notable publications
Competitive Strategy: Techniques for Analyzing Industries and Competitors, Free Press, New York, 1980; 2nd edn, Free Press, New York and London, 1998
Competitive Advantage: Creating and Sustaining Superior Performance, Collier Macmillan, London, 1985; 2nd edn, Free Press, New York and London, 1998
"Strategy and the Internet", Harvard Business Review, March 2001
With Kramer, M., "Strategy and Society: The Link Between Competitive Advantage and Corporate Social Responsibility", Harvard Business Review, December 2006
With Kramer, M., "Creating Shared Value", Harvard Business Review, January/February 2011

Notable quotations
The essence of strategy is choosing what not to do.

Billions are wasted on ineffective philanthropy. Philanthropy is decades behind business in applying rigorous thinking to the use of money.

Background
Michael Porter is the doyen of living management gurus, a professor at Harvard Business School whose office is a whole on-campus house, home of his own Institute for Strategy and Competitiveness. A talented sportsman (like Frederick Winslow Taylor, see page 309), Porter could have became a professional golfer.

The Economist once said: "His work is academic to a fault. Mr Porter is about as likely to produce a blockbuster full of anecdotes and boosterish catchphrases as he is to deliver a lecture dressed in bra and stockings." He has been criticised for his willingness to boil his thoughts down into a series of bullet points, each of them with a ploddingly unmemorable title. Unlike many of his colleagues, Porter is frustratingly unquotable. Charles Handy (see page 249) once said: "Influence, not popularity, is what Michael Porter wants." He never, for example, allows his books to be published in paperback.

Nevertheless, Porter effectively redefined the way that businessmen think about competition, largely by introducing the language and concepts of economics into corporate strategy. He began by simplifying the notion of competitive advantage (see page 37) and then created a new framework for companies to think about how to achieve it.

Later he moved on to advising countries about how they too could gain competitive advantage, and this led him to another field of interest, clustering (see page 35) – the extent to which industries old and new (from diamond dealers to nanotechnologists) stay geographically close to each other, and the reasons for this. Porter maintained that countries do well economically in large part because of this clustering of specialised skills and industries that, through dynamic competition between them, produce superior products and processes.

After that, Porter started to write about health care and corporate social responsibility (see page 45), applying his thinking about competition to social issues. Indeed, so broad did his interests become that in 2000 he was made a professor of Harvard University, with a free-ranging remit, only the fourth Harvard Business School faculty member ever to be so honoured.

Like many leading management thinkers, Porter trained first as an engineer. Then, after a doctorate in economics, he moved to Harvard Business School. Aside from being a bestselling author, he found time to set up a successful global consulting firm called Monitor. He also commands top-dollar fees for personal appearances – his own competitive weapon being differentiation (see page 61), not low cost.

C.K. Prahalad

BORN: 1941
DIED: 2010
NATIONALITY: Indian

Notable publications

With Hamel, G., "The Core Competence of the Corporation", *Harvard Business Review*, May–June 1990

With Hamel, G., *Competing for the Future*, Harvard Business School Press, 1994

The Fortune at the Bottom of the Pyramid: Eradicating Poverty through Profits, Pearson Education, 2004

With Brugmann, J., "Co-creating Business's New Social Compact", *Harvard Business Review*, February 2007

Notable quotations

I get extremely energised when there is an extremely complex problem to be solved. But management is a lot of blocking and tackling.

The typical pictures of poverty mask the fact that the very poor represent resilient entrepreneurs and value-conscious consumers.

Background

C.K. Prahalad is an unlikely guru. Born one of nine children in the teeming Indian city of Madras (now Chennai), he was once described by *Fast Company* magazine as "a moustachioed, bespectacled, slightly round man" with a rich baritone voice. He first studied physics at university before being persuaded by his father, a senior judge and a noted Sanskrit scholar, to work for Union Carbide, a chemicals company. He stayed there for four years, a time he has described as a major inflexion point in his life.

Then he went to Harvard Business School before returning to India for a number of years to teach management. But he found the protectionist Indian economic environment of the time unaccepting of his ideas about multinational companies and multinationalism. He returned to the United States to teach with, as he once put it, $18 in his pocket. A quarter of a century later he had topped at least one widely respected poll of the world's leading management gurus.

He first made his reputation with work he did with Gary Hamel (see page 245), then a colleague at the University of Michigan. Their 1990 *Harvard Business Review* article on core competencies (see page 41) is one of that magazine's bestselling articles of all time. Later Prahalad became better known for his ideas about what he called "the bottom of the pyramid", the idea that poor people around the world can be a good and profitable market for businesses and should not be ignored.

In 2000 Prahalad left his university post and moved to California to work for a high-tech start-up called Praja, a Sanskrit word meaning "the common people". The company created software that organised data not by words (as, for instance, Google or any encyclopaedia does) but by experience. It then intended to allow the "common people" unlimited access to its information. Prahalad argued: "We are still operating as if we never left Gutenberg. If you look at keyword searches, the document is still going to be the organising idea. But now the metaphor is not going to be the document – it's going to be the experience."

Prahalad's experience with Praja, however, was not a complete success. The company was forced to lay off a big chunk of its workforce and was then sold to TIBCO, a software company. Prahalad returned to his university post in Michigan and turned some of the ideas he had developed at Praja into his book *The Fortune at the Bottom of the Pyramid*, which was voted top business book of the year (2004) by amazon.com.

Richard Rumelt

BORN: 1942
NATIONALITY: American

Notable publication
Strategy, Structure and Economic Performance, Harvard Business School
    Press, 1974; revised edn, 1986
"How Much Does Industry Matter?", *Strategic Management Journal*, 1991
Good Strategy/Bad Strategy, Crown Business, 2011

Notable quotations
Most analysts overestimate the importance of scale and underestimate the inertia of buyers.

Using bullet points so much drives out thinking. One of the nice features of PowerPoint is how fast you can create a presentation. But that's the trouble. People end up with bullet points that contradict one another, and no one notices. It is simply amazing.

Background
An electrical engineer by training, Richard Rumelt has been at the Anderson School of Management at the University of California in Los Angeles since 1976, rising to be professor of business and society. For a three-year period (1993–96) he was on secondment to INSEAD, near Paris. His chief area of interest (and of influence) has been corporate strategy.

Throughout his long career Rumelt published little. But his influence grew slowly, and interest in his ideas was reignited in 2007 by a widely read interview published in *McKinsey Quarterly*. His most influential thoughts were contained in just two articles published some ten years apart. In 1982 he demonstrated that there was a statistical link between corporate strategy and profitability, showing that somewhat diversified companies performed better than highly diversified ones. And in 1991 he published a controversial paper arguing that neither the ownership of a business nor the industry that it was in could explain the bulk of the difference in profitability between different businesses. Being good at what you do, he maintained, counted for a lot more.

Rumelt argued that strategic planning (see page 173) should be separated from annual resource budgets. "Changes don't come along in nice annual packages," he said, "so the need for strategy work is episodic, not necessarily annual." He recommended that companies separate their long-term resource plans (their budgets) from a separate "non-annual, opportunity-driven process for strategy work".

A bit like Michael Porter (see page 295), Rumelt came to the conclusion that there are only two ways for companies to attain long-lasting success. They must either invent their way to it, or they must exploit some change in their environment – "in technology, consumer tastes, laws, resource prices or competitive behaviour, and ride that change with quickness and skill". This second way, he claims, is how most companies make it.

In the *McKinsey Quarterly* interview, Rumelt told the story of how he had asked Steve Jobs, the boss of Apple, in 1998, just after Jobs had successfully turned Apple around, what his longer-term strategy was. Jobs, he recalled, "just smiled and said, 'I am going to wait for the next big thing.' ... he was waiting until the next moment for that predatory leap, which for him was Pixar and then, in an even bigger way, the iPod. That very predatory approach ... is what distinguishes a real entrepreneurial strategy."

In his own life, however, Rumelt was not a great one for predatory leaps. He moved around the academic world relatively little, and his favourite pastime was mountaineering, in which he achieved a number of first ascents by sheer, dogged persistence.

E.F. Schumacher

BORN: 1911
DIED: 1977
NATIONALITY: German

Notable publication
Small is Beautiful: A Study of Economics as if People Mattered, Blond and
Briggs, 1973; HarperPerennial, 1989; Hartley & Marks Publishers, 1999

Notable quotation
*Maybe what we really need is not either/or but "the one and the other at the
same time". This very familiar problem pervades the whole of real life.*

Background
A bit like Laurence Peter (see page 291), E.F. Schumacher is remembered for
the one book that he wrote – or, more accurately, for the title of that book,
a title that was both accidental and misleading. First published in 1973,
the book was called *Small is Beautiful*. But that was not the title originally
conceived by its author. It was added as a last-minute afterthought by the
publisher.

The book's subtitle is the less engaging *A Study of Economics as if People
Mattered*, but it is more true to its content. For the book is not a paean to
smallness. It is more a polemic against industry's brutality and (among
other things) its despoiling of the environment and of the human spirit.
Schumacher was strongly influenced by the Buddhism he encountered
on a trip to Burma. His book's frontispiece quotes the historian R.H.
Tawney:

> *Since even quite common men have souls, no increase in
> material wealth will compensate them for arrangements which
> insult their self-respect and impair their freedom. A reasonable
> estimate of economic organisation must allow for the fact that,
> unless industry is to be paralysed by recurrent revolts on the part
> of outraged human nature, it must satisfy criteria which are not
> purely economic.*

If a more caring industry and "the humanisation of work" could be achieved only by breaking big firms up into a number of small firms, then (in Schumacher's schema) small would, indeed, be beautiful. But Schumacher never attempted to show that meanness of spirit bears any relationship to the size of the organisation in which it is being exercised.

The phrase "small is beautiful" caught on at a time when industrial gigantism had been the dominant trend for decades, fuelled partly by the need for industry to satisfy the thirst of two world wars. With the wars well ended, it was time for a swing of the pendulum. After the book was written, a number of countries set up government bodies to look at ways in which the disadvantages faced by small firms, particularly in financial markets, might be removed.

Schumacher was an economist who was born in Germany and studied at Oxford University as a Rhodes scholar in the 1930s. With the rise of Nazism he fled back to the UK, only to be interned as an enemy alien during the war. After the war, he became briefly chief economics editorial writer for *The Times* before he joined the National Coal Board, a large organisation where he spent most of the rest of his working life. Based on his experience there, he later wrote: "Organisations should imitate nature, which doesn't allow a single cell to become too large ... The fundamental task is to achieve smallness within large organisations ... The great achievement of Mr Sloan of General Motors was to structure this gigantic firm in such a manner that it became in fact a federation of fairly reasonably sized firms."

He used the National Coal Board as an example of a big organisation that had set up a number of "quasi-firms" within it. These quasi-firms, he said, had to have a large amount of freedom "to give the greatest possible chance to creativity and entrepreneurship".

Peter Senge

BORN: 1947
NATIONALITY: American

Notable publications

The Fifth Discipline: The Art and Practice of the Learning Organization,
   Currency/Doubleday, New York, 1990; 2nd revised edn, Random
   House Business Books, 2006
*The Dance of Change: The Challenges of Sustaining Momentum in Learning
   Organizations*, Nicholas Brealey, 1999

Notable quotations

*You can only understand the system of a rainstorm by contemplating the
whole, not any individual part of the pattern ... business and other human
endeavours are also systems ... systems thinking is a conceptual framework,
a body of knowledge and tools, that has been developed over the past 50
years to make the full patterns clearer, and to help us see how to change
them effectively.*

*Mutual reflection. Open and candid conversation. Questioning of old beliefs
and assumptions. Learning to let go. Awareness of how our own actions
create the systemic structures that produce our problems. Developing these
learning capabilities lies at the heart of profound change.*

Background

Peter Senge studied aerospace engineering at Stanford University before
moving into the field of organisational behaviour and becoming director
of the Centre for Organisational Learning at MIT's Sloan School of Management. He is credited with developing the idea of the learning organisation,
based on his study of social systems and the relationship of the whole to
its constituent parts. A learning organisation, he once said, "is continually
expanding its capacity to create its future".

Senge's message is that organisations obtain competitive advantage
(see page 37) from continuous learning, both individual and collective.
Learning new ways of doing things, however, also necessarily involves a
continuous process of unlearning, of forgetting old ways of doing things.

The technology of the information age is radically changing the way in which such processes take place.

Senge rose to prominence with the publication in 1990 of *The Fifth Discipline*, the book in which he laid out his thoughts about organisational learning. There he described the five essential ingredients ("disciplines") of the learning organisation:

1 Personal mastery – continuous learning by each individual, "expanding the ability to produce the results we truly want in life".
2 Mental models – to develop awareness of the acquired patterns of thinking within organisations, and to constantly challenge them.
3 Shared vision – creating "pictures of the future" that all members of a group can identify as their own.
4 Team learning – learning together through dialogue and discussion so that the members of a team are more effective than they would be as solitary individuals.
5 The "fifth" discipline, the ability to see the organisation as a whole, as something with its own behaviour patterns separate from those of the individuals who are its constituent parts.

Organisations work as a set of interconnected subsystems, said Senge, so decisions made in one part of the business have implications for the other parts. Managers, therefore, need to embrace the complexity of organisations rather than embracing what he calls "the pervasive reductionalism" of Western culture, whereby simple answers to complex questions are always sought. Senge says that a non-threatening dialogue needs to be carried out among the employees of an organisation in which some sort of consensus is reached as each employee comes to see the points of view of all the others, and begins to learn from them.

Senge's ideas have been criticised as being "utopian", the fruits of a man who spent the late 1960s at a university in California and who has dabbled subsequently in Eastern philosophies. Nevertheless, they have been enormously influential, which is surprising if only because the book in which they are laid out has never been described as an easy read.

Herbert Simon

BORN: 1916
DIED: 2001
NATIONALITY: American
ACHIEVEMENT: Awarded the Nobel Prize for economics in 1978, to considerable surprise, since by then he had not taught economics for two decades

Notable publications
With March, J.G., *Organizations*, John Wiley & Sons, 1958; 2nd edn, Blackwell, 1993
Administrative Behaviour: A Study of the Decision Making processes in Administrative Organisation, The Macmillan Co, New York, 1948; 4th edn, Free Press, 1997

Notable quotations:
Satisficing fits pretty well our introspective knowledge of our own judgmental processes, as well as the more formal descriptions of those processes made by the psychologists who have studied them.

In an information-rich world, the wealth of information means a dearth of something else: a scarcity of whatever it is that information consumes. What information consumes is rather obvious: it consumes the attention of its recipients. Hence a wealth of information creates a poverty of attention and a need to allocate that attention efficiently among the overabundance of information sources that might consume it.

Background
Simon is most famous for what is known to economists as the theory of bounded rationality, a theory about economic decision-making that Simon himself preferred to call "satisficing", a combination of two words: "satisfy" and "suffice". Contrary to the tenets of classical economics, Simon maintained that individuals do not seek to maximise their benefit from a particular course of action (since they cannot assimilate and digest all the information that would be needed to do such a thing). Not only can they not get access to all the information required, but even if they could, their

minds would be unable to process it properly. The human mind necessarily restricts itself. It is, as Simon put it, bounded by "cognitive limits".

Hence people, in many different situations, seek something that is "good enough", something that is satisfactory. Humans, for example, when in shopping mode, aspire to something that they find acceptable, although that may not necessarily be optimal. They look through things in sequence and when they come across an item that meets their aspiration level they go for it. This real-world behaviour is what Simon called satisficing.

He applied the idea to organisations as well as to individuals. Managers do much the same thing as shoppers in a mall. "Whereas economic man maximises, selects the best alternative from among all those available to him," he wrote, "his cousin, administrative man, satisfices, looks for a course of action that is satisfactory or 'good enough'." He went on to say: "Because he treats the world as rather empty and ignores the interrelatedness of all things (so stupefying to thought and action), administrative man can make decisions with relatively simple rules of thumb that do not make impossible demands upon his capacity for thought."

The principle of satisficing can also be applied to events such as filling in questionnaires. Respondents often choose satisfactory answers rather than searching for an optimum answer. Satisficing of this kind can dramatically distort the traditional statistical methods of market research.

Simon, born and raised in Milwaukee, studied economics at the University of Chicago. "My career," he said, "was settled at least as much by drift as by choice", an undergraduate field study developing what became his main field of interest – decision-making within organisations. In 1949 he moved to Pittsburgh to help set up a new graduate school of industrial administration at the Carnegie Institute of Technology. He said that his work had two guiding principles: one was the "hardening of the social sciences"; and the other was to bring about closer co-operation between natural sciences and social sciences.

Simon was a man of wide interests. He played the piano well – his mother was an accomplished pianist – and he was also a keen mountain climber. At one time he taught an undergraduate course on the French Revolution.

Alfred Sloan

BORN: 1875
DIED: 1966
NATIONALITY: American

Notable publications
My Years with General Motors, Doubleday, 1964; revised 1990
"The Sloan Legacy", *Business Strategy Review*, Winter 2009

Notable quotation
The business of business is business.

Background

Alfred Sloan was not only arguably the most original CEO and organisational thinker of the 20th century, but he was also clever enough to set his record down in a book that became a management classic: *My Years with General Motors*, written with the help of John McDonald, an editor from *Fortune* magazine, and a rising young historian called Alfred Chandler (see page 225).

Sloan studied electrical engineering at MIT before joining a small company that manufactured ball bearings. By the age of 24, at the dawn of the 20th century, he was already president of the company and steering it towards making anti-friction bearings for the then fledgling market for automobiles. Four years later the company, which had been close to bankruptcy, was making profits of $60m. Sloan was soon in close touch with many of the pioneers of the car industry, men such as Henry Ford and William Durant.

Before long his ball-bearing business became part of General Motors, and in 1923 (in the midst of a dire slump in the car industry) Sloan became president of GM. It was there that his reputation was made. He reorganised the company in a way that became the template for virtually every corporate entity for the rest of the century. He divided the company into separate autonomous divisions that were subject only to financial and policy controls from a small central staff.

This "federal decentralisation", as he called it, is said to have taken only a month to set up, but its results were enduring and dramatic. Within six years the company had moved from being a laggard in the industry (way behind Ford with its famous Model T) to being the market leader with a turnover of $1.5 billion and a share price that had in the meanwhile almost quintupled.

Sloan also introduced a systematic strategic planning (see page 173) procedure for the company's divisions, the first CEO ever to do such a thing. Each GM model was changed and updated annually, and models were designed not to compete with each other – a strategy that effectively made Sloan the inventor of the second-hand car market. His aim was to produce a car "for every purse and purpose", unlike Ford, which stuck with its single model – understandably since, when Sloan took over at GM, Ford had some 60% of the market, compared with GM's 12%.

He was president of the company from 1923 to 1937, chief executive from 1923 to 1946, and chairman from 1937 to 1956, over 30 years with his hand effectively on the helm of one of the largest companies in the world. However, he was known as "Silent Sloan" to the company's workers because he preferred to run the business from behind the scenes. Management by walking about (see page 123) was not one of his methods. His management style is well illustrated by his famous summing up at the end of a GM senior executive meeting. "Gentlemen, I take it we are all in complete agreement on the decision here," he started, and everyone nodded their heads in agreement. "Then," he went on, "I propose we postpone further discussion of this matter until the next meeting to give ourselves time to develop disagreement, and perhaps gain some understanding of what the decision is all about."

In his later years Sloan gave large sums of money to his alma mater, MIT, which in gratitude named its business school after him. He also helped fund the Sloan-Kettering Institute for Cancer Research in New York.

Frederick Winslow Taylor

BORN: 1856
DIED: 1915
NATIONALITY: American

Notable publications
The Principles of Scientific Management, Harper and Brothers, 1911;
    reprint, Hive Publishing Company, 1986
*Two Papers on Scientific Management: A Piece-rate System and Notes on
    Belting*, George Routledge, 1919

Notable quotations
*The principal object of management should be to secure the maximum
prosperity for the employer, coupled with the maximum prosperity of each
employee.*

In the past, the man has been first; in the future the machine must be first.

*In our scheme, we do not ask the initiative of our men. We do not want any
initiative. All we want of them is to obey the orders we give them, do what
we say, and do it quick.*

Background
Frederick Winslow Taylor was a Quaker whose tombstone in Pennsylvania
bears the inscription "The Father of Scientific Management". He was born to
a wealthy family in Philadelphia and, as a teenager, travelled round Europe
with his parents, whom he referred to formally as "thee" and "thou".

Like many management theorists after him, Taylor trained first as an
engineer. He started his working life on a factory floor as an appren-
tice pattern-maker, an experience that infused everything he achieved
thereafter. He then worked at Midvale Steel Works in Philadelphia,
where he became chief engineer, before moving to Bethlehem Steel
Company. There he pioneered time and motion studies which analysed
how specific jobs might be done more efficiently. He took to walking
round with a stop-watch and a notepad breaking down manual tasks
into a series of components that could be measured. Out of this grew the
idea of piece work. At the same time he managed to win the American

national tennis doubles championship, using a spoon-shaped racquet of his own design.

His larger purpose was to prove that "the best management is a true science, resting upon clearly defined laws". This he called scientific management (see page 159). Peter Drucker (see page 235) said that Taylor was "the first man in history who did not take work for granted, but looked at it and studied it. His approach to work is still the basic foundation". Drucker maintained that Darwin, Freud and Taylor between them were the makers of the modern world.

Taylor's greatest work, *The Principles of Scientific Management*, was the very first business bestseller. Its influence spread to unlikely places. It was translated early into French and inspired Henri Fayol (see page 237). In Russia, Lenin at one stage exhorted Soviet workers to "try out every scientific and progressive suggestion of the Taylor system". Subsequent failure to achieve Taylor-like production targets led many Soviet workers to the gulag.

Today scientific management, sometimes known as Taylorism, is often seen as a system that has no room for the nuances of human nature in its urge to find ever greater manual efficiency. But Taylor himself is universally acknowledged to have been one of the most original and influential management thinkers of all time. His biographer, Robert Kanigel, wrote: "After Ford and Taylor got through with them, most jobs needed less of everything – less brains, less muscle, less independence."

Taylor lived at a time when industrialisation was being fuelled by massive movements of labour from the land to the factory. His main achievement was to devise a way whereby totally unskilled sharecroppers could, as Drucker put it, "be converted in 60 to 90 days into first-rate welders and shipbuilders".

Alvin Toffler

BORN: 1928
NATIONALITY: American

Notable publications
Future Shock, Bantam Books, 1970; Pan Books, 1979
The Third Wave, Morrow 1980
Powershift: Knowledge, Wealth, and Violence at the Edge of the 21st Century,
     Bantam Books, 1990
With Toffler, H., *Revolutionary Wealth*, Alfred A. Knopf, 2006

Notable quotation
*We cannot cram the embryonic world of tomorrow into yesterday's
conventional cubby holes.*

Background

Alvin Toffler was the most famous futurologist of his generation. He
coined the term "future shock" in an article that first came out in 1965
and then published a book of the same name in 1970. The phrase has now
entered the vocabulary, referring to what happens to society when too
much change happens in too short a time, when the ensuing confusion
causes normal decision-making processes to break down.

Future Shock was the first of a trilogy, followed at ten-year intervals by
the *Third Wave* and *Powershift*. All three books are about change: the first
about how it affects organisations; the second about where it is taking
them; and the third about who controls it. Managers today can scarcely
string a sentence together without using the word "change", and Toffler is
largely responsible for that. He was the first to point to the acceleration of
change in business life.

In his second book, Toffler came up with another profound insight
that we all now more or less take for granted. The first and second waves
he refers to are the agricultural and the industrial revolutions. The third
wave is the information revolution, brought about by the invention of
computers, and still running its course. "The advanced economy," wrote
Toffler, "could not run for 30 seconds without computers."

His understanding of the implications of information technology was

311

extraordinary for a man who began his adult life writing poetry, long before he knew that not all chips were made from potatoes. His special skill was not just that he could see technology with an outsider's eye, but that he could also write about it with a poet's ear. He has not, however, been infallible. One of his predictions was that we would all by now be working in a "paperless office".

The considerable contribution of Toffler's wife, Heidi, to his work has been more openly acknowledged in recent years, and their later publications have been under their joint names. They first met when they were both studying English at New York University. For a while they were journalists for a number of different publications, including *Fortune* and *Playboy*, before being invited by IBM in 1960 to write a paper on the long-term implications of the computer – a paper that was the genesis of everything they wrote thereafter.

Their later book, *Revolutionary Wealth*, built on an earlier concept of theirs, the idea of the "prosumer", the consumer who is also part-producer of what he or she consumes. For example, a person who designs a kitchen with IKEA's online templates and then buys the necessary kits from an IKEA shop to be assembled in his or her own home is a prosumer. The book ranges widely in its predictions for the future – from the rise of a Christian fundamentalist Chinese leader to the creation of a low-fat-food-only credit card that won't allow you to buy butter.

The *Washington Post* said it is unfortunate that "the Tofflers have little time for history and less still for economists, whom they dismiss as 'inerrantist' and overfond of jargon. But *Revolutionary Wealth* contains more jargon than a dozen economic papers, including such gems as 'obsoledge', 'complexorama' and 'producivity'".

Robert Townsend

BORN: 1920
DIED: 1998
NATIONALITY: American

Notable publication
Up the Organisation, Michael Joseph, 1970; reprinted as *Further Up the Organisation*, Coronet, 1985

Notable quotations
Consultants are people who borrow your watch and tell you what time it is, and then walk off with the watch.

If you don't do it excellently, don't do it at all. Because if it's not excellent, it won't be profitable or fun, and if you're not in business for fun or profit, what the hell are you doing there?

Managers must have the discipline not to keep pulling up the flowers to see if their roots are healthy.

Background
Robert Townsend was a rare specimen – a man who succeeded in corporate life, becoming a director of American Express and then president of Avis, a car-rental company, before debunking it all in a book that became a classic, the extremely amusing (and still relevant today, though now out of print) *Up the Organisation*. In it Townsend mocked many of the sacred cows of corporate life. The book's subtitle is effectively a short summary of its contents: *How to Stop the Corporation from Stifling People and Strangling Profits*. It joins a select line of corporate mickey-takers – a line which includes Laurence Peter's famous "principle" (see page 291) and the more recent "Dilbert" cartoons of Scott Adams.

Townsend's book had the benefit not only of being jargon-free, but also of being easily digestible – it ran to around 250 pages and was broken up into small sections, none of which was longer than three pages. Its praises continue to be sung to this day, more than 40 years after it was first published. It was particularly harsh on the vanity and stupidity of executive leaders, and it argued that a wide range of the perks of the leader's job should be abolished – from the reserved space in the corporate car park, for instance, to the corporate jet and the company shrink.

Townsend's view of the big picture was that companies had remained under the influence of military and ecclesiastical organisational role models for far too long. He argued that tight control from above had left people in the lower ranks of organisations trapped in mindless slavery. Employees from executive vice-presidents down to secretaries in the typing pool had, he said, three things in common: they were docile; they were bored; and they were dull. He suggested that chief executives should try calling themselves by phone to find out how impossible it is to communicate with them (and for them therefore to receive information from the outside world).

In a sense, Townsend anticipated the empowerment (see page 73) movement and the idea of "flattening" the organisation in order to diffuse responsibility and authority more widely.

Not all of his advice has been taken to heart. He was, for example, keen to tell companies not to hire Harvard Business School graduates, arguing that they lacked some of the essential requirements for corporate success, such as humility and a track record for fairness and honesty under pressure. Harvard Business School graduates continue to be in great demand.

Dave Ulrich

BORN: 1954
NATIONALITY: American

Notable publication
Human Resource Champions: The Next Agenda for Adding Value and Delivering Results, Harvard Business School Press, 1997

Notable quotation
Moving toward service centres, centres of expertise, or outsourcing does not mean that HR has been transformed. If new delivery mechanisms provide basically the same old HR services, the function has changed but not transformed itself. HR transformation changes both behaviour and outputs. The changes must improve life for key stakeholders in ways that they are willing to pay for.

Background
Dave Ulrich illustrates one of the biggest shifts in corporate focus at the turn of the century. An academic at Ross School of Business at the University of Michigan, he pioneered a new way of looking at corporations' human resources departments. He was named as the most influential person in human resources by *HR Magazine* for every year from 2006 to 2009.

Starting with the widely accepted idea that human resources were becoming the most valuable asset in a knowledge-based economy where talent was at a premium, Ulrich argued that traditional corporate HR departments were entirely inadequate for the task of ensuring that companies got the right talent when they needed it. HR personnel were so involved in the detail of pay, pensions and disputes that they had no time for the higher strategic thinking required by the knowledge economy.

Ulrich suggested that companies should transform their HR departments, and he proposed a three-part model that has since been widely adopted around the world – so much so that it has come to be known as the Ulrich Model. At its core, the model tries to free HR staff to think strategically about their organisation's human resources. Ulrich says they must "grasp and master the concept of value". People in HR departments have too little understanding of how a business actually works.

Ulrich's father was a park ranger in Nevada and Ulrich, brought up a Mormon, studied first at Brigham Young University in Utah. An inspiring teacher, he established a wider reputation in the business world when working with Jack Welch at GE, where he impressed the legendary boss by pointing out the dangers of recidivism – sending people off on courses where they feel inspired and uplifted, only for them to return to the same old working environment, where they inevitably revert to their bad old ways. This risk had been brought home to him as a boy when he had seen children from poor inner cities be transformed by a stay in the parks he grew up in, only for them to change back again on their return to the city.

Ulrich became in such demand as a speaker and consultant that he clocked up 8m frequent-flier air miles keeping in touch with clients all over the world. However, after an embolism in his leg nearly prevented him from attending a daughter's wedding, he retired for three years (2002–05) to "answer the church's call" and to run a Mormon mission in Quebec. He also kept his feet on the ground for a while.

Pierre Wack

BORN: 1922
DIED: 1997
NATIONALITY: French

Notable publication
"Scenarios: Shooting the Rapids", *Harvard Business Review*, 1985

Notable quotation
Scenarios deal with two worlds; the world of facts and the world of perceptions. They explore for facts but they aim at perceptions inside the heads of decision-makers. Their purpose is to gather and transform information of strategic significance into fresh perceptions. This transformation process is not trivial – more often than not it does not happen. When it works, it is a creative experience that generates a heartfelt "Aha" ... and leads to strategic insights beyond the mind's reach.

Background

Pierre Wack was an unconventional French oil executive who developed the use of scenario planning (see page 157) at Royal Dutch Shell's London headquarters in the 1970s. So successful was he that the Anglo-Dutch oil giant was able to anticipate not just one Arab-induced oil shock during that decade, but two.

By the standards of Shell executives, Wack was wacky. He almost invariably had an incense stick burning in his office and his own favourite guru was not Peter Drucker (see page 235) or Douglas McGregor (see page 273) but a bizarre bald Russian called Georges Gurdjieff.

Gurdjieff was a spiritual teacher who died in France in 1949. He studied Sufi mysticism in his youth and brought some of its ideas to the West. Wack visited him regularly during the second world war when Gurdjieff was based in Fontainebleau, south of Paris, today the home of INSEAD, one of Europe's leading business schools. After Gurdjieff's death, and while employed by Shell, Wack continued to spend several weeks a year meditating in India with another guru.

Gurdjieff taught that with special insight it was possible to "see" the future. But he did not mean literally to see with your eyes. Wack explained this form of seeing by telling the story of a gardener he had once met in Japan. The gardener had pointed to a thick bamboo stem and explained that if a pebble was thrown at it and it hit the trunk slightly off-centre, it would bounce off and make hardly any sound. But if it hit the trunk dead centre, it would make a distinctive "clonk". He then said that to be sure to hit the stem in this way, it was necessary to hear the distinctive sound in your own mind in advance of throwing the pebble – and then to concentrate intensely on that sound. According to one of his colleagues, Wack believed that anticipating the future involved a similar discipline. It is, he said, "about being in the right state of focus to put your finger unerringly on the key facts or insights that unlock or open understanding".

That is not to say that Wack was a kind of clairvoyant. He was also well versed in the facts of the real world. He analysed them and the vast range of possible futures that they presented. Then, with the help of a spiritually heightened awareness, he was able to focus on those particular facts that would help him to see, in a metaphorical sense, the future. He once described the future as "the rapids" – traversable terrain that required intense concentration on the task in hand.

Wack's last years were spent at his home, a 14th century chateau, in the Dordogne region of France.

Max Weber

BORN: 1864
DIED: 1920
NATIONALITY: German
ACHIEVEMENT: A member of the committee set up to draft the constitution of the Weimar Republic in 1918

Notable publications
The Protestant Ethic and the Spirit of Capitalism, Allen & Unwin, 1930; Unwin Paperbacks, 1985
The Theory of Social and Economic Organisation, William Hodge & Co, 1947; reprint, Free Press of Glencoe, New York, and Collier Macmillan, London, 1964

Notable quotation
Bureaucratic administration means fundamentally the exercise of control on the basis of knowledge.

Background
Max Weber was a German sociologist who taught both before and during the first world war at the universities of Freiburg, Heidelberg and Munich. He would probably be slightly bemused by the influence he has come to wield in the corporate world. For in his lifetime he was best known for his political ideas, in particular for his enormously influential definition of the state as a community "that successfully claims the monopoly of the legitimate use of physical force within a given territory".

Weber's fame in the field of management rests essentially on the ideas put forward in two books: first, *The Protestant Ethic and the Spirit of Capitalism*, in which he linked the morality of puritanical Protestantism, especially Calvinism, with the drive behind entrepreneurship (see page 77) and capitalism; and second, *The Theory of Social and Economic Organisation*, which was not published until four years after his death.

The second book is the one that bears most on the theory of management. It was an attempt to examine why people obey orders, and in it Weber described three types of leadership: the charismatic, the hereditary and the bureaucratic. Each of these, he claimed, can generate obedience, but each is suitable for a different stage in an organisation's development.

The charismatic leader suits an organisation in its early days, when it relies on the vision of a single person to push it towards its goal. The hereditary leader, who comes with authority that has been vested elsewhere (either because his father was chairman before him, or because of success in another organisation), is suitable for an organisation whose rules and precedents are well established. In the third bureaucratic stage, everything runs with machine-like efficiency, and authority and control are exercised "on the basis of knowledge". The military is one example of an organisation in this stage.

Weber was in no doubt that the third type of leadership was the most efficient. "Precision, speed, unambiguity, knowledge of files, continuity, discretion, unity, strict subordination, reduction of friction and of material and personal costs – these are raised to the optimum point in the strictly bureaucratic administration," he wrote. However, he warned against the dehumanising effects of these bureaucracies. He came to believe that the only way to escape the mechanical existence they imposed was for a charismatic leader to come along and transform the organisation through a sort of rebirth.

In the meantime, Weber laid down certain features that he felt the most efficient bureaucratic organisations should possess. These included a career structure with a system of promotion dependent on the judgment of superiors within a formal hierarchy; a permanent fixed office for each career employee; selection on the basis of technical qualifications; and remuneration in the form of a fixed cash salary with the right to a pension. In return, the employee would be subject to discipline and control from his or her superiors.

Looked at today, this list seems almost banal. But this is only because of Weber's extraordinary influence on some of the most powerful corporate leaders of the inter-war period. They took his ideas, transformed them into the corporate arena and, through their subsequent success, persuaded almost every large corporation on the planet to follow.

William Whyte

BORN: 1917
DIED: 1999
NATIONALITY: American

Notable publications

The Organisation Man, Jonathan Cape, 1957
The Last Landscape, Doubleday, 1968, reprint, University of Pennsylvania
  Press, 2002
City: Rediscovering the Center, Doubleday, 1988

Notable quotations

*We are not hapless beings caught in the grip of forces we can do little about,
and wholesale damnations of our society only lend a further mystique to
organisation. Organisation has been made by man; it can be changed by man.*

*Unless one believes poverty ennobling, it is difficult to see the three-button
suit as more of a straitjacket than overalls, or the ranch-type house than old
law tenements.*

Background

William Whyte was an editor at *Fortune* magazine when he wrote the book
on which rests his fame. In *The Organisation Man*, published over 50 years
ago, he brilliantly captured the nature of corporate life in the mid-1950s, at
exactly the same time as cinema audiences were watching Gregory Peck
playing the archetypal organisation man in *The Man in the Gray Flannel
Suit*. Whyte not only defined a phenomenon of contemporary working
life, he named it too.

Whyte's thesis was that the American people (who, he said, "had led in
the public worship of individualism") had recently turned into a nation of
employees who "take the vows of organisation life". "Blood brother to the
business trainee off to join DuPont", he wrote, "is the seminary student
who will end up in the church hierarchy." These business trainees lived in
"the new suburbia, the packaged villages that have become the dormitory
of the new generation of organisation men". The *New York Times* praised
Whyte for recognising that "the entrepreneurial scramble to success has
been largely replaced by the organisational crawl".

Only after the second world war did society fully recognise the size and influence of the massive corporations that had been built up between the wars, organisations such as Ford, General Motors, Unilever and Procter & Gamble. Organisation man, who turned the cogs of these corporate giants' wheels, was ruled with a discipline and sense of loyalty not uninfluenced by the second world war – which, significantly, also hovered like a dark cloud over the man in the grey flannel suit.

Whyte's book preceded by several years both Alfred Chandler's *Strategy and Structure* (see page 225) and Alfred Sloan's *My Years at General Motors* (see page 307), two works that put corporate gigantism well and truly on the map. *The Organisation Man* was a huge success, selling over 2m copies at the time.

It was after *Fortune* had commissioned Whyte to interview the bosses of a number of large companies (including Ford and General Electric) that he wrote the book. But the company that became most closely associated with the way of life he described was of younger stock. It was IBM, rapidly becoming the largest private company the world had ever seen on the back of its dominance of the market for mainframe computers. IBM's managers for many years wore only dark blue suits, white shirts and dark ties, symbols of a lifetime's allegiance to the company that was known as Big Blue. In their devotion to their employer they probably most closely resembled the seminary students that Whyte had in mind.

Whyte's greatest passion, however, was not for corporations or seminaries, but for urban planning. He worked for a while for the New York City Planning Commission and was instrumental in the rejuvenation of Bryant Park, one of central Manhattan's rare green spaces. He wrote a number of books on town planning (including *Securing Open Spaces for Urban America* and *City: Rediscovering the Center*) which were based on meticulous observation of the way that people and vehicles moved around cities. He used time-lapse photography to record how pedestrians used public spaces and is described in Wikipedia as "an urbanist, journalist and people-watcher".